Gateways to the Southwest

Gateways to the Southwest
The Story of Arizona State Parks

JAY M. PRICE

The University of Arizona Press
Tucson

The University of Arizona Press
© 2004 The Arizona Board of Regents
First printing
All rights reserved
♾ This book is printed on acid-free, archival-quality paper.
Manufactured in the United States of America

09 08 07 06 05 04 6 5 4 3 2 1

Library of Congress Cataloging-in-Publication Data
Price, Jay M., 1969–
Gateways to the southwest : the story of Arizona state parks / Jay M. Price.
p. cm.
Includes bibliographical references and index.
ISBN 0-8165-2287-1 (Cloth : alk. paper)
1. Parks—Arizona—History. I. Title.
SB482.A7 P75 2004
333.78'09791—dc21
2003014291

British Library Cataloguing-in-Publication Data
A catalogue record for this book is available from the British Library.

Contents

List of Illustrations   vii
Preface   ix
Introduction   xiii
List of Abbreviations   xix

1   From Dream to Reality: Establishing State Parks in Arizona   3

2   Local Landmarks under New Management: The Historic Parks   26

3   Water in the Desert: Lakes Become Parks   58

4   Ambitions and Setbacks: The Natural Parks   88

5   The Babbitt Era: Creative Approaches   111

6   New Directions and Old Challenges: Redefining the State Park   140

Conclusion: Finding the Right Niche   172
Appendix A. Arizona State Officials   177
Appendix B. Five-Year Plan, 1960–1965 (as Proposed in 1959)   179
Appendix C. Ten-Year Plan, 1965–1975 (as Proposed in 1959)   181
Notes   183
Bibliography   213
Illustration Credits   233
Index   235

Illustrations

Papago Park   10

Governor McFarland Signs House Bill 72   19

Map of Arizona State Parks   27

Tubac Presidio State Historic Park   28

Tombstone Courthouse   31

Yuma Territorial Prison State Historic Park   34

Jerome State Historic Park   37

Picacho Peak State Park   40

Fort Verde State Historic Park   42

McFarland State Historic Park   51

Riordan Mansion State Historic Park   54

Lyman Lake State Park   64

Buckskin Mountain State Park   67

Lake Havasu State Park   69

Alamo Lake State Park   73

Roper Lake State Park   75

Patagonia Lake State Park   78

Painted Rocks State Park   80

Tonto Natural Bridge   95

Dead Horse Ranch   97

Boyce Thompson Southwestern Arboretum   99

Lost Dutchman State Park   102

Catalina State Park   104

Governor Bruce Babbitt   112

Homolovi Ruins State Park   119

Red Rock State Park   125

Slide Rock State Park   128

Oracle State Park   133

Ken Travous, director of Arizona State Parks   141

Kartchner Caverns State Park   144

Fool Hollow Lake Recreation Area   151

Yuma Crossing State Historic Park   155

San Rafael Ranch Natural Area   164

Spur Cross Ranch Conservation Area   168

Preface

When I told people that I was writing the history of Arizona's state parks, the response usually involved something along the lines of "Oh, how interesting. I love the Grand Canyon." Occasional responses included references to Casa Grande, Canyon de Chelly, Monument Valley, or Lake Mead. When I mentioned the names of Tonto Natural Bridge, Yuma Territorial Prison, Lake Havasu, or Kartchner Caverns, the response was sometimes one of familiarity but usually followed by "Oh, I didn't know that was a state park." I recall friends and colleagues asking me, "How is that book on the national parks of Arizona coming along?" Pointing out that the book was on *state* parks got a little old after a while, but I was amused by the comments. They confirmed the need for this book.

Confusion about state versus national parks is a familiar situation in the West. The National Park Service is such a prominent fixture in the region that the general public often assumes that the only parks in the West are national parks. When the public visits places like Homolovi Ruins, Alamo Lake, Lost Dutchman, or Dead Horse Ranch, they follow the familiar chocolate-colored road signs, pay a person in a khaki uniform, and enjoy the site—often oblivious to whether the word "state," "national," or even "county" is on the markers and brochures. The confusion increases when there is access to an adjacent national forest or a place operates with the support of Arizona Game and Fish or the

Nature Conservancy. To the public, a place is simply a "park." It doesn't matter who runs it.

Arizona's state parks, like those of other states in the intermountain West, emerged in a region where well-known federal agencies already controlled most of the land and where counties and cities operated many local attractions. The attitude was "If it was worth saving, the National Park Service would already have done it." The region was also a place where powerful industries shaped nearly every aspect of society and politics. Not until after World War II did outdoor recreation, let alone environmental issues, find significant numbers of supporters. Finding a role in this arena took several decades. Part of the challenge was that early park promoters and staff were dealing with a definition of "park" that was a century old and increasingly ill suited to the nature of preservation and recreation in the late twentieth century. In the years since its creation in 1957, Arizona State Parks has evolved from a competitor for sites to a partner with agencies, communities, and organizations. The very nature of a park, let alone state park, has had to be redefined.

The inspiration for this study started with an oral history project that I conducted for Arizona State Parks in the mid-1990s. In the years since, I have been fortunate to have support from scores of people, without whom this research would not be possible. First, I want to thank the Arizona State Parks Board and the staff of Arizona State Parks who have allowed me to go through agency records, scour clippings files, and make more than my fair share of photocopies. Thanks also to Arizona State Parks for providing many of the photographs for this book. In particular, I want to thank Charles Eatherly, Jay Ziemann, Ken Travous, Jim Garrison, and Ellen Bilbrey for helping me in my research and putting up with what surely must have seemed like an endless stream of questions and requests. Thanks also to the staff at the park sites themselves who took the time to help me, show me their clippings files, and answer my questions. Thanks to the people who agreed to be interviewed for the oral history project and later research. I am also indebted to the staff of several repositories, including the Arizona State Library and Archives; Special Collections at the University of Arizona, Arizona State University, Northern Arizona University, and Wichita State University; the Arizona Historical Foundation; the National Archives; the National Recreation and Park Association; the Arizona Historical Society; and the many county and local historical societies that I visited. Furthermore, I want to thank Larry Landry, Jason Gart, E. Lendell Cockrum, Robert McKittrick, Dave Diamond, Don Charpio, Randy Tufts, Gary Tenen, Gwen Robinson, E. Charles

Adams, Thomas Cox, Tere Ireys, the Friends of Oracle State Park, John D. Wilburn, Vic and Joy Robeson and the Tombstone Restoration Commission, members of the Hopi Tribe, Edward Collins, Lyle Matzdorff, and the many others who allowed me to come into their homes and offices, put up with my phone calls, answered my e-mails, and read the drafts of this text. Finally, I want to say thank you to the faculty of Arizona State University, colleagues at Wichita State University, and the many friends and family members who supported and encouraged my work over the years. I could not have done it without all of your help.

Introduction

The American West is famous for its parks, monuments, and historic sites. For many foreign visitors these places are the embodiment of everything "American." Each year, millions of people from around the world experience the stunning natural beauty of Yosemite, Yellowstone, Zion, the Great Sand Dunes, and the Grand Canyon. They are drawn to the blending of nostalgia and history at Little Bighorn. They marvel at the rich cultural legacy of Chaco Canyon and Mesa Verde. In many cases, these are national parks. Although state and local parks fill the West, national parks get the attention.

Historians who study tourism and environmental issues in the American West naturally look at the national parks. Earl Pomeroy's study suggested that the parks embodied the Golden West image that the region developed in the twentieth century. Alfred Runte's history of the National Park Service pointed to the parks as examples of a society trying to make all land in the West "useful." Even "worthless lands" could be made productive by allowing tourists to explore them. Roderick Nash, in *Wilderness and the American Mind*, explored how the concept of wilderness started with eastern writers such as Thoreau and Muir but took root and developed in the American West, especially in Alaska. In recent years, David Wrobel, Patrick Long, and Hal Rothman have wrestled with the ways in which national parks and monuments allow tourists to connect with a

West of rugged beauty and Cowboys and Indians heritage. Originally these parks were set up as refuges for the elite, who stayed in grand lodges and traveled on the "Detours" of the Fred Harvey Company. In the 1920s, 1930s, and later, the National Park Service and the tourist industry promoted and advertised parks to a larger segment of society. Such marketing, along with improvements in road travel and general economic prosperity, allowed a flood of middle- and working-class visitors to inundate the western parks, prompting many within and outside the National Park Service eventually to wonder if some parks had become too popular.[1]

In the shadow of these large and impressive national parks exists an even bigger collection of state, county, local, and private parks, museums, and monuments. Some, such as the missions of California and Texas or the museum at the O.K. Corral, have reputations that rival the major locations of the National Park Service. More commonly, however, these places provide recreation and education for residents within the region itself, many of whom, admittedly, were transplants from outside. These visitors are more likely to drive to a place hours away than to a destination days away. They come from the region's suburbanized cities for day trips or weekend getaways, often with campers and boats in tow. For them, a park is more of a brief escape from urban life than a cross-country experience into a mythic West.

Management of these state and local attractions has been a complex and dynamic story during the twentieth century. In the first half of the century, the management of natural, recreational, and cultural resources in the intermountain West took place primarily on two levels: the federal and the local. On the federal level, those lands tended to belong to the National Park Service, the U.S. Forest Service (USFS), the Bureau of Indian Affairs, or the entities that eventually became the Bureau of Land Management (BLM). Architectural historian Norman Newton has observed that these sites involved "creating something for all the people from land already owned by them."[2]

At the other end of the spectrum were the parks and museums of cities and counties. These parks ranged from modest picnic areas to Phoenix's South Mountain Park, one of the world's largest city-owned parks. Cultural features were often local responsibilities. Outside of a handful of important archaeological and cultural sites managed by the National Park Service, historic locations were usually the responsibility of local bodies, either cities themselves or local citizens groups.

State-level parks did not have that same presence until well after World

War II. One reason involved state governments, which in the West served the interests of extractive industries such as mining, timber, and cattle. For western legislatures and the agencies they funded, developing the region's resources was the main concern. "Protecting" land from "development" seemed counterproductive at best and a threat to livelihoods and tax dollars at worst. Advocates for environmental issues and outdoor recreation found it easier to work with federal agencies than with state ones, a situation that Samuel P. Hays has shown extended well into the 1970s.[3]

For decades, parks at the state level seemed irrelevant in large parts of the West because national and local institutions seemed to meet existing needs. It took the concerted efforts of parks advocates in the 1920s and New Deal support in the 1930s to create state parks in Idaho, Nevada, Utah, and New Mexico. Yet the energy to maintain interest in state parks, let alone expand systems, could not compete with the far more organized efforts of the extractive industries nor with public indifference. State park movements stagnated and even retreated during the late 1930s.

After World War II, however, outdoor recreation assumed an unprecedented importance for the region. Growing numbers of visitors sought places to camp and explore. Tourism expanded from a colorful but minor endeavor to a major contributor to the region's economy. Tourists became sources of revenue, especially for places where mining, timber, and cattle industries ceased or were no longer as profitable as they had been. State governments began to find tourism and parks to be useful industries in their own right. As a result, state park agencies emerged in Colorado, Utah, Nevada, and Arizona or were greatly expanded in Idaho, Montana, and Wyoming. By then, many of the choice sites had already been developed, and there was competition for those that remained. Meanwhile, federal agencies such as the BLM and the USFS began developing their own campgrounds, lakes, and trails, as did cities and counties.

State park agencies in this region found themselves operating in the awkward and contentious arena between federal agencies, local bodies, and private interests. If they tried to acquire or develop large and significant sites, they faced resistance from established—and territorial—federal agencies that already owned the land. If they tried to develop recreation-based parks, they often ran into similar competition from county or local governments. Meanwhile, even other state agencies, such as a game and fish department or the state historical society, might prove to be rivals in acquiring and managing sites. Agencies fought to keep land under their authority and competed with each other over privately owned parcels when opportunities to buy or lease them came up. The years after World War II also saw the rise of nonprofit organizations, such as the Nature Conservancy and the Defenders of Wildlife, who themselves started purchasing land or receiving donations from sympathetic landowners.

This struggle to find a role for state parks was common throughout the intermountain West, such as in Arizona. Arizona's case provides insight into challenges of creating a state park system in the West after World War II. As home to some of the region's most stunning national parks and monuments, Arizona has had a long tradition of strong federal agencies. There is also a tradition of city and county governments acquiring, developing, and managing large parcels of land for the benefit of their citizens. Some of the smaller of these communities also developed historic and recreational sites to stimulate the tourist trade.

Chapter 1 explores the challenge of creating state parks in Arizona. Like other states in the intermountain West, Arizona had a large amount of federal land, a small urban population, and a state government dominated by extractive industries. Like the movements of neighboring Utah and Colorado, Arizona's state park movement did not become visible until after World War II. Urbanization, the rise of automobile tourism, and growing concern that development was erasing natural and cultural features made state parks seem useful to at least a segment of Arizona's social and political leaders. By the late 1950s, Arizona's lack of state parks was an embarrassment to a society that prided itself on being a recreation destination. Responding to these demands, Arizona established a parks board with the passage of House Bill 72 in 1957, but Arizona's parks board also began with a number of restrictions and limitations that proved fateful in the agency's later development.

Chapters 2, 3, and 4 examine the challenges of creating state parks in the 1960s and 1970s. Throughout, the stories of the places that did not become state parks are just as revealing as the stories of the parks themselves. As chapter 2 demonstrates, the first state parks were often historic sites whose operations were beyond the resources of the historical societies and communities that ran them. Even so, Arizona State Parks[4] did not develop into the sole manager of historic sites on the state level, in part because of the emerging competition from the Arizona Historical Society.

Chapter 3 discusses an area where Arizona State Parks had some success: water-based recreation. As with historic sites, many lakes became state parks because their previous owners no longer wanted to manage them. Parks along the Colorado River, however, emerged because Arizona State Parks was able to get involved early enough in the negotiations. Cooperation with the Army Corps of Engineers produced additional parks in western Arizona.

Chapter 4 illustrates, by contrast, the agency's more limited legacy in establishing recreational and natural parks that were not lake-based. In addition to the political and financial constraints on state park issues, many sites that might have become state parks were already under some form of federal, state, or local management. The BLM and the USFS were not willing to part with their premier locations. Arizona State Parks had to look elsewhere, again acquiring sites that previous owners no longer wanted to manage. Where there was local support for a state park project, however, the process could take on an energy of its own, as with the decade-long campaign to create Catalina State Park.

Chapter 5 illustrates how Arizona had become part of what historian Samuel Hays has called the "new environmental West," referring to a growing sensitivity among urbanized westerners to the environmental threats to the region. The administration of Bruce Babbitt energized and transformed nearly every aspect of Arizona State Parks in the late 1970s and early 1980s. Even Babbitt, however, had to work around and through the state legislature to get things done. Babbitt's techniques included land exchanges and creation of the Arizona Parklands Foundation, a nonprofit organization set up to acquire land for state parks. Babbitt was also skilled at shaping and using public opinion to promote projects he felt were valuable, such as at a series of ruins by Winslow called Homol'ovi.

Chapter 6 discusses the opportunities and challenges that the board and staff of Arizona State Parks faced in the wake of the Babbitt administration. The late 1980s and 1990s saw the development of two major sites, both originally on private land: Tonto Natural Bridge and Kartchner Caverns. Meanwhile, the dynamics of park development and creation were changing. Partnerships between different federal and state agencies began to replace earlier rivalries. Money from the Arizona Heritage Fund gave Arizona State Parks an unprecedented financial independence, but in many cases, it was no longer cost-effective to purchase land for parks. Partnerships and cooperative ventures became the hallmarks of park development. Land exchanges, partnerships, conservation easements, and other arrangements have brought in more significant and noteworthy sites. The results include the Sonoita Creek Natural Area, San Rafael Ranch, and Spur Cross. Consequently, state parks in Arizona have become much more complicated entities than the phrase "state park" might initially suggest.

As opposed to the "direct stewardship" of actually owning and operating a natural, recreational, or historic site, institutions such as Arizona State Parks came to rely on what can be called "indirect stewardship": guiding the use of resources that are owned or managed by others. Examples of indirect stewardship include public awareness campaigns, incentive programs, cooperative ventures, advisory councils, sponsorship of workshops, and planning projects. During its history Arizona State Parks changed from relying solely on direct stewardship to employing a combination of direct and indirect forms.

Space considerations preclude this study from covering in detail the myriad other activities that Arizona State Parks has engaged in. For example, in the 1960s, the director of State Parks took on the role of state historic preservation officer (SHPO). Although that role changed in the 1970s, historic preservation activities still take place out of Arizona State Parks. A natural areas program emerged when a number of scientists felt that certain parts of Arizona should be preserved—not as parks for the public to visit, but as areas that should be maintained and protected for the unique habitat they contain. In the 1980s, Bruce Babbitt launched a program that encouraged average citizens to become aware of and involved in the preservation of archaeological sites and to curb pot-hunting. Meanwhile, the agency has taken on the responsibility for coordinating the development of trails and off-road vehicle recreation. Arizona State Parks has also played a role in administering grant programs, such as the Land and Water Conservation Fund (LWCF), the State Lake Improvement Fund (SLIF), and the Heritage Fund. Future writings will ideally capture these aspects of Arizona State Parks because they, too, mirror the issues that have faced state park systems regionally and nationwide.

Abbreviations

ACGA	Arizona Cattle Growers Association
AHS	Arizona Historical Society
AORCC	Arizona Outdoor Recreation Coordinating Commission
ARA	Arizona Recreation Association
ASPA	Arizona State Parks Association
ASPB	Minutes of the Arizona State Parks Board
BLESF	Boating Law and Safety Enforcement Fund
BLM	Bureau of Land Management
BOQ	bachelor officers' quarters
BOR	Bureau of Reclamation
CCC	Civilian Conservation Corps
COQ	commanding officer's quarters
CVHS	Camp Verde Historical Society
CVIA	Camp Verde Improvement Association
ECW	Emergency Conservation Work program
FOSP	Friends of Oracle State Park
HMB	Homolovi Management Board
LCRLUP	*Lower Colorado River Land Use Plan*
LWCF	Land and Water Conservation Fund

MNA	Museum of Northern Arizona
NACP	National Archives, College Park Site, Maryland
NYA	National Youth Administration
OEPAD	Office of Economic Planning and Development
ORGC	Oracle Road Greenbelt Committee
ORRRC	Outdoor Recreation Resources Review Commission
OSP	Oracle State Park
RRSP	Red Rock State Park
SAEC	Southern Arizona Environmental Council
SCORP	Statewide Comprehensive Outdoor Recreation Plan
SES	Southwest Environmental Service
SHPO	state historic preservation officer
SLD	State Land Department
SLIF	State Lake Improvement Fund
TCSHP	Tombstone Courthouse State Historic Park
TRC	Tombstone Restoration Commission
USFS	U.S. Forest Service
VVRRIG	Verde Valley Recreation Resource Information Group
YCSHP	Yuma Crossing State Historic Park

Gateways to the Southwest

Chapter 1 **From Dream to Reality**
Establishing State Parks in Arizona

During the nineteenth century, state parks *were* the national parks. With the exception of a handful of places such as Yellowstone, states took the lead in setting aside locations to preserve natural or scenic features, creating parks such as the Adirondacks and Niagara Falls in New York and Itasca in Minnesota. Park management was generally a state, not federal, responsibility. Even though Yosemite was established as a national park, the state of California had the duty of managing it for the first several decades. Likewise, cultural sites tended to be the wards of states or local organizations. For example, Texas preserved the Alamo and the Battlefield of San Jacinto as state monuments beginning in the 1880s.

These arrangements made sense in an era when the federal government was in the business of distributing the public domain to other owners. This policy governed expansion into the South, the Ohio Valley, the upper Midwest, and the Great Plains. By 1890, most land from the Atlantic Ocean to the Rocky Mountains was in the hands of states, counties, municipalities, or private entities. Parks and cultural sites in those regions had to be established from those holdings.

Conservationists east of the Rocky Mountains and west of the Sierra Nevadas and Cascades often looked to state parks and state conservation organizations as outlets for their endeavors, especially in the nineteenth and early twentieth centuries. For this reason, states such as Minnesota, Iowa, Indiana, and New York became early leaders in the state park movement. For example, Rebecca Conard's study of the Iowa Conservation Commission illustrates the vast array of activities with which a state institution could be involved. Even California was part of this movement early on. State parks in California developed among private and local holdings along the coast, with national parks in the interior, where most land was federal. Although the forest-conservation tradition of New York differed from the preservation of scenic beauty along the Pacific Coast, the park movement in the nineteenth century and into the Progressive Era included a strong state-level component.[1]

Then a shift took place. Rather than selling off or giving away the public domain land to others, the federal government began to retain ownership of the land and allowed other individuals or organizations to lease it. It was a new ethic in stewardship. Professional managers, not private landholders, supposedly knew the best ways to manage the land and the resources on it. The federal government became the permanent manager of the remaining public domain instead of a temporary distributor. It so happened that most of the remaining public domain was in the intermountain West, concentrated in the Rocky Mountains, Great Basin, desert Southwest, Sierra Nevadas, and Cascades. Some lands were often too rocky, too steep, or too dry to lend themselves to farming. Other parcels and resources seemed too vulnerable to be left to private enterprise. Land was still considered a resource to be used and not to be wasted. The issue was who determined the rate and dynamics of that use.

Most states in the intermountain West contained a patchwork of mostly federal holdings along with some state and private tracts. Only a small amount of state land was available. The amount of private land was sometimes even smaller. Recent figures illustrate trends that hold for the twentieth century. Although nationwide, 27.7 percent of the land in the United States was government owned, for the intermountain states, that figure was often much higher, with Arizona at 44.6 percent (70.7 percent including Native American reservations), Colorado at 36.5 percent, Idaho at 62.5 percent, Montana at 27.6 percent, Nevada at 82.9 percent, New Mexico at 34.2 percent, Utah at 64.5 percent, and Wyoming at 49.8 percent.

In states such as Arizona, land distribution was mainly federal, followed by a complex array of state, local, tribal, and private holdings. In 1891, 75.7 percent of the land was part of the public domain. In 1912, some of that land went to the newly created state government. The land that remained federal became the responsibility of a number of major agencies. By 1945, almost 66 percent of the land in Arizona was federal, made up mostly of Native American reservations, land under BLM control, and nearly 11.5 million acres of national forests. The State of Arizona owned more than 11 percent of the state's land, most of which was under the control of the State Land Department (SLD). This left 19 percent of the state's land in private hands (a figure that in more recent years has declined to 16 percent).[2]

In western states such as Arizona, the use of public domain lands has been a major political issue. Members of the ranching, mining, and timber industries feel the purpose of federal management should be to enable mining companies, timber companies, ranchers, and farmers to use the public domain lands with enough care to ensure use of these resources in the future. To these industries, "conservation" means regulating use so that development can continue without using up the resources in the process.

Arizona accommodated this viewpoint as well. For much of the twentieth century, Arizona's economy had the nickname "the three C's": copper, cotton, and cattle. Individuals connected with those industries had long had influence in Arizona government. Of the fifty-two delegates to the Arizona Constitutional Convention, in 1910, five were connected with the mining industry, thirteen were ranchers, two were farmers, and several others had ties to more than one of those industries. In the years that followed, as in rest of the West, legislators and governors in Arizona focused on promoting growth, development, and business. Moreover, these state leaders were committed to keeping taxes low and government small.

As scholars of western state politics have noted, legislators and governors in this region have tended to be either from or at least sensitive to industries such as cattle, farming, ranching, and mining. To many twentieth-century cattlemen and other rural westerners, tourism was a frivolous and wasteful use of the land. Parks and recreational sites were for city dwellers to visit. As one historian noted, "Though ideas about saving scenic beauty and using the state as a vehicle to do so were 'in the air' nationally [in the 1920s], the same could hardly be said of the Rocky-Mountain-Intermountain Basin states."[3] Samuel Hays has noted that state and local governments nationwide have traditionally been concerned with development instead of environmental and recreational issues. Support of development is especially strong in rural constituencies with recreational and environmental issues more likely to be important to urban voters. With such a strong rural presence in western state government in the years before World War II, it is hardly surprising that environmental and recreational uses of public lands received little sympathy from western politicians. In Colorado, legislators scoffed at state parks as mere playgrounds for the motoring rich, forcing cities such as Denver to create a large-scale system of city parks in the nearby mountains. This was the same basic dynamic that stifled the ambitious park plans of Governor James Scrugham in Nevada, that caused Utah's State Board of Park Commissioners to fade away, and that tolerated only isolated state parks in Idaho. Scholars of Idaho history, for example, have noted that the state lacked a "park-spirited citizenry until the 1950s and 1960s." In Montana, efforts of state forester Rutledge Parker and other park supporters pushed for state parks in the 1920s but with little success. State parks were an urban concept that had relatively low support in what were still predominantly rural states.[4]

In places such as Arizona, money from the sale or lease of state lands was intended to fund education. To facilitate this goal, Article X of the Arizona State Constitution specifically noted that state lands had to be sold or leased to the highest bidder. The administrator of that process, the land commissioner, had the responsibility of developing the lands in such as way as to maximize the revenue to the state. The act clearly implied that the proper use of lands was for development, not preservation.[5]

With state governments so focused on development, it was in the federal holdings where preservation and recreation efforts took place. The national parks at Yosemite and Yellowstone were among the first sections of the public domain in the West set aside for preservation and recreation. The 1906 Antiquities Act authorized the president to set aside parts of the public domain as national monuments, again with recreation as a key use of the sites. Rather than having land devolve to state or territorial governments, it made sense to carve a national park or monument out of the existing federal lands. The results were parks such as Bryce Canyon and Zion in Utah, and Mesa Verde in Colorado. By the 1910s, Arizona monuments included the Grand Canyon (soon to become a national park), Walnut Canyon, Tumacacori, Tonto, and Papago. In 1916, a new agency, the National Park Service, emerged as part of the Department of the Interior to manage these sites and the national parks. Meanwhile, the Bureau of Reclamation (BOR) established itself in the West to channel the region's meager water supply into reservoirs and projects that irrigated otherwise unfarmable land. Access to these reservoirs was limited but still provided opportunities for outdoor recreation for growing numbers of westerners. Local residents soon began using the logging trails in the national forests to get into places for hiking, hunting, camping, and fishing. Agencies such as the USFS, Fish and Wildlife Service, BLM, U.S. Army Corps of Engineers, and Bureau of Indian Affairs all had land holdings, each containing natural or cultural features that the public felt were worth visiting.

Consequently, land use and social dynamics made western park development different from that of the East. In the interior West,[6] conservationists often worked though federal agencies such as the National Park Service. The federal government proved a more supportive outlet than development-oriented state governments. Predictably, most of the early national parks, and all of the early national monuments, lay in the West. Had these dramatic natural and cultural features existed back east, some likely would have become state parks rather than national ones.

In terms of outdoor recreation and wildlife preservation, local activists supported and worked with the federal agencies. Arizona, for example, had established a group of officials to regulate hunting and fishing since territorial times. By the 1920s, the Arizona Game Protective Association and other groups had reshaped this body into the Arizona Game and Fish Commission. Although Game and Fish ran hatcheries and other facilities, it primarily worked out cooperative arrangements with other agencies, federal and state, to regulate the hunting and fishing of the general public, rather than to acquire game preserves to operate.[7]

By World War II, a relatively set pattern had developed throughout the region. National parks preserved major scenic features and were the main hosts for out-of-state visitors. County and municipal parks provided recreation for locals. Cities and local historical societies managed historic sites that the National Park Service did not own. State game and fish agencies managed activities on federal, state, and local lands.

State parks seemed irrelevant in a region with so much federal public land, where local bodies handled most recreation and preservation activities. State park advocate Raymond Torrey, in his 1925 survey, found that Arizona, for example, contained no state parks and that there was little sentiment to create any. He quoted Governor George W. P. Hunt as saying that "the number of National parks and the large amount of public land which are available for recreation and vacation purposes does not justify creating them [state parks]."[8] Another advocate, Beatrice Ward Nelson, came to a similar conclusion when she looked at Arizona for her 1928 assessment of state parks, also citing Hunt as a source. In this regard, Arizona was not unique. Nelson attributed the lack of state park development in New Mexico, Colorado, Montana, Wyoming, and Utah to the large presence of federal land as well.[9]

In Arizona and the other states of the intermountain West, state parks have usually faced an uphill battle. For example, when the Arizona Good Roads Association proposed creating a state park at Mormon Lake near Flagstaff in January 1925, the Flagstaff Junior Chamber of Commerce passed a formal resolution denouncing the action. The resolution argued: "The establishment of the proposed park would be of no advantage to the people of Arizona, but would work a great hardship upon Flagstaff and Coconino county, in that lumbering would be stopped and a big industry practically paralyzed."[10] The resolution went on to say that the Forest Service, with its policies of multiple use and forest management, was a competent steward of the local timber resources. This policy of multiple uses allowed industries to extract resources, including timber, from public lands. A park would restrict such activities. The issue was a matter of access to these resources.[11]

Cattlemen in Arizona were especially vocal in their opposition to parks. Freeman Tilden, in his book *The State Parks: Their Meaning in American Life,* concluded that the park movement in Arizona was stifled by "a small segment of the population, pioneer-minded people of unquestionable merits, yet convinced that the hoofed animal was still the state's greatest heritage."[12] Cattle families respected the beauty of the land that gave them their livelihood. However, they also distrusted the public ownership of resources and believed that stewardship was best accomplished by keeping resources in private hands when possible. They also distrusted political leaders from urban areas who came to represent entirely different views on how resources should be used.[13]

Population was another factor. Arizona, like the rest of the interior West in the 1920s, lacked a large urban middle class who would have used state parks. Before World War II, Arizona's population was under five hundred thousand and could take advantage of the Grand Canyon, fifteen national monuments, more than 11 million acres of national forests, thirty thousand acres of county parks, and more than fifteen thousand acres of metropolitan parks. Even the National Park Service, in its 1941 survey of outdoor recreation in the United States, remarked that most urban Arizonans "are fairly well served by municipal, metropolitan, or county parks and nearby forest areas. There is no state park system and there does not appear to be a need for one."[14] Another 1941 study, produced by the Arizona Resources Board, came to a similar conclusion.[15]

State Parks and the New Deal

Not even New Deal funding and support could stimulate state parks in Arizona. The New Deal was a crucial catalyst for creating state parks around the country, especially in the South. Parks became popular work projects, and states often jumped at the infusion of federal dollars into their Depression-era economies. Advocates for state parks in the interior West hoped these resources would overcome the inertia that had doomed state park endeavors in the 1920s. Some were successful. New Mexico and Montana used New Deal programs to jump-start their state park systems. Nevada re-established its state parks program in 1935. After creating its first state park at Lewis and Clark Caverns in 1936, Montana established its state park system in 1939. Meanwhile, Colorado gave its Board of Land Commissioners responsibility for state parks, although little came of the effort. Throughout the West, the catalyst to state park creation was the New Deal's Emergency Conservation Work (ECW) Act, which established the Civilian Conservation Corps (CCC).[16]

Part of the New Deal's effort to provide work and to improve the nation's infrastructure, the ECW/CCC established work camps on federal and state projects around the region, from the Spanish missions of New Mexico to Heyburn State Park in Idaho. However, many of these endeavors gained the designation of "state park" simply to qualify as ECW/CCC projects. In Arizona, for example, Colossal Cave State Park and Tucson Mountain State Park were both under the jurisdiction of the Pima County Park Board. Hualapai Mountain State Park was under the jurisdiction of Mohave County. The University of Arizona owned Saguaro Forest State Park, itself an inholding within Saguaro National Monument. Although ECW Procurement Officer Aaron L. Citron concluded that "Saguaro Forest, Tucson, Arizona . . . is really the only true State Park in Arizona,"[17] even Saguaro was a state park in name only. It became a park when University of Arizona President Homer Schantz called it such to take advantage of ECW funding. There is no record that the state legislature, the governor's office, or the state land commissioner seriously worked to make Saguaro a legitimate state park.[18]

The 1930s did see the creation of the first real state park in Arizona: Papago. Sandwiched between Phoenix and Tempe, the federal government established Papago Park as a national monument in 1914. In 1930, at the request of several individuals, including Senator Carl Hayden, Congress officially abolished Papago's national monument status, dividing the resulting land between the state, Phoenix, and Tempe. ECW/CCC camps developed the site starting in 1933 and continued into 1937, first under the National Park Service and later under the BOR. Papago Park fell under the authority of the SLD in 1936 after certain parcels had been leased to a number of state and local organizations, including the Arizona Game and Fish Department and the Cactus Floral Society of Arizona.

10   Chapter 1

Papago Park went from national monument to state-run facility, ultimately being divided among several communities. Although technically Arizona's first state park, Papago had primarily served the populations of Phoenix, Tempe, and Scottsdale. By the late 1950s, the Arizona State Park Board confirmed that fact when it oversaw the transfer of Papago to local governments.

Papago Park remained popular with the people of Phoenix and Tempe. The park was reasonably well developed, with picnic areas, a rifle range, botanical gardens, and a fish hatchery. Although it did preserve some natural scenery, the site was essentially a large city park similar to Phoenix's South Mountain and Squaw Peak. By the 1950s, the cities of Phoenix and Tempe began pushing for Papago Park to be divided between them.[19]

New Deal projects had encouraged neighboring New Mexico and Nevada to create state park systems. To some, it seemed time for Arizona to join in. Starting in the late 1930s, several bills authorizing a state parks commission emerged. All failed, victims of a legislature dominated by cattle interests. Arizona missed a prime opportunity to establish a state park system and had to wait another twenty years to create one—with no CCC camps to help in the development.[20]

Arizona after World War II

In the years after World War II, the American West, and the Southwest in particular, had gone from an isolated region dominated by cattle, timber, and mining interests to the embodiment of the Sunbelt. Millions of people moved to the

West, dramatically transforming the society. These new residents were often professionals or workers with the region's now prominent defense industries or related technology firms such as Motorola. Their numbers transformed modest regional centers, such as Las Vegas, Albuquerque, and Denver, into major metropolises with suburbs extending out into former farms and grazing areas. They traveled out there on the federally funded highways that had replaced the crude roads of earlier years. Government housing loans and financial aid from the GI Bill enabled former World War II veterans to move to the places where they were once stationed. States such as Utah, Colorado, New Mexico, and Nevada were part of this trend. So was Arizona, with the percentage of the population living in urban centers rising from 34.8 in 1940 to 74.5 in 1960.

In addition to Arizona's general prosperity during the 1950s, the lifestyle attracted both visitors and residents to the state. Americans in general had by now rejected the Puritan-inspired association of recreation with sloth. Decades of advertisements, messages in the popular culture, and even government programs helped encourage working classes to join the middle classes in seeing outdoor recreation, day trips, and vacations as rights rather than luxuries. For those who lived out west, reaching lakes, hiking trails, and parks was often a matter of riding a few hours in a car instead of traveling across the country. As the *Arizona Republic* columnist Ben Avery remarked in 1962: "Outdoor living is a cultivated way of life with Arizona. It begins at the patio of nearly every home, extends to the outdoor barbecue, the poolside, and finally out into the millions of acres of public lands. Here camping and picnicking . . . can be a year round pleasure."[21] With many of Arizona's scenic places within a relatively short drive from Phoenix and Tucson, outdoor recreational activities, especially camping, hunting, fishing, and even boating became popular.[22]

Throughout the West, tourism blossomed from an afterthought into a cornerstone of the economy. In Arizona, tourism became the state's fourth largest industry. Communities in Arizona, as elsewhere in the American West, became especially interested in developing roads, historic sites, tourist attractions, and a wide range of facilities to meet the needs of these primarily automobile-oriented travelers. The tourist of the 1950s was a different breed from the elite traveler of the previous century. Rather than traveling by train to elegant resorts, these vacationers loaded families into cars to drive to campgrounds and picnic areas. They expected, and demanded, the exotic flavor of the Wild West but with the amenities of home. Motels and restaurants along Route 66 offered attractions such as fake Hollywood-inspired forts and concrete tipis—with air-conditioned comfort and convenient service. Communities struggled to redefine themselves to take advantage of the tourist dollar.

In the southern part of Arizona, for example, resorts and dude ranches were popular, especially in the winter. In the northern part of the state, the public traveled to the popular national parks and monuments, camped and picnicked in the national forests, and visited the Hopi and Navajo reservations.[23]

Tourists inundated the parks and forests. By 1957, attendance at the Grand Canyon was at a record 1,101,817. By the mid-1950s, more than 4 million persons visited national parks, national monuments, and other sites around the state, with 2 million of them visiting just Lake Mead.[24]

The nature of recreation was changing as well. Outdoor recreation had long since abandoned the ruggedness of early camping and hiking but retained the image of "roughing it." Companies such as Coleman produced dozens of gadgets, from coolers to portable stoves, to make the camping experience comfortable. Hiking miles into the mountains on logging trails had given way to camping at campgrounds and picnic areas with ample parking, water fountains, flush toilets, and ranger talks at night. The National Park Service spent more than $43,600,000 on its facilities in Arizona alone. Roughly half of these funds went toward construction and improvement of utilities while the other half went toward developing roads and trails. Even the Forest Service, traditionally more concerned about timber harvests than summer visitors, began to provide outdoor recreational opportunities such as campgrounds. By the 1960s, the Forest Service provided the slopes for the infant downhill skiing movement. Even the BLM started to provide facilities for visitors. In Arizona, the Game and Fish Commission and the Arizona Highway Commission also expressed growing interest in outdoor recreation. By the 1950s, a growing number of roadside parks appeared in the state. Meanwhile, cities and counties became more interested in park issues, and municipal and regional parks emerged, especially in the Phoenix and Tucson areas.[25]

Compared to previous generations of westerners, these individuals had very different views of the land and how it was to be used. For those whose livelihoods did not directly depend on the land, the mountains, lakes, rivers, and forests of the West were for recreation and enjoyment. Beautiful scenery became a value worth protecting in its own right. Cutting timber, grazing rangeland, flooding canyons, and mining mountains destroyed the natural areas that many traveled miles to see. For earlier generations, developing the West's resources was an obvious necessity. The only question was to what extent and for what purposes.

Federal agencies such as the Forest Service or the BLM had grown accustomed, however imperfectly, to working with these goals in mind. After World War II, development in the West was no longer the unquestioned benefit that it was just a few years earlier. Recreation, and with it preservation, became legitimate uses for land in their own right.

The growing environmental movement found a sympathetic voice in the urban West. By the 1950s, David Brower and groups such as the Sierra Club marshaled public opinion against development-oriented projects such as occurred with the Echo Park Dam controversy. Such activities helped inspire the next generation of environmental thinkers and writers, such as Edward Abbey or Secretary of the Interior Stewart Udall.[26]

Some began to realize that prosperity and development also had negative effects on the state's cultural heritage. Secretary of the Interior Stewart Udall summarized the situation: "While we have watched Arizona mature and while we have great faith in its future, we also have watched bits and pieces of its great natural beauty and historic legacy disappear. Many of its historic buildings have been razed without care. Its towns and cities have spread without concern for preserving nearby open spaces."[27] Cities and towns tore down historic structures to put up high-rise buildings, parking lots, and housing developments. Many other historic buildings fell into neglect as people and communities focused on new construction. Looters ransacked prehistoric sites for pots and artifacts. Many sites fell to construction and development. Urban sprawl obliterated large expanses of desert and the traces of those who once lived there.[28]

By the mid-1950s, even elected officials began to take notice. In Arizona, Governor Ernest McFarland noted that "homes were being built on desert and farm lands. The encroachment of civilization was rapidly restricting the natural areas."[29] McFarland was not alone. Others pointed out problems related to the state's growth and expansion, from reduction of air quality to loss of scenic beauty.[30]

The Arizona State Parks Association

It was during this period of economic expansion, boom in outdoor recreation, and growing concern over the loss of cultural and natural resources that Arizona's first true state park movement emerged. Historian Thomas Cox noted that after World War II, "state parks systems became standard in the region [of the West]—albeit on a more limited scale than in other parts of the country."[31] In Arizona, state parks bills appeared in the legislature, starting in 1952. Individuals including state senators Robert Morrow and J. Morris Richards sponsored them. These measures failed as their predecessors of the 1930s did, victims of a legislature preoccupied with growth and development.[32] By 1955, journalist Ben Avery lamented that "the failure of Arizona to set up a state parks and recreation department is a sad commentary on the interest taken in government by citizens of the state. Some of the most beautiful sections of the state are seriously threatened because of this failure."[33]

These bills represented the emergence of a diverse state park constituency. Some saw state parks as a way to conserve Arizona's scenic and recreational resources. Others viewed state parks as good business. In 1955, the Arizona Legislative Council, recently established to advise and assist the legislature, commissioned the also new Arizona Development Board to do a study on the possibilities of a state park system for the state.[34]

The report concluded that state parks could provide both a means of preserving historic and scenic places and opportunities for recreation and tourism. The report stated that "the Arizona Development Board firmly believes that Arizona should have a state park system; that the time to plan for and enact laws relating to the establishment of a state park system is now; that Arizona is richly endowed with outstanding scenic and recreational resources which should be set aside, preserved and developed for the enjoyment of the people of Arizona as well as the visitors to the state."[35] The authors also believed that state parks would boost local economies by drawing tourists. With Colorado establishing a state park system in 1955, Arizona was now the last state in the country (Hawaii and Alaska still being territories), without a system of state parks.[36]

These observers looked around and saw other states in the interior West making strides to develop their state parks. Individuals such as Idaho's governor Robert E. Smylie pushed for more to be done to revitalize that state's moribund park system. The Utah State Parks Commission replaced the defunct State Board of Park Commissioners. Colorado's legislature overcame decades of resistance to establish a state park and recreation board. New Mexico started adding several new parks to its system, such as Bluewater Lake and Conchas Lake. Meanwhile, popular movements pushed for more state parks in Nevada and Wyoming.[37]

In January 1956, Governor Ernest McFarland suggested to the twenty-second legislature that a state parks and recreation commission be created for Arizona. Meanwhile, another bill, House Bill 20, was put before the legislature, which called for the creation of a state parks board. As with previous state parks bills, the powerful cattle interests in the legislature defeated both measures. Ben Avery noted that "in the last legislature the house passed a watered-down state parks and recreation bill, but the senate is so completely dominated by the Arizona Cattle Growers Association that even though two of the cattlemen senators pleaded with association leaders, it would have been impossible to build a single picnic table under the bill passed by the senate."[38] In disgust, the proponents of the bill scuttled their own legislation rather than let a watered-down version pass. Although there was growing support for state parks, opposition to state parks from legislators interested in protecting the interests of the powerful cattle industry remained an obstacle.[39]

By 1956, some individuals realized that an organized campaign was needed to get a state park system created in Arizona. Soon after the defeat of the 1956 state parks bill, Joseph F. Carithers, the manager of Tucson Mountain Park, and Ben Avery took on the responsibility of organizing a state park movement. Ben Avery was a journalist for the *Arizona Republic* who had long been interested in outdoor recreation and conservation in Arizona. In his column "Rod and Gun" (which appeared several times a week in the *Republic*), he tracked the policies and actions of the Arizona Game and Fish Department and the Arizona Game Protective Association, commented on outdoor recreation and land use issues in Arizona, and promoted the selling of hunting and fishing licenses as wildlife management.[40] Joseph Carithers headed the local chapter of the Audubon Society and chaired the Arizona Conservation Coordinating Committee, an organization that united several conservation groups in the state.[41] Carithers was also involved in the movement opposing the building of dams in northern Arizona, such as Glen Canyon Dam. He knew from experience that efforts to conserve Arizona's natural and scenic places required organized campaigns that marshaled massive public support. He noted that opponents to state parks "are organized and have funds at their disposal to use against such a move. We are going to have to be as well organized as they are to succeed."[42] It was going to take a substantial campaign to challenge the traditional opponents to state parks.[43]

On June 22, 1956, the two men called a meeting of thirty persons at the Westward Ho Hotel in Phoenix. Many who attended were professionals with parks and recreation in some capacity. Wayne O. Earley of the state highway department was in charge of the state's growing number of roadside parks. Dennis McCarthy of the Maricopa County Parks and Recreation Department (and president elect of the Arizona Recreation Association) attended, as did Henry T. Swan of Phoenix's park system. People outside of the recreation profession included Bert Fireman of the *Phoenix Gazette*. Interested in Arizona's history, politics, and society, Fireman wrote several articles for *Arizona Highways* and delivered a program on Arizona history called *Arizona Crossroads* for Phoenix radio station KTAR. There were prominent local archaeologists, including Dale S. King, Lyndon Hargrave, Luis Gastellum, and Odd S. Halseth. Although not in attendance, Emil Haury of the University of Arizona and head of the Arizona State Museum became a prominent supporter of the state park movement. Groups as diverse as the Arizona Automobile Association, the Arizona Farm Bureau Federation, the Oak Creek Canyon Lions Club, and the National Park Service, came together to lobby their legislators for a bill creating a state parks agency.[44]

Those who pushed for state parks in 1956–1957, led by the Arizona State Parks Association (ASPA), consisted of an unlikely assortment of partners. The coalition included the Arizona Recreation Association (ARA), which was interested in state parks to meet the growing need for outdoor recreation in Arizona; the Arizona Development Board, which wanted state parks as tools to promote and develop tourism in the state; and individuals such as Ben Avery and Joseph Carithers who saw parks as a means to preserve scenery, natural areas, and historic sites.[45]

The state park movement gained momentum throughout the rest of 1956. On August 10, 1956, the ASPA formally organized, complete with constitution and bylaws.[46] At that meeting, Robert M. Jaap, vice president of Valley National Bank in Phoenix, became the organization's first official president. These individuals embarked on a vigorous publicity campaign, sending letters to legislators, holding public meetings, and contacting directly various organizations and individuals. Contacts with civic and professional groups around the state were also important. Meanwhile, journalists wrote articles in favor of state parks. In November 1956, the association set up a booth at the Arizona State Fair, bringing more publicity to the state park cause.[47]

Of particular importance was the association's work to make friends among the state's cattle ranchers. Although other industries had their reservations about state parks, the cattle growers were the most powerful and influential opposition in the state legislature. For any state parks bill to pass, it needed the support of the cattle growers and their representatives.[48]

The cattlemen's concerns were similar to those of Flagstaff's timber industry back in 1925 when the Arizona Good Roads Association proposed a state park be created in the area: Designating a site a park restricted the use of natural resources on that site to those related to outdoor recreation. It was vital for the ASPA to convince the state's cattlemen that state parks would not be a threat. Thus, five individuals from the Arizona Cattle Growers Association sat on the

ASPA's advisory board. Leading the cattlemen's delegation was Earl Platt, president of the Arizona Cattle Growers Association. Platt once noted that "the cattlemen are not opposed to state parks legislation but want to protect the industry from any laws that might be harmful. 'We are jealous of our waterholes and a little jealous of our pastures.'"[49] Platt worked closely with the cattle industry on drafting the state parks bill to go before the legislature. By including the cattle industry in the development of state parks legislation, the ASPA hoped to gain the support of the pro-cattle segment of the legislature.[50]

Yet people such as Joseph Carithers were concerned that the state park movement was far too accommodating to the interests of the cattle industry. In a letter to Jaap, Carithers said:

> the Association has ignored the experienced opinion of every park expert who has been asked to give advice.... When a problem arose the leadership of the Association always, with few exceptions, turned to the cowboys for advice, instead of the general public represented by the membership of the Association.... This attitude of 'if you can't fight 'em, join 'em' is a bit ridiculous.... I [along with others, whether they say so or not] are hoping that you, Bert [Fireman], Stan [Womer] and the others there in Phoenix who have taken on the responsibility of determining what is best for the future of State Parks here in Arizona, will stop being led around by the cow-boys.... I have been in this conservation-preservation business for most of my adult life, and I have found out, as has everyone else in the business, that when you fall off the high road of public interest and get in the rut of special interest you soon find out that you miss the boat all the way around: the special interest boys start taking advantage of you (Platt already has) and those who were for you in the beginning soon lose interest. Play it down the middle and you can't go wrong.[51]

To Jaap and the leadership of the movement, however, compromise was necessary to get a bill passed; previous attempts that did not compromise had failed.[52]

In addition to gaining the support of the cattle industry, Jaap, Earley, and others made a conscious attempt to bring the leadership of the state legislature into the process. The advisory board went to legislators for suggestions and guidance on drafting the state parks bill. The ASPA worked with such legislators as Senator Charles "Chick" Orme to persuade his colleagues that state parks would not hurt the cattle business. Senator Orme later said that "probably our own group [of cattlemen] in Yavapai County was the most hostile group two or three years ago . . . but by my going around—man to man—and explaining to those gentlemen that the Legislature had no intention of setting up a board which would damage their interests."[53]

The result of these months of work, negotiation, and compromise was House Bill 72, which was introduced into the state legislature on January 28, 1957. An identical piece of legislation, Senate Bill 61, was introduced simultaneously in the senate. House Bill 72 contained compromises to reassure the cattle industry. The bill called for the creation of a state parks board of seven members, appointed by the governor and serving without compensation. At least two members of the board had to be from the cattle industry and one had to be a recreation professional. One of the seven was the state land commissioner, who, as an ex officio member, could vote but not serve as chair. Except for the land commissioner, whose term on the board lasted for his or her tenure, the other members had six-year staggered appointments.[54]

Perhaps the greatest concession to the cattle industry was the amount of land that the board could acquire. The law stipulated that the parks board could not acquire any land for state parks over 160 acres without the permission of the state legislature, although the board could accept gifts of larger acreage. The 160-acre limitation satisfied the cattle industry. The size restrictions and other provisions also satisfied a legislature that did not want to spend large amounts of money creating state parks. As Senator J. Morris Richards, one of the bill's supporters, noted to the board, "We want you to get as many of those park areas by gift as you can. The legislature is not interested in spending a lot of money. . . . We would like parks and places that are now suitable for state parks to be given to the State wherever the owners are willing to do that—and many of them, I think, will do that."[55] House Bill 72 seemed to have enough provisions to satisfy the cattlemen and their sympathetic legislators while also allowing supporters of the state park movement to have a park system develop.

Unlike the earlier state parks bills that either died in committee or were amended to death, House Bill 72 was introduced in the house by the Committee on Livestock and Public Lands and in the senate by a group that included several cattlemen. Some in the livestock industry, including Earl Platt, were genuinely interested in the state parks bill. Once he warned the senate that if it did not pass the bill, "you might not see the light but you will feel the heat."[56] Other supporters among the cattlemen had different motives. To some it was safer to create a state parks board now than have one created later that was in total conflict with cattle interests. E. B. Thode, one of the representatives who guided the bill through,

State Senator M. O. Lindner (right) and Arizona State Parks Association leader Bert Fireman (left) are with Governor Ernest McFarland as he signs House Bill 72 into law.

made it clear that "primarily my interest was to protect the cattlemen. If the bill had not passed the Legislature it might have been referred to the people in a form that the cattlemen might not be able to accept."[57] The bill also had the support of several important members of the legislature, including Senators "Chick" Orme and Senator Harold G. Giss. House Bill 72 passed both houses of the legislature unanimously and the ASPA's compromises with the cattle industry played a major role in the bill's success. On March 25, 1957, Governor Ernest McFarland signed House Bill 72 into law. The Arizona State Parks Board was born.[58]

House Bill 72 gave the state park movement what it wanted: an organization to establish and manage state parks. Yet it also contained several fateful provisions that limited state park development for decades. One was the provision that parks over 160 acres needed the permission of the legislature to be created. Moreover, revenues from entrance fees did not stay with Arizona State Parks. They reverted to the general fund. The agency did not have control over its own finances. Money to purchase, lease, or develop parks had to come from the legislature. Thus, every state park project became intensely political.

The provision to have an autonomous state parks board was fateful as well. Arizona, like all other states, had a variety of boards, agencies, and commissions that handled state-level recreation and conservation matters, from the projects of the Game and Fish Commission to the roadside parks of the Arizona Highway Commission to the resources of the SLD. This was at a time when most states were starting to consolidate these activities into a handful of larger departments. This consolidation allowed for more coordinated policies among institutions, reducing conflict between them. "It would seem advisable for the welfare of the state park movement if all state parks had a definite form of administration," observed state park advocate Beatrice Ward Nelson as early as 1928. "Probably the most practical system is a department in which are grouped all the recreational, development and conservation activities of state government."[59] As Rebecca Conard has shown with respect to the Iowa Conservation Commission, organizations that oversaw a number of different activities, from state parks to game and fish issues, were able to tap into a wide range of constituencies and could play influential roles in conservation and preservation matters.

By the 1950s, most states had started to replace their separate state parks commissions and departments of state parks under larger administrative units, often natural resources or even highway departments. With a handful of exceptions it was in the states of the western South and Southwest where autonomous state parks commissions remained: Nevada, Utah, New Mexico, Colorado, Texas,

Kansas, Missouri, Arkansas, Louisiana, Wyoming, and now Arizona. Of these, Wyoming, Colorado, New Mexico, and Kansas had split the administration of historic sites and natural and recreational parks into two different arenas. Arizona's state parks board handled both areas, making it a potential competitor with a host of historic, recreational, and natural resource agencies.

House Bill 72 did not clarify the role of the Arizona State Parks Board with that of other state agencies such as Arizona Game and Fish, which by the 1950s had also acquired and leased recreational sites, usually from the federal government. In Arizona, Game and Fish and Arizona State Parks were separate entities whose boundaries were ill defined and overlapping. Meanwhile, ill-defined boundaries between the Arizona Historical Society and Arizona State Parks led to problems in later decades. The potential for rivalry existed with other state agencies as well as with federal or local bodies.

House Bill 72 also reflected a concept of land stewardship that was at the time nearly a century old. To protect natural, cultural, scenic, and recreational resources, the Arizona State Parks Board was to acquire land to turn into parks and monuments to be run as tourist facilities. House Bill 72 noted that the purpose of the board was to "select, acquire, preserve, establish and maintain areas of natural features, scenic beauty, historical, and scientific interests, and zoos and botanical gardens, for the education, pleasure, recreation, and health of the people."[60] Acquisition was key. Management of a location and its resources implied ownership. Thus an agency that wanted to manage certain resources had to look for parcels of land that contained those resources and try to acquire them. While management of resources was a pressing issue, acquiring parcels of land to accomplish that goal would prove to be far more problematic.

The First Board and First Challenges

For reasons still not entirely clear, McFarland, a Democrat, appointed to the newly formed Arizona State Parks Board political supporters rather than individuals from the state park movement. Only one appointee was a major figure in the ASPA: Charles J. Reitz, the superintendent of the City of Yuma's Recreation and Park Department. Others in the association, such as Bert Fireman, were disappointed that they were not selected to be on the first board. The board did include cattlemen Ezekiel B. Taylor and Virgil Mercer. Mercer had been a director of the Arizona Cattle Growers Association in the early 1950s and had even supported the association's 1954 resolution against making the Cochise Stronghold site a national park.[61] Max Connolly was a local publisher affiliated with newspapers in Kingman and the Phoenix area. Frances B. Weedon was an active member of the Arizona Democratic Party and had served as vice president of the Maricopa County Democratic Central Committee, president of the Arizona Federation of Democratic Women's Clubs, and an Arizona delegate to the Democratic National Convention. Ricki Rarick was an executive of Tucson Newspapers, Inc., and later became involved in real estate. The only Republican on the board, Rarick had some experience with park and recreation issues in that he was president of the Tucson Golf Association, vice president of the Sportsmen's Fund, and a member of the Tucson Chamber of Commerce's park committee. Responsibility for implementing House Bill 72 rested on a group who now had to learn by trial and error the complex and daunting task of setting up a state park system. Given the challenges that they faced, it is remarkable that the first members of the parks board accomplished as much as they did.[62]

One of the first jobs of the board was to select a parks director. After looking through several applications, the board selected Dennis McCarthy. Then head of Maricopa County's park system, McCarthy was also president of the ARA and had been involved with the ASPA's efforts to pass the state parks bill. He began his work as state parks director on October 16, 1957, and held that position for nearly twenty years. Joseph Carithers, who had long been suspicious of the cattle industry's influence upon state parks, wrote to Wayne Earley, concurring with his misgivings about having McCarthy as state parks director. He wrote: "I can't help but feel this whole thing would not have happened if the ASPA had fought it out with the cow-boys and not have given them a majority on the Board." To Carithers, Dennis McCarthy was "the very type of person they want; someone who does not grasp the state park idea at all, and who will leave the larger areas alone. He will be content to have small playground type parks." Carithers felt that the activities of the years to come would prove "*conclusively* that they picked the wrong man."[63]

Partly, this concern reflected differences within the recreation profession. On one side were those who saw parks primarily as places to gather for organized recreation (the "bats and balls boys" according to one parks board member), and on the other side were those who thought of outdoor recreation in terms of fishing, hiking, and other activities that related to nature. The fear was that McCarthy would favor the former.[64]

Debate over McCarthy's appointment was also a symptom of a growing rift between the Arizona State Parks Board and the ASPA. In the months that followed, animosity between the association's activists and McFarland's board appointees had deteriorated to such an extent that the board was known to refuse ASPA members access to meetings. In 1958, then ASPA President Dale S. King was astonished to learn from the board that while he was welcome to attend board meetings, other members of the ASPA were not. After a year as president, King, too, became critical of the board and outlined his complaints in his final presidential speech. He felt that none of the board's members was competent to deal with state-level parks. Even Charles Reitz, though qualified to work with recreational parks, did not have enough experience dealing with parks of natural, historic, or archaeological significance. He also sharply criticized the board for not taking stronger initiatives for acquiring parks and for being far too timid. King even suggested that the entire board be replaced.[65] Not everyone agreed. Odd Halseth felt that the association was too hard on the board. He remarked that "in our impatience to get a well balanced park system established overnight, almost, we disregarded at times the fact that . . . this board [is] a body of laymen who had to feel their way around areas where many of us had long experience."[66]

Not long afterward, the ASPA found that it had enough trouble keeping itself alive as a functioning entity, let alone as a source of advocacy for state parks. Once the state parks bill passed and work began on identifying and setting up state parks, the association had served its main purpose. With none of its leaders appointed to the first Arizona State Parks Board, the association's voice in state park matters was severely limited. The organization did little to lobby for more state park funding or work to acquire specific sites. The ASPA's membership proposed to the board sites that could be examples of state parks but did not take an active role in, for example, persuading the owners to donate their land to the state park system once it was created. By 1960, newsletters ceased being published, and correspondence between the members stopped, although letters occasionally reached individual members into the very early 1960s. The ASPA had always been a coalition of individuals and organizations rather than a single, focused entity. As the state parks issue faded into the background, the various recreational, cultural, environmental, and community groups went their separate ways to focus on other issues. By early 1963, the ASPA ceased to exist. Arizona lost the one organization that had made the public aware of the need for state parks and that had used that awareness to persuade the legislature and the Arizona State Parks Board to take more of an interest in Arizona's natural and cultural resources. Arizona State Parks was on its own.[67]

Finding a Role

Ironically, the board's first task was to dispose of the one state park already in existence: Papago Park. The City of Phoenix had tried to acquire Papago Park for several years, but the legislature and the state government refused to hand over the property. The city hoped that the newly created state parks board could help get the property transferred. The board held hearings on the issue months before it even hired a state parks director. The issue was complicated. It took several months just to determine who had the authority to transfer the park from the SLD to the parks board. When that issue was resolved, negotiations resumed, with the board listening to representatives of the Phoenix City Council, the Papago Park Commission, the Arizona Game and Fish Commission, and a host of other agencies and organizations. After several years of negotiations, all parties agreed to sell Papago to the City of Phoenix with the condition that the city update the Arizona State Parks Board on the park's development.[68]

With Papago gone, the main goal of the Arizona State Parks Board became to acquire new state parks. Determining what to acquire was problematic. In Arizona there was no central, threatened site for the parks movement to rally around, as existed in some other states. Rather, the 1950s was an era when having a state park system, or at least a body to coordinate one, was the status symbol. Although recreation and the preservation of threatened sites were legitimate goals of the state park movements in the region, there was a good measure of state pride in the matter as well. By the 1950s, increasingly vocal citizens of Arizona and Colorado felt ashamed that they were from the only two states in the continental United States without a state park system. They created their state parks authorities not just to meet actual needs but also because the other states had them.

What these park systems should contain was less clear. Most of the discussion around House Bill 72 centered on the methods and dynamics of acquisition, not on what a state park should be. House Bill 72 made no mention of what made a place worthy of being a state park instead of a national or county one. There were no specific qualities that made a site a good state park candidate. There was no conclusion on whether a state park should be like a large-scale city or county park, geared toward recreation, or a small-scale national park, focused on protecting major scenic, natural, or cultural features. Any place could be a state park if the parks board and legislature deemed it so.

Once created, Arizona State Parks quickly found that many of the places that might become state parks were already under some form of public ownership or management, usually by the federal government. Dennis McCarthy recognized this situation when he wrote to Ernest Allen of the National Park Service stating that "those most desirable recreation areas in the State are located in the National Forests," that "we have agreed that the State of Arizona has scenic areas 'coming out of its ears,'" and that "most of the state's scenic areas are now in some form of public reservation, either in National Forests or under control of the Bureau of Indian Affairs." In regard to prehistoric sites, he noted, "for the present, and for at least five years, the Pre-historic Sites program is adequately taken care of by the National Parks Service, by the Arizona State Museum, and by other organizations interested in the particular field." McCarthy suggested that the state parks board might acquire some national forest land in the future as state parks but admitted that those prospects would take considerable negotiation.[69]

This situation showed up in the first state parks plans, drafted in the first years after McCarthy came on board. There were three documents: a one-year plan for the 1959–1960 fiscal year, a five-year plan of sites to be acquired by 1965, and a ten-year plan consisting of sites to be acquired by 1975. Perhaps the most common characteristic of the sites listed was how many were already under public ownership. For example, the Salt River Project's Canyon, Apache, and Saguaro Lakes were surrounded by USFS land and the Forest Service was already planning some development for the sites. Possible state parks included Monument Valley, located on the Navajo Reservation. Sites already administered by the state included Arizona Game and Fish lakes and Indian ruins still owned by the University of Arizona. Municipally owned sites included Pueblo Grande Ruins in Phoenix, Ft. Lowell in Tucson, and Ft. Verde in Verde Valley. Pima County operated Colossal Cave as a county park. Only a handful of suggestions, such as Tonto Natural Bridge, were in private hands, and even Tonto was already in operation as a recreational facility.[70]

Thus in Arizona, the key issue was often not whether a place should be set aside to protect it. That was already done for most of the major sites identified in the initial plans. Arizona State Parks had to argue that it would be a better steward than the current managers. For some organizations, especially those that ran historic museums, the appearance of Arizona State Parks was a welcome relief. For other institutions, however, transferring land to Arizona State Parks was harder to sell.

Chapter 2 **Local Landmarks under New Management**
The Historic Parks

Preservation writer William Murtagh has noted that in contrast to England, "America has tended to keep her interests in natural conservation distinct from those of [historic] preservation."[1] This attitude has filtered down to state-level policies. In many states, including three of the eight states of the interior West, parks authorities oversaw only recreational or natural sites—often lakes. Historic and cultural sites were the responsibilities of other organizations. In New Mexico, for example, historic sites fell under the same agency that oversaw historical museums. In Colorado, the state historical society managed historic sites. In those states, the lines between the stewardship of cultural resources and those of a recreational or natural character were distinct and relatively clear. In states such as Arizona, the state parks authority managed both cultural and natural areas. Initially, the Arizona State Parks Board was to be the one organization that oversaw the management of historic and cultural sites. Yet as the Arizona Historical Society started to become more active in site preservation as well, the ill-defined distinction between the two organizations became awkward.

Major archaeological or historic sites might have been beyond the reach of Arizona State Parks, but the agency in its early years found itself inundated with suggestions for places that would make great state parks. Many involved a local historic site that the given community had decided to develop as a tourist attraction and local shrine. Frequently, volunteer citizens groups operated them as

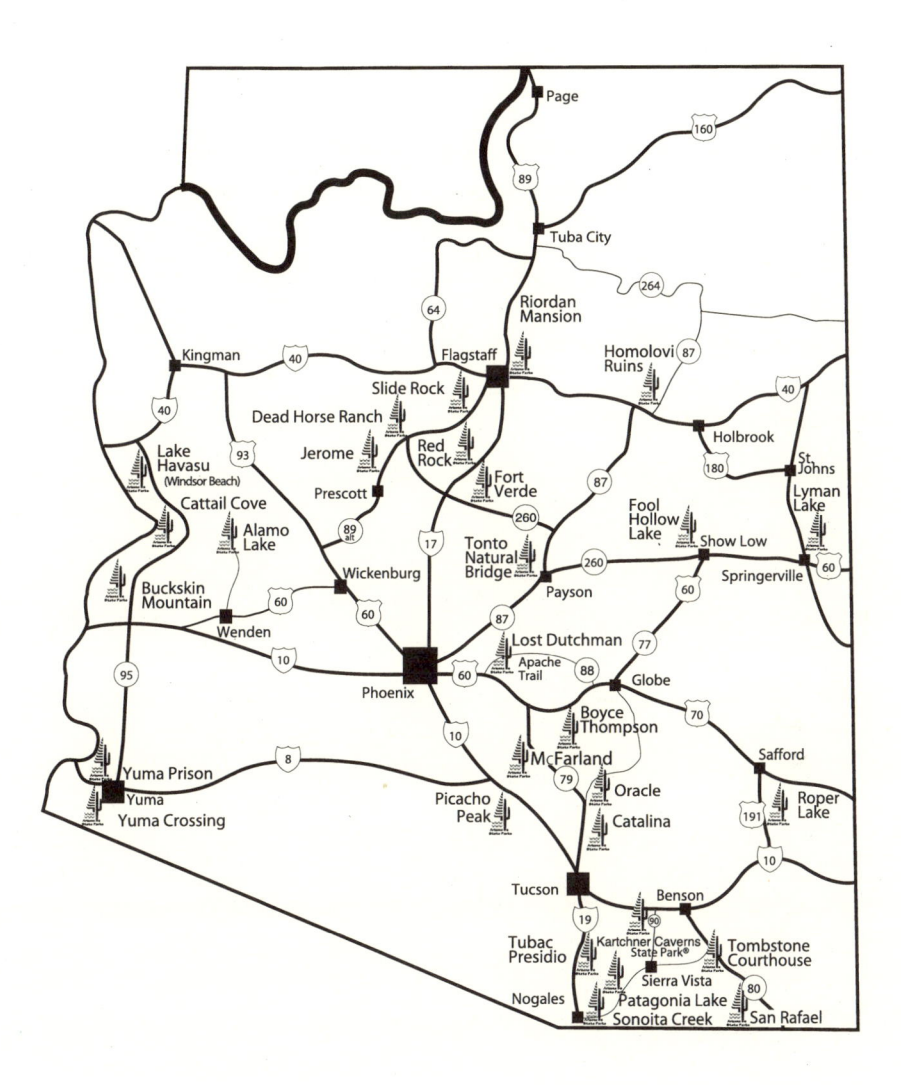

Arizona State Parks

The ruins of Tubac Presidio became the Arizona State Parks Board's first acquisition. In the years that followed, Tubac Presidio State Historic Park expanded to include adjacent sites that told the story of one of Arizona's oldest communities.

museums. However, these groups soon realized that the costs, efforts, and resources involved in operating even a small museum proved greater than what they could muster. Rather than shut down a local icon, these groups preferred to donate their museum to someone who could take care of it. In other instances, communities were in the process of rehabilitating their historic structures to cater to the tourist trade. Some of these structures were still privately owned but had owners who were willing to sell or donate their property to help their community preserve a part of its history. The Arizona State Parks Board seemed to be a perfect new manager for these sites.

Tubac

The first site to become a state park contained the ruins of the Spanish presidio in Tubac. Founded as a Spanish presidio in 1752, it was the first European settlement in what is today Arizona. Tubac was abandoned or nearly abandoned several times only to be reborn through a new set of occupants. One rebirth was in 1948, when artist Dale Nichols purchased five adobe buildings in the center of what had been a dying agricultural community to establish an art school. Although the costs of running the school proved too great and Nichols had to close his dream in 1949, the institution brought Tubac to the attention of several of Nichols's friends and students. Two of these were Will Rogers, Jr., and his wife, Collier, who moved to Tubac after restoring an old adobe house there.[2]

Frank and Olga "Gay" Griffin were another pair of migrants to Tubac. Originally from Indiana, the Griffins came to Arizona for health reasons, settling initially in Tucson. They quickly became interested in local history and were intrigued by the story of Tubac. Upon visiting the tiny community, they fell in love with the place and purchased a lot in the center of town in the fall of 1956. Within a year of arriving, they had revived the *Weekly Arizonian,* a local newspaper that took its name from the original town paper published in the 1850s. They also helped form the Tubac Restoration Foundation, Inc., to encourage the restoration of the community's remaining historic structures.

The creation of the Arizona State Parks Board coincided with the Griffins' interest in Tubac's history. Inspired by the prospect of establishing the presidio as a state park, the Griffins purchased the original presidio site in September 1957. Three months later, the Santa Cruz County Board of Supervisors recommended that the Tubac presidio be the number one site in the county to promote as a state park and designated Frank Griffin as the official representative for the endeavor. It was Gay Griffin, however, who sped up the process by offering the presidio parcel to the Arizona State Parks Board. To the board, the presidio seemed a logical choice for state park status. On January 24, 1958, the Arizona State Parks Board voted and agreed to accept the Griffins' donation.[3]

Meanwhile, one of Tubac's most prominent local developers became involved in the creation of the park. William Morrow, a Philadelphia businessman who owned the Morrow's Nut House chain, came to Tubac in 1957 to engage in real estate and soon became an active booster of the town. One of his activities included acquiring a parcel of land across the street from the original presidio site. In April 1958, Morrow donated this parcel to the Arizona State Parks Board for the location of a museum. Together, these parcels formed the core of what became Tubac Presidio State Historic Park, formally dedicated on September 28, 1958. At the ceremony, Governor Ernest McFarland spoke to a crowd of two thousand people.[4]

The site contained no facilities for tourists and, after months of development, was open only on Sundays. It was not a fully operational state monument until 1961. In the meantime, work began on rehabilitating the adobe on Morrow's donation as a temporary museum and visitor's center. Initially, the community hoped for a complete reconstruction of the presidio site, but those plans quickly fell through. In 1961, the board began construction on a permanent museum and visitor's center. On February 2, 1964, the board dedicated the new museum of the Tubac Presidio State Historic Monument. Sadly, Frank Griffin was not there to witness the event, having passed away in September 1961.[5]

The initial acquisition of the land for Tubac was relatively easy, involving willing donors and a community interested in promoting the area's historic character. Subsequent acquisitions, however, were sometimes more complicated and drawn out. One of these was the Tubac school. The original schoolhouse was too small for the needs of the district, and the school board announced in 1964 that it wanted to sell the school. Many in the local community, including the Santa Cruz Art Association and the newly formed Tubac Historical Society, encouraged the Arizona State Parks Board to take on the site. Arizona State Parks, in response, contacted the school district about the matter. To the school board, however, this was just one of many possible outcomes, ranging from donating the building to the county to selling it to a private buyer. For example, one of the school board members, Josephine Bailey, wanted the school preserved but felt she should sell it at a price that would bring in the most money for the school district. (Bailey later became a member of the Arizona State Parks Board in the 1970s.) It took several more years before the parks board, through the condemnation process, was able to purchase the school for thirty-five thousand dollars, using federal Housing and Urban Development funds. Today serving as the park's visitor's center, the school became one of several additional properties and parcels that the Arizona State Parks Board acquired for the site.[6]

Tombstone Courthouse

Another early state park is that of the Tombstone Courthouse. In 1881, the citizens of Tombstone voted to separate from Pima County and establish Cochise County, with Tombstone as its county seat. Soon afterward, construction began on a county courthouse. What rose out of the desert was a two-story, cruciform brick building that contained the county jail, a courtroom, and all other county offices. In 1903, the building underwent an expansion that lengthened the rear wing. In spite of Tombstone's legacy as the site of the shoot-out at the O.K. Corral, the Cochise County Courthouse served a relatively mundane career as a jail, court facility, and county office building. Although there were colorful events, including a local controversy over whether to have grandstands for public hangings, the housing and trying of criminals was a largely routine operation, lasting

The Tombstone Courthouse was a cornerstone of the town's historic preservation efforts in the 1950s. Many of Arizona's early historic parks, such as Tombstone Courthouse State Historic Park, Yuma Territorial Prison State Historic Park, Jerome State Historic Park, Fort Verde State Historic Park, and McFarland State Historic Park, began when communities looked to the state for assistance in managing local landmarks.

until 1929, when Cochise County voters moved the county seat to Bisbee. In the years that followed, the county first leased and then sold the obsolete courthouse to the City of Tombstone.[7]

As did many towns whose economic base was in jeopardy, Tombstone looked to the growing tourist industry as an economic base. During the 1940s and 1950s, city officials, local business people, and boosters worked to transform Tombstone into a major tourist attraction for southern Arizona. The community entered into what Hal Rothman has called a "devil's bargain" in which tourism seemed at the time like a panacea for economic development but often at the risk of distorting actual history in favor of a manufactured past geared to tourists. In November 1949, a group of interested citizens, several of whom were recent transplants to the area, came together to form the Tombstone Restoration Commission (TRC). The commission had several goals that centered on promoting the town's western image. A speech at a 1950 TRC event noted that tourists "come here to see a show. They come to see part of the old West. A definite, and important part of Tombstone Restoration is the restoration of a western atmosphere." This same speech encouraged local citizens to dress in western-style outfits to reinforce that atmosphere.[8]

Because so many of the town's pre-1900 buildings still stood, the commission saw historic preservation as a key to the development of a tourist industry. By the mid-1950s, the restoration of the town was under way. For example, in 1956, the Lions Club approached the 180-member TRC to restore the O.K. Corral. The members of the commission were especially interested in the restoration of the old Cochise County Courthouse, which, in spite of attempts to convert it into a hotel, had been largely vacant since its closing in 1931.

In August 1955, the City of Tombstone leased the courthouse to the TRC for use as a museum. Fixing up the building was slow, and the TRC opened up the structure to the public bit by bit as restoration progressed. By 1956, the first floor of the building had been restored (money had run out before the second floor could be finished), and the TRC opened at least part of the structure as a museum.[9]

Although many men and women were involved in the restoration of Tombstone, one lady became an especially visible part of the process to save the Tombstone Courthouse: Edna Louise Landin. A native of Ohio, Landin came to Tombstone in 1947. In the 1950s, Landin became a tireless advocate for the promotion and restoration of her adopted community. She served as president of the chamber of commerce from 1952 to 1953, president of the TRC from 1955 to 1960, and served on the city council from 1958 to 1960. An enthusiastic publicist and letter writer, Landin had a vision for Tombstone that combined the town's history with its already well-known Old West mythology. She traveled all over the country as well as overseas promoting Arizona and Tombstone to public officials and dignitaries, whom she "installed" as deputy marshals of the City of Tombstone." By the early 1960s, fewer than fifteen years after first moving to the community, Landin's promotional efforts brought her the title of "Mrs. Tombstone."[10]

It was as president of the TRC that Edna Landin did most of her work to get the Tombstone Courthouse restored and established as a state park. For Landin, the courthouse was more than just a site of territorial justice. It was a "shrine to our pioneers who helped in the building of the West."[11] She wrote constantly to state and national representatives to find money to complete the restoration of the courthouse. Each request received a polite but firm no. There seemed to be no way that the state of Arizona or the federal government could finance the restoration.[12]

Landin and the TRC saw the creation of a state park system as the solution to their financial dilemma. When House Bill 72 passed, she quickly began corresponding with the board, with State Parks Director Dennis McCarthy, and with the ASPA about having the courthouse become a state monument. In April 1958 a delegation of TRC members, including Landin and TRC historian Ethel Macia, attended the Arizona State Parks Board's meeting in Tubac. For the next several months, McCarthy and the board discussed the matter with advisors from the National Park Service. In August, the Arizona State Parks Board included the Tombstone Courthouse in its first year plan (1959–1960), to be classified as a state monument. In September, the TRC hosted a meeting of the ASPA to further promote the development of a state park in Tombstone.

The Arizona State Parks Board ultimately agreed to take over the courthouse as a state monument. In spite of a disappointing financial situation in its early years, the board proposed accepting the courthouse with three thousand dollars for limited maintenance and with salaries for staff to come from donations. In the agreement, the building would revert to the City of Tombstone should the board fail to fulfill its duties. The formal transition took place on August 1, 1959. Ironically, Edna Landin, the woman who had spearheaded the campaign to restore the building and establish it as a state park, was on vacation in Europe and was not present at the signing. Because of the work of the TRC, the site was already set up for use as a museum and could be opened to the public almost immediately. It was Arizona's first operational state park.[13]

Yuma Prison

Like the Tombstone courthouse, the third state park in Arizona was also a well-known landmark: the Yuma Territorial Prison. From 1875 to 1909, the territorial prison housed criminals from all over the territory, including a handful of female convicts. In spite of its twentieth-century reputation as the Hellhole of the West, the penitentiary was a progressive and modern facility for its time. It had electric lights, running water, and forced-air ventilation, amenities that many residents in Yuma did not have. Yumans sometimes called the facility the country club on the Colorado. The prison served the needs of Arizona until a new facility opened in Florence in 1909. Thereafter, it was up to the City of Yuma to find a use for the former prison.[14]

Although visitors to Yuma Territorial Prison State Historic Park sometimes expect the prison's "Hellhole of the West" reputation, the park interprets a facility that was quite modern and advanced for the late nineteenth century.

The first move toward preserving the old prison was in 1931, when the local chapter of the Veterans of Foreign Wars leased the guardhouse from the city for a clubhouse. The prison seemed a promising tourist draw, attracting an estimated one hundred visitors a day, although some of them were actually Depression-era transients. Eventually, a citizens committee formed to help promote the renovation of the site. In late 1939, the National Youth Administration (NYA) agreed to take up the project. To oversee the process, the city created a committee that included among its members the last prison doctor. By 1940, a unit of the NYA was well under way to stabilize the ruins and construct a new museum building on the site of the former mess hall. The prison was not restored to its original condition but enough remained to give a sense of life as a territorial convict.[15]

The task of outfitting the museum fell to Arizona native Clarissa Winsor. She had a passion for the state's history, a history that she often remembered personally, having been born in the 1880s. Her father was the sheriff who brought outlaw Pearl Hart to the penitentiary. She was also very active in community affairs, prompting State Senator Harold Giss to conclude that "not a single civic club, fraternal organization, or social society in Yuma was started without help from Clarissa." In later years, she became known in the community and to those who met her as "the Prison Lady." Thanks to her efforts, the prison museum opened on March 28, 1941. The prison quickly became one the state's best-known historic attractions, attracting three hundred thousand visitors in the first fifteen years.[16]

As with Tubac and Tombstone, Arizona State Parks seemed a promising steward for the property. Yumans such as Harold Giss were instrumental in the creation of the Arizona State Parks and saw a local institution such as the prison as a logical addition to the system. It helped that Charles Reitz, the superintendent of Yuma's parks and recreation department, was on the first Arizona State Parks Board. As early as January 1958, Arizona State Parks and the city had tentatively agreed to make the prison a state monument. It took several years for the City of Yuma to work out the details of the land ownership with the federal government, but in September 1960, the City of Yuma had acquired the property to sell to the Arizona State Parks Board for one dollar. During the negotiations, however, the VFW's building, the guardhouse, burned down. The structure was to have been the visitor's center, and Arizona State Parks' staff had to scramble to revise its plans, causing a delay in the park's opening. The Yuma Territorial Prison State Historic Park opened on a limited basis on January 1, 1961, once a temporary center had been created.

One feature that had not changed, however, was Clarissa Winsor. Now wearing a uniform of Arizona State Parks, she remained curator until she retired at the age of eighty-five in 1965. During her tenure at the museum, Winsor greeted more than five hundred thousand visitors to the facility.[17]

In 1966, the Arizona State Parks Board acquired an additional site in Yuma: the office of the depot quartermaster at Yuma Crossing. Constructed in 1867, this building served as the main office that the U.S. government had set up at the depot to coordinate traffic, trade, and development along the Colorado River. The office of the quartermaster was one of the earliest Anglo-built structures remaining in Arizona. The Arizona State Parks Board acquired the site from the U.S. Boundary Commission, which had operated out of the structure since the 1950s. Until the creation of Yuma Crossing State Historic Park, the quartermaster depot was a satellite museum of the territorial prison. The Yuma County Historical Society helped with the maintenance of the facility but neither the historical society nor State Parks had the resources to manage the historic structures of the former depot.[18]

Jerome

Another town that capitalized on the developing tourist economy was Jerome. In its heyday, Jerome was one of the largest towns in Arizona, its mines producing $800 million worth of copper. The wealth from the mines enabled James S. "Rawhide Jimmy" Douglas to construct a massive adobe mansion on an outcropping in front of the town in 1916. At eight thousand square feet, it ranked as one of the largest adobe houses in the country. The mansion was more of a place to entertain guests than an actual residence; Mrs. Douglas stayed in California, and the children were grown by the time the home was built. In the 1930s, however, Douglas had moved out of town. In 1953, Phelps Dodge, which had acquired the United Verde Mine, concluded that the facility was no longer cost effective and closed down the operation. By then, the town's population had dwindled from fifteen thousand residents in its peak to around two hundred.

If the community was to survive at all, the residents who were left had to find a new source of income. Entering into another of Rothman's devil's bargains, some suggested that perhaps the town would survive by promoting its historical significance to tourists. In response, a group of concerned residents formed an organization in March 1953 called the Jerome Historical Society to establish a historical museum and promote the town through its history. Within a few months, the organization's membership stood at 239. Members began to develop a pro-

The town of Jerome embraced tourism when the mines shut down. In the process, Arizona State Parks acquired the mansion of the Douglas family to create Jerome State Historic Park.

gram for attracting tourists to Jerome and concluded that the town's future resided in its history, or at least in the romanticized images of it. Jerome gained a new reputation as "America's largest ghost city," consisting of old, abandoned, run-down buildings, shadows of the glory days of the mining era. If Tombstone was "the town too tough to die," Jerome decided that death wasn't so bad after all. Attractions often emphasized Jerome being haunted over being historic. To some promoters, the terms seemed interchangeable. Even though the town had several residents who were very much alive, the ghost town theme permeated the Jerome Historical Society's early activities.

In June 1953, only three months after the organization formed, the society opened a museum in a former drugstore and saloon leased from the Verde Exploration Company. The following year, Verde Exploration Company sold the museum building to the society for a nominal fee. This acquisition became the first in a series of buildings that the historical society purchased and preserved. In 1956, the society purchased a deed from Verde Exploration for much of the downtown, consisting of forty properties—for ten dollars. The society later sold or rented some of these properties to entrepreneurs and the artists who began to move into Jerome. Yet what the society considered a "satisfying trickle" of visitors could not provide enough income to fix up a whole town. To promote development, the Jerome Historical Society looked at a variety of ideas, including having automobile races up the winding hills to the town.[19]

The creation of the Arizona State Parks Board seemed to be perfect timing. In August 1957, the Jerome Historical Society contacted the board, suggesting that the town of Jerome itself become a state monument. The board felt that Jerome had possibilities and even listed the town as a proposed state monument in its first five-year plan.

What that state monument entailed quickly changed, however. At the same time as Jerome was struggling to transform itself, the Douglas family was looking for a new use for the old family mansion. When Jimmy Douglas died in 1945, the family considered several prospects, none of which were successful. As did the Jerome Historical Society, the Douglas family felt that the Arizona State Parks Board would be a suitable new owner for their property. Spearheading the effort was Rawhide Jimmy's son, Lewis Douglas. Another supporter was State Representative M. O. Lindner, who represented the Verde Valley and who was a major force behind Arizona's state park legislation. The Douglas family approached the board about turning the adobe mansion into a mining museum. The board liked the idea from the start, with members such as Ricki Rarick considering the site a good tribute to the state's mining past. In 1960, parks staff did a feasibility study on Jerome and concluded that the mansion, with its fantastic views of the town, was the best choice to be the state monument. In August 1962, Lewis, James, Marcelle, and Peggy Douglas signed a deed selling the mansion to the Arizona State Parks Board for ten dollars, and the Arizona State Parks Board accepted the mansion as its newest monument. Soon afterward, Arizona State Parks drew up plans to develop the site. The plans called for a museum that discussed mining in Arizona and Jerome as a mining center. The park itself was named Jerome State Historic Park but the museum inside was the Douglas Memorial Mining Museum.[20]

Although disappointed by the smaller scale of the park, the society was glad to have a state-sponsored attraction in the city. Yet Arizona State Parks' suggestion that the society's mining museum relocate to the Douglas Mansion and consolidate the two museums into one facility sparked an instant and visceral rejection from the community. As the society's newsletter explained, "Most of our readers are sure that OUR Museum has this summer completed fully ten years of successful operation . . . and as to the question that if we would perhaps give up our Mine Museum, I think the Parks Board couldn't have taken away any other meaning than a firm N O–NO."[21] The society was proud of its achievement and did not want to give it up. Jerome was small but seemed big enough for two museums.

During the next two years, Arizona State Parks staff worked at turning a long-unused mansion into a museum. On July 16, 1965, Jerome State Historic Park officially opened to the public at a ceremony with James and Lewis Douglas in attendance. The date happened to coincide with the Jerome Historical Society's annual Spook Night, enabling a connection between the community events of the society and the activities of Arizona State Parks. Although the park was complete, the museum inside was not. The Douglas Memorial Mining Museum opened the following May. Thanks to such efforts, the Ghost City was stirring back to life.[22]

Picacho Peak

Two factors that helped a site become a state park were fame and access. Picacho Peak had both. The peak has long been a sentinel to travelers in southern Arizona. It was fitting, therefore, that one of the westernmost clashes in the Civil War took place there. In August 1861, Confederate Captain Sherod Hunter led company A of the Arizona Rangers west from Mesilla (next to today's Las Cruces, New Mexico) to solidify Confederate control in the region. Hunter marched into Tucson, at the time a bastion of pro-Confederate sentiment, and began plans to invade deeper into the territory. This move, however, prompted alarm from Federal forces stationed along the Colorado River. Captain William Calloway led a detachment of Federal cavalry from Fort Yuma across the Arizona desert to stop the Confederate advance. The first engagement between the two sides took place at Stanwix Station, but the main conflict in Arizona took place at Picacho Peak. On April 15 (some sources suggest 16), 1862, Union troops attempted to capture Picacho. Although the fighting lasted an hour and a half, the action was really little more than a skirmish and probably involved no more than twenty-four troops. The result was two Federal dead and four wounded, one of whom died later. The Confederacy had three of its troops captured as prisoners but by most accounts did not have any dead or wounded. One of the captured troops said that they would have surrendered had the Union troops asked them to instead of firing first. The result was a nominal victory for the Confederacy, but Picacho represented only the beginning of a wave of Federal soldiers coming from California. Unable to defend his position, Hunter retreated back to Mesilla the following month.[23]

The actual location of the engagement remains in dispute, but during the

Although the site of the Battle of Picacho Pass is uncertain, generations of Civil War enthusiasts have associated the peak with the battle. Picacho Peak State Park has also become famous for its wildflowers.

twentieth century, the peak itself became associated with the battle. In 1928, the Southern Pacific Railroad, whose tracks ran nearby, and the Arizona State Historical Society replaced a dilapidated cross and grave-marker (dating from around 1900) with a substantial stone monument to the Union soldiers killed in the battle.[24] Several years after the Southern Pacific erected its monument, a local chapter of the Sons of Confederate Veterans erected a monument to the Confederate soldiers who served in the battle. Because the peak was also an important landmark for the Mormon Battalion of the 1840s, a local group of Latter-day Saints also erected a monument.

In the years that followed, Picacho Peak and its monuments became one of the major landmarks along the highway between Phoenix and Tucson. The collection of stone monuments was a convenient roadside stop, but in the 1960s, the interstate came through and bypassed the site. As motorists sped past Picacho instead of stopping, the area around the monuments became overgrown and desolate. It became the haunt of drinking parties instead of Civil War buffs. Erosion and vandals began to threaten the monuments themselves.[25]

Because of the site's historical significance, Picacho Peak was included in the early state park plans of 1958. In 1960, Arizona State Parks' staff conducted a feasibility study on a 640-acre parcel of federal land whose grazing lease was due to expire in 1962. In 1962, as part of the centennial celebration of the battle, a reenactment took place on the slopes of Picacho Peak. That same year, the board began seriously looking into acquiring the site as a state park.

The BLM had leased a significant part of the property to Tucsonans Robert and Mary Barber for grazing purposes. Fortunately, the Barbers were willing to work with Arizona State Parks. In 1965, the state legislature authorized the creation of Picacho Peak State Park and the purchase of 640 acres of land around Picacho Peak to make the park possible. Negotiations with the BLM continued over the next year, with the Barbers relinquishing their leases, and the patent for the property was officially turned over to Arizona State Parks in early 1966. Construction began soon after. Six years after Arizona State Parks first seriously began the project, Picacho Peak opened to the public on Memorial Day, May 30, 1968.

Land expansion at the park has continued steadily ever since. In 1970, the board purchased another 2,760 acres for the site, with an additional 597 acres added in 1974, and eight hundred acres in 1978. With its location next to a major highway, the park drew a lot of visitors, who came for the dramatic scenery of the peak as much as for its Civil War history. Springtime wildflowers became the main reason for visitation. In particularly good years, visitors were so numerous

After its decommissioning, the site of Fort Verde became part of the community of Camp Verde. In the 1950s, the community embarked on a restoration of the surviving buildings to create a museum. Arizona State Parks later acquired the site to tell the stories of both the Indian Wars and local history.

that the park itself could not handle the cars and people parked along the roads outside the main gate.[26]

Fort Verde

During the nineteenth century, the U.S. government established forts in Arizona to quell Native American resistance to white settlement in the region. Fort Verde, established initially as Camp Lincoln in 1864, was perhaps most famous as the staging point for Lieutenant Colonel George Crook's 1872–1873 campaign against Apache resistance in the central part of Arizona. By the 1890s, however, the Apache threat to American settlement was over, as was the need for so many forts in the Southwest. The end for Fort Verde came with its closing in 1891. Settlers in the adjacent community of Camp Verde acquired various parcels soon afterward. Gradually, the old fort got absorbed into the town. The quarters became homes or took on other uses. Many structures were torn down or abandoned. The parade ground became a park for the town, with the local high school at one corner. Pathways in the old fort became public streets and roads. By World War II, only four original structures remained. These were the bachelor officers' quarters (BOQ), the commanding officer's quarters (COQ), the surgeon's quarters, and the former administration building.[27]

In 1940, Harold and Margaret Hallett of Camp Verde purchased the administration building as a temporary residence while they built a new home. They soon discovered that erosion and neglect had undermined the eastern half of the building. By 1953, the Halletts were ready to tear down the structure. Then, as Mrs. Hallett later remarked, "Call it what you like—a change of heart, sentiment, or civic pride, we changed our minds, and helped get a group of interested people together to discuss the possibility of a museum to preserve the historic past of Fort Verde." This change of heart turned them into crusaders for the fort.[28]

Shortly thereafter, the Halletts proposed turning the building over to the Camp Verde Improvement Association (CVIA) as a museum. The CVIA, which had formed to help develop the tiny community, agreed to the effort. In 1956, the CVIA created a group, the Fort Verde Museum Committee, to look into preserving the original buildings and establishing a museum in at least one of them. Work began on restoring a couple of rooms in the former administration building, still under the private ownership of Harold Hallett. It took another year for the building to be fixed up and filled with artifacts that told the story of the army in territorial Arizona. Later that year, Harold and Margaret Hallett sold the administration building to the CVIA for one dollar. The transfer stipulated that should the building cease being a museum, it would revert back to the family. The museum opened to the public in November, telling the story of the fort and of the community that grew up around it. In 1961, a new organization, the Fort Verde Museum Association, took over the museum from the CVIA's committee. Work continued. The association purchased the BOQ in 1964. In 1965, local resident Hank Wingfield purchased the COQ for the Fort Verde Museum as a memorial to his wife.[29]

By the late 1960s, however, the operation of the museum proved more than local efforts could handle. To protect the site fully would entail purchasing the surgeon's quarters, the parade ground, and adjacent properties, all of which was estimated to cost around $1 million—a price well beyond the capacity of the community. With the Halletts' stipulation about needing to keep a museum at the site as a part of their gift, the association had to look for an alternative. In early 1968, the museum association began talking with the Arizona State Parks

Board, the Arizona Pioneers Historical Society, and members of the state legislature about making Fort Verde a state park. The museum's supporters noticed that nearby Jerome received twelve thousand visitors a month, compared with three thousand a month to Fort Verde. As a statement from the museum association pointed out, "This decision is not lightly taken. . . . We feel we have done this to the best of our ability. But we realize it is time for Fort Verde to take its rightful place in the larger picture of our nation's history."[30]

Meanwhile, the Arizona State Parks Board had been interested in army forts as potential parks, with Forts Bowie, Buchanan, and Crittenden appearing on the original five-year plan, and Fort Apache and Camp (Fort) Verde on the ten-year plan. Because of the work of the CVIA, Fort Verde did not need extensive development to become a public facility. It was what Dennis McCarthy called an instant state park. The Arizona State Parks Board voted in September 1969 to add Fort Verde to its roster of state parks. Then the enabling legislation creating the park passed the legislature. In July of the following year, the board of the Fort Verde Museum, with Margaret Hallett now as president, agreed to the transfer and sold Fort Verde to Arizona State Parks for one dollar. On October 10, 1970, coinciding with the annual Fort Verde Day celebration, Arizona State Parks opened Fort Verde State Historic Park.[31]

Further development of the fort continued under State Parks management, although developments sometimes strained relations with a community who still felt a sense of pride and connection to the fort. When changes at the park were made and the community not notified, local citizens were concerned that the state was tinkering with "their" fort without their input. For example, although the contents of the museum had gone to the state as part of the transfer, the community now wondered if they could have back some of the items that no longer related to the museum's current mission. To add insult to injury, the brochures about the park did not even mention the role that the community had in saving the fort, implying to one resident, "for all anyone reading the brochures would learn, the State started the park from scratch in 1970."[32]

Things came to a head in a November 1975 meeting, when nearly all the members of the former museum association board met with the Arizona State Parks Board to vent their concerns. The now frustrated CVHS announced that it had approached the Arizona Historical Society as a new manager for the fort because the Arizona State Parks Board seemed too recreation-oriented to adequately manage a historical site. The state historical society's president, Sidney Brinckerhoff, had already declined the offer. In many ways, the root of the problem was whether the museum was fundamentally for the community that moved to protect and preserve it or for the people of the state of Arizona. As one speaker put it, "I guess the local folks are not quite so compulsive as your staff members, the professionals, compulsive in the sense of talking in terms of plans and schemes and just so, you know, some of the homey sort of things, some of the exhibits that come right out of the people. There are people that are still living here and still making history who are quite important to the local community." To Camp Verde, the fort, even though a state park, was primarily a community institution, and the community needed to remain a part of its operation. Yet the state had a responsibility to a larger audience as well. As the museum's curator noted, "I just wanted to point out one of our primary obligations now that we are a State institution is not only to the local people, but to the public at large, and this means people in other parts of the state, from other parts of the country." Ultimately, the two sides promised to work more closely, although some misgivings on the part of the community continued.[33]

The Fort Verde Museum Association, under Hallett's presidency, recast itself into the Camp Verde Historical Society (CVHS) and donated four thousand dollars to the Arizona State Parks Board to help with work on the fort. The board acquired parts of the parade ground in the early 1970s. With the help of the CVHS, State Parks purchased the final surviving structure of the fort, the surgeon's quarters, in 1972. Using state funds, State Parks also acquired parcels along officer's row, so that the whole row was part of the park with the three buildings that remained. In the years that followed, restoration work and land expansion gradually continued. By 1990, most of the parade ground and the land along officer's row had been acquired. Although only four original buildings stood, the fort was still the best-preserved Indian Wars fort in Arizona.[34]

A New Rival

In the 1960s, another state entity started acquiring and operating historic sites: the Arizona Pioneers Historical Society (later the Arizona Historical Society, or AHS). The society had been an Arizona institution for decades and was one of the premier organizations that preserved the state's history. At first, respective responsibilities seemed clear. The society managed documents, photographs, and artifacts, displaying them in museums it operated. Arizona State Parks managed sites such as Tubac, Tombstone Courthouse, and Yuma Territorial Prison.[35]

That changed in the 1960s, when the society began to expand its scope to acquiring and operating historic structures while Arizona State Parks took responsibility over grant programs and the resulting historic preservation efforts.

During the 1960s and 1970s, the two organizations sparred over who would guide the stewardship of the state's cultural heritage.

For example, the passage of the 1966 National Historic Preservation Act sparked debate over who would administer the act's responsibilities. The Arizona State Parks Board was initially ambivalent about taking on this responsibility, but Director McCarthy was not and helped persuade Governor Goddard to assign him the role of state historic preservation officer (SHPO).[36] As SHPO, McCarthy was responsible for three major tasks: to nominate properties in the state to be included on the National Register of Historic Places; to oversee a grants-in-aid program in which federal money would go to public or private landowners for the preservation of historic sites; and to ensure that the whole process complied with guidelines and standards set up by the National Park Service. The state legislature did not even fund the program in its first year, so there was little McCarthy could have done to fulfill this role.[37]

McCarthy, as state parks director, was the official liaison between the state of Arizona and the National Park Service. The real work of implementing the National Historic Preservation Act went to the assistant director of state parks, a position that Wallace Vegors filled for many years. In its early years, the historic preservation component of state parks developed slowly. Support for historic preservation in Arizona was not particularly strong outside of such historical societies as the Arizona Pioneers Historical Society. As Vegors recalled in the late 1970s, "It seemed to me, ten years ago [in 1967], that there was very little interest in preserving historic sites in Arizona, and I met actual antagonism to the idea. Preservation was definitely 'anti-progress' then. 'It would take property off the tax rolls,' people said. The general attitude was that 'if it was worth saving, the National Park Service would already have done it.' A cadre of vitally interested citizens existed, but it was not yet visible."[38]

As the home of Arizona's SHPO, the Arizona State Parks found itself having to serve a new role. Instead of reacting to proposals to create parks, the agency now had the obligation to go out into the community to raise awareness of historic preservation issues. In 1970, parks staff started publishing a newsletter, *Arizona Preservation News,* to inform a growing historic-preservation constituency of relevant news from the office of the SHPO. Topics included the status of sites to be nominated to the National Register, discussions of historic preservation philosophy, and information about permanent state and federal legislation. The SHPO's office also began offering workshops on historic preservation and worked with county and local historical societies in identifying and preserving historic properties. In fact, some considered these public relations efforts to be among the SHPO's most important activities. Vegors again mused, "Looking back from the vantage point of eight years experience, the labyrinthine critical-flow-path charts, the agonized-over target dates, the laboriously developed strategies, and the academically-oriented lists of sites were all inconsequential. What counted was the talks and the meetings and the newspaper articles that got the word around that State Parks was concerned with historic preservation."[39] By the late 1970s, the staff of the historic preservation program had grown to five persons who were working to make preservation policies possible.[40]

Meanwhile, the president of the AHS, Harold Steinfeld, led his organization to become involved in acquiring historic properties. The organization established a historic sites committee to look for threatened sites. The committee focused its attention initially on the 1860s-era Charles O. Brown house in Tucson, which was in danger of being lost to urban development. After a months-long public campaign, the AHS persuaded the owner to deed the property to the society in 1960. Over time, the society also became involved in restoration work at Fort Lowell, including designing and furnishing the museum at the site. Subsequent acquisitions included the Century House in Yuma, donated in 1969; the Oro Belle mining campsite, donated in 1970; the Empire Ranch in the Sonoita Valley, also donated in 1970; and the John Charles Fremont House in Tucson, which was dedicated in 1972 as a museum.[41]

Initially, the Arizona State Parks Board was not especially bothered by these acquisitions, which were mostly small urban sites. With the acquisition of Empire Ranch, however, the board became alarmed that AHS was trying to take over its responsibilities. In fact, some in the AHS argued that their organization should be the sole steward for historic properties in Arizona. These issues became more visible in the early 1970s, when the legislature introduced a bill to create a centralized department of natural resources, of which State Parks was to be a part. AHS used this opportunity to push for the transfer of the existing state historic parks to its jurisdiction, leaving State Parks to handle recreational and natural sites. At the request of Dennis McCarthy and State Senator Sandra Day O'Connor, the AHS and Arizona State Parks met to discuss the possibility. Soon afterward, the legislation for a centralized natural resources department failed to pass and the issue was dropped. However, the rivalry between Arizona State Parks and AHS continued to simmer.[42]

The next conflict took place when a real estate development company donated two sites, Guevavi and Calabasas, to the AHS instead of to Arizona State Parks. *Los Santos Angeles de Guevavi* was a small mission, now in ruins, built in the 1700s along what is now the Arizona-Mexico border. Calabasas (officially

San Cayetano de Calabazas) was a branch, or *visita,* of Guevavi. Both sites had been on the board's original ten-year plan, but there is little evidence that the board had followed up on the matter. In 1969, the owner of the two ruins, Rio Rico Development Company, approached State Parks about donating the sites to the agency. In the years that followed, however, Arizona State Parks board and staff did little to follow up on the offer. In early 1974, Governor Jack Williams had learned of the rapid deterioration at the sites. A group of concerned citizens, headed by journalist Ben Avery, approached the governor and suggested that an agency be designated to take the lead in preserving these sites. The most immediate concern was preventing further deterioration. Once the sites were stabilized, the state could then find a suitable agency to manage them. The group suggested that the Arizona State Parks Board look into the matter and Williams concurred. Soon afterward, staff began a feasibility study on the project.

Later that year, Dennis McCarthy contacted Rio Rico to look into a possible transfer. He received a notice that they had already created an arrangement with the AHS. The Arizona State Parks Board protested with a formal resolution warning about the danger of creating two park systems in the state. Lester Ruffner, president of the AHS, responded that his organization was the legitimate custodian of historic sites and Arizona State Parks should concern itself with "catfish farms, ponds, and boat docks." In October, the Arizona State Parks Board passed a resolution stating that it felt "there is a definite trend on the part of the Historical Society to create its own Historic Park System." Later that year, the next AHS president, T. G. Chilton, suggested that a "poorly written and inaccurate newspaper story" mistakenly suggested that his organization was interested in creating a rival system of parks. Instead, AHS was interested in acquiring the ruins purely to prevent further vandalism. The culmination of the struggle was in 1975, when a senate bill appeared in the legislature that, had it passed, would have given the Arizona Historical Society the legal authority to acquire and maintain historic sites. Among the supporters was then attorney general Bruce Babbitt. Ralph Burgbacher, chair of the board, wrote a formal protest to the legislature, noting that "if the Society implements this program on a major scale, another Park system would be created."[43] After Senate Bill 1202 failed to pass, AHS backed off acquiring new sites, and the tensions between the two organizations cooled down. While the AHS has not since been in conflict with State Parks over a major cultural site in recent years, the controversy over Calabasas proved that Arizona State Parks was not the only body to whom a donor could give a historic or prehistoric property.[44]

Other Challenges

Logistics also plagued several historic site projects for Arizona State Parks, as in the case of Fain Castle, a Victorian house near Prescott Valley and a nearby archaeological ruin known as Fitzmaurice Ruins. In 1969, vandalism at the ruins site prompted cattleman Norman Fain to approach the board about making the site into a state park. This site had considerable potential, both because of what it contained and because of its proximity to Prescott. In September 1971, the board agreed to meet with Fain at the ruins to discuss ways of acquiring the place.[45]

State Land Commissioner Bettwy and Fain were especially interested in setting up a land trade, and at first things looked positive. By early 1972, the Fain Land and Cattle Company put forth the paperwork exchanging 130 acres of land with the state. Things began to change, however, when the Fains suggested that in exchange for their lands, they receive 1,300 acres of state land near Prescott. This 10 to 1 ratio of exchange raised a red flag to the SLD. As negotiations between the SLD and Fain deteriorated, Dennis McCarthy began working with State Senator Boyd Tenney about having the legislature purchase the Fain property outright.[46]

By 1973, the land exchange proposal had fallen through, but State Parks encouraged sympathetic legislators to introduce House Bill 1136 into the legislature. This bill authorized state funds for the acquisition of the Fain lands, but the timing of the bill was poor. This was the session when House Bill 2068, creating Dead Horse Ranch, also appeared. Once projects on the Hassayampa River and for a Graham County lake had been added to the Dead Horse Ranch legislation, the fate of the Fain Castle program was sealed. There were just too many state parks projects going before the legislature at the same time. The Fain Castle–Fitzmaurice Ruins bill failed. Later that year, the Arizona State Parks Board considered trying again for the 1974 legislative session but, in the face of other issues such as Catalina, decided to not actively pursue the matter further. A handful of later attempts were equally unsuccessful.[47]

Even having a willing donor or seller did not guarantee that a place would become a state historic park. In 1972, the Northwestern Mutual Life Insurance Company approached Arizona State Parks about donating a parcel of land near Gila Bend containing a stage stop and a Hohokam platform mound called the Gatlin Ruin, another portion was on state land. The Arizona State Parks staff looked into the matter and concluded that it would be an excellent archaeological park, with Vegors suggesting that perhaps the neighboring

Fortaleza archaeological site be added to make a possible park even more attractive. The local community concurred with the park idea in general. In the years that followed, however, State Parks found itself involved in a number of other major projects, including nearby Painted Rocks, and did not follow up on the matter. Ultimately, the City of Gila Bend took on the lease for that part of the Gatlin site that was on state lands.[48]

Nor was having a site on state land a guarantee that it could become a state park. One such parcel of state land was the Adamsville site near Florence. Adamsville was not as large or significant as other Hohokam sites, such as Casa Grande, but it did have the ruins of a ball-court. In 1966, State Land Commissioner Obed Lassen withdrew the site from public sale with the hopes of protecting it. Eventually, the board, at the request of the next state land commissioner, Andrew Bettwy, directed McCarthy to draft an application for the Adamsville commercial lease, which went into effect in January 1971. However, the agency could not fund the staff needed to manage and develop the location. Adamsville was never opened to the public as a state park. The site was not even fenced. Protection did not seem to be as pressing an issue. Adamsville's remote location seemed to make it relatively secure. In the face of other projects and endeavors, State Parks Director Michael Ramnes proposed that Arizona State Parks not renew its lease when it expired in 1979. The board agreed. Ironically, this action took place just as the plight of Homolovi Ruins emerged to help renew an interest in archaeological preservation.[49]

McFarland

Sometimes, however, the opposite situation occurred when pressure to create a state park was so strong that the Arizona State Parks Board had to agree to the project. One such endeavor was that of the first Pinal County Courthouse, dating from the late 1870s. When the courthouse was constructed, Florence was still very much a desert town with strong ties to Mexican Sonora to the south. Architecturally, the building reflected these Sonoran roots: a one-story adobe structure in the shape of a U, surrounding a central courtyard. This humble building served as the county courthouse until 1891, replaced by a larger Victorian structure that looked similar to its counterpart in Tombstone.

In the years that followed, the original courthouse had a number of different uses but remained part of the county government. It served as the county hospital until the 1930s. During this period, the building received its now prominent surrounding portal. From the 1930s through the 1960s, the hospital became a

The first territorial courthouse for Pinal County had been a hospital and museum by the time Governor Ernest McFarland suggested it become a state park. The development at McFarland State Historic Park included restoration of the structure and the construction of the archives for McFarland's papers.

public health center and a boarding house for elderly dependents in the county. In 1963, the medical facilities moved, and the county had to find a new use for its now historic old structure. The county turned the old courthouse into a museum, a home for the Pinal County Historical Society. The museum occupied one wing of the building—the other still housing the county nursing home until the late 1960s. The historical society ran the museum at the site until they constructed a new museum down the street. With its last tenants gone, the old building seemed to have outlived its usefulness for the county.[50]

The building soon found a friend, however, in the form of Governor Ernest W. McFarland. Originally from Oklahoma, McFarland moved briefly to Arizona in 1919 and then went on to law school at Stanford. When he graduated, Mac, as he became known, returned to Arizona. Eventually, he found his way to Florence, in part due to his interest in county politics. Gradually, Mac's career took off, first through the court system in Pinal County and later at the state and national levels. In 1940, he became a senator in Congress and eventually became majority leader of the Senate. After serving twelve years in the Senate, he turned his attention to state politics. Arizonans elected him governor in 1954. He served two terms, and it was during his second term that Mac signed into law House Bill 72, creating the Arizona State Parks Board. Following his term as governor, McFarland gained a seat on the Arizona Supreme Court, finally retiring from public life in 1971. In addition to his political career, McFarland was also interested in media. For many years, he served as president of KTVK in Phoenix. McFarland's career was one of the most dramatic in Arizona history.[51]

In 1972, McFarland announced to the Arizona State Parks Board that he wanted to purchase the old Pinal County Courthouse and donate it to the state as a historical monument and as a repository for his personal papers. Why he wanted to place his personal collection in a little prison town miles away from the state's major urban centers remains a mystery. The structure had long ceased being a courthouse by the time McFarland came to Florence. Several universities had already contacted him about being the repository for his papers. In fact, Mac's time in Florence was relatively short given his lengthy and varied career. McFarland simply summarized his intentions as wanting to "preserve the history of the state and to research the history of the state, particularly for the boys and girls in school."[52]

The Arizona State Parks Board was initially wary. They were already working on a number of projects, such as Dead Horse Ranch, Boyce Thompson Arboretum, and Tonto Natural Bridge. They were just getting involved in the creation of Catalina State Park. Even so, it was just too awkward to turn down the former governor of Arizona who had signed the bill that created the Arizona State Parks Board. Arizona State Parks went ahead with the project.

McFarland purchased the old courthouse in late 1974. In December of that year, he donated the building to the Arizona State Parks Board along with a thirty-seven thousand dollar endowment and thirty thousand dollars' worth of Mountain Bell telephone bonds to help fund the maintenance and operation of the park. As a condition of the gift, the Arizona State Parks Board agreed to the creation of a seventeen-member advisory board to guide the rehabilitation of the building. This advisory board seemed to represent McFarland's life in miniature. The membership of this first board included the presidents of Arizona State University and the University of Arizona (where he had received honorary law degrees), a representative from the Stanford University, representatives of the University of Oklahoma and the East Central State College in Oklahoma (schools Mac had attended), the mayor of Florence, McFarland's sister, a representative of the local historical society, and several individuals who had been on one of his staffs or had worked with him over the years.[53]

It took four years for Arizona State Parks' staff to rehabilitate the former courthouse into a museum. Part of the delay involved funds. The money McFarland had given the board for restoration work did not cover daily operating expenses. When the state legislature did not allocate funds for the park for the 1976–1977 fiscal year, the opening date had to be pushed back. Gradually, however, reconstruction work continued. In March 1977, parts of the old courthouse opened to the public as part of Arizona State Parks' twentieth anniversary celebrations. In addition, the agency constructed a separate building to house McFarland's papers. On January 27, 1979, Governor Bruce Babbitt paid tribute to former Governor McFarland in a ceremony that officially dedicated the completed park.[54]

Riordan

In a few instances, board members were active participants in the creation of a given state park. One such member was Duane D. Miller, a Sedona rancher who played a key role in establishing Riordan State Historic Park. In the late nineteenth century, the lumber industry in Flagstaff boomed, with the dominant family being the Riordans. Not long after arriving in Flagstaff, two brothers, Timothy and Michael Riordan, quickly became among the wealthiest members of Flagstaff society. Their financial success enabled them to build an impressive mansion on a small knoll near downtown. In 1904, they commissioned Charles Whittlesey, the architect of the Grand Canyon's El Tovar Hotel, to design the home. Constructed of logs in an arts and crafts style, the building was actually a duplex of two separate mansions connected by a common billiard room, or "rendezvous wing." The Riordans entertained guests with a wide range of novelties and features. Among the amenities were a series of windows in the billiard room that were not just window glass—they were photographs of the Southwest on glass plates taken by photographer Jack Hillers. The Riordans gave their home the Navajo name of Kinlichi.[55]

Over the years, the two families of Timothy and Michael grew up in the duplex. By the 1970s, however, Blanche Riordan Chambers (Michael's daughter) and her brother-in-law, Robert L. Chambers, found themselves in possession of a complex that required a lot of maintenance and upkeep. Robert Chambers approached the family's long-time friends Duane and Beverly Miller about donating the house to the Arizona State Parks Board. Although preliminary discussions

Close relations between the Riordan family and that of state parks board member Duane Miller enabled Arizona State Parks to acquire the Riordan mansion in Flagstaff. The home at Riordan Mansion State Historic Park is actually a duplex, and for many years only one half was open to the public while the other half remained a residence.

on the matter began in 1972, it was not until late 1977 that Miller, State Parks Director Michael Ramnes, and Chambers renewed efforts to consider a state park at the mansion. Chambers proposed donating the home and the surrounding five acres to the board on the condition that he be allowed to live in his half of the house until his death. After only a few months of deliberation, the board willingly accepted the gift in December 1977. After Director Michael Ramnes and staff member Charles Eatherly met with Blanche Chambers in her bedroom on the estate, she agreed to donate her interest in the property after reserving a life estate for herself.

In December 1978, the board acquired the property and much of its contents. However, the Chambers had also sold forty-five acres surrounding the house to a development firm. As the firm developed its holdings, Arizona State Parks' staff had to work to ensure there would be appropriate access to the site. Like many state parks, the Riordan estate was increasingly surrounded by urban development. It maintained a slice of the original landscape in the face of encroaching strip malls and gas stations.

After Robert Chambers's death in 1980, work began on restoring the east wing of the house. The process took several years, with the park finally open on August 4, 1983. During this time Blanche Chambers continued to live in the west wing of the house but seldom left her quarters. Staff could work at the site for months without ever seeing their housemate, leaving some of them to wonder if she had, in fact, already passed on. After Blanche Chambers's confirmed death in the 1980s, staff worked on Michael Riordan's side of the house, a process that took over fifteen years. The west wing opened in January 2002.[56]

Rivalries and Connections

Although the story of historic preservation in the United States has centered on organizations such as the National Trust for Historic Preservation and federal policies such as the National Historic Preservation Act, historic preservation in the United States has often been a local endeavor. Prior to the passage of the National Historic Preservation Act, it was usually up to communities and individuals to identify significant historic sites and move to preserve them. In an era without tax credits and federal grants to promote preservation, the way to fund restoration efforts at historic sites often involved turning the place into a museum to attract tourist business. Tourism was the initial spark for historic preservation in places such Tombstone. In Arizona, as elsewhere in the region, local boosters saw community development and a restoration of that community's past as intertwined. Downplaying agricultural and industrial development, they reshaped the public memory of their communities to focus on the Old West, a mythologized world of cowboys and outlaws. Their preservation efforts often focused on buildings that reinforced that image, such as courthouses and prisons. The early park promoters often included Ernest McFarland and others whom Hal Rothman has called "neonatives": people who moved in from the outside, were captivated with the romance and character of their adopted community, and worked to ensure that character was maintained and promoted. Creating museums or monuments was a common way for these neonatives to reinforce the community image as they saw it. These parks came about because they enshrined the image that the local leaders wanted to promote but could not afford to maintain. In each case, the community found that running a historic site was costly and demanding.

Many of the people behind these first state parks were women. They ranged from Edna Landin to Gay Griffin to Clarissa Winsor. Some were neonatives, but others came from a long line of Arizonans. It was these women, working through community organizations, who helped push for parks in a number of Arizona communities. While women's clubs were active in preservation in earlier generations, by the 1950s and 1960s, it appears that, at least in Arizona, women played important roles in directing community-wide groups and efforts to preserve historic structures and designate prominent buildings as parks and museums.[57]

Arizona State Parks emerged just as these individuals, organizations, and communities were looking for options in restoring or operating their respective sites. As these boosters saw it, Arizona State Parks could be an important partner in helping them redevelop their communities. Having a place designated a "park" also gave a site, and therefore a community, a legitimacy of being especially important to experience. State parks, like their federally operated counterparts, served as important fixtures in several towns' attempts at drawing tourists—akin to an "anchor store" in a shopping mall. With communities and individuals willing to donate or sell these structures at low cost to the state, the process for acquiring these earliest parks was relatively easy.

The result was that most of the historic sites that the Arizona State Parks Board acquired already had histories, even in a limited form, as monuments or museums. Riordan Mansion and the Douglas Mansion, which had been private residences until becoming state parks, were the exceptions. Tombstone, Yuma Territorial Prison, and Fort Verde were community museums by the time Arizona State Parks was involved. Picacho Peak had been a noted landmark since the nineteenth century. Even McFarland had been a county museum at one point. Those sites that were not already museums, such as Jerome and Tubac, emerged in the context of communities establishing themselves as tourist sites.

Yet Arizona State Parks was only one of a number of organizations involved in saving historic structures. One of the main challenges in creating historic parks in Arizona involved the presence of rival organizations, especially the AHS. This meant that donors had options in deciding to whom to give or sell their historic properties. The State Parks Board's often reactive nature in these early years made room for the AHS to move in to acquire several sites, including Guevavi and Calabasas.

Meanwhile, the entire concept of managing historic structures was changing. Programs such as those established under the National Historic Preservation Act reduced the need to turn every historic structure into a museum in order to save it. Instead, tax incentives and education programs encouraged private property owners, community organizations, and local governments to manage historic sites on their own. Arizona State Parks was still a factor in helping communities save their historic structures. What changed was that the agency oversaw grant programs and other endeavors to help communities maintain the museums and historic sites that they had. It was more than a potential foster home for museums and historic monuments.

Chapter 3 **Water in the Desert**
Lakes Become Parks

For much of the interior West, and for many other parts of the country, "state park" has become nearly synonymous with "lake." The eloquent writings of early state park advocates have traditionally described parks as preserving stunning scenery or perhaps saving a historic site for future generations. Yet the humble recreational park located along a lake or river emerged as the lifeblood of many state park systems. New Deal–era work to develop recreational facilities at lakes launched state park systems in the South and the Midwest. After World War II, the rise of tourism and boating resulted in lakes being standard features of state park systems nationwide, including the West. No longer just a hobby for those who lived on the coast or had vacation cabins, boating had become a pastime even for people who lived in the desert.

Gone were the days of portaging everything into the back woods. Boating itself had become more than just taking canoes and small aluminum boats out for a day of fishing. "Boating" now included water-skiing and even houseboating, which enabled people to take mini-cruises for days or even weeks. This new generation of boaters also demanded more facilities. There needed to be docks, ramps for launching, and parking lots for cars and trailers. Boaters demanded convenient gasoline outlets and grocery stores at which to stock up on supplies.

The development of lakes and the rise in boating complemented each other. The years after World War II witnessed the creation of reservoirs throughout the

West. These ranged from minor flood-control projects and local efforts at storing water for agriculture to nationally known projects such as Lake Mead and Lake Powell. Much to the chagrin of a growing environmental movement, once-dry canyons filled with the contents of flood-control and water-storage projects.

There were two major agencies in the dam-building business. The first was the BOR, whose main objective was to build reservoirs for commercial and development purposes, often related to agriculture. The second was the Army Corps of Engineers, which was primarily concerned about issues of flood control. In addition to providing water storage and power, these bodies of water came to serve an additional role: recreation. Although certainly the biggest builder of dams, the federal government was not alone. Private investment and community endeavors developed countless smaller lakes for flood control and water storage, or exclusively as recreational sites in their own right.

As the water levels rose throughout the West, so did the numbers of people visiting them from the burgeoning cities of the region. By the 1960s, there were so many lakes in the West that a pressing question became who could manage the recreational facilities that adjoined them. The Corps of Engineers and BOR were more interested in constructing dams than managing the boaters and picnickers who used the resulting impoundments. While the federal government managed some of the largest reservoirs, much of the work of managing water-based recreation fell to state and local governments.

State park systems emerged in the interior West just as construction of artificial lakes reached a near-frenetic pace. In some instances, state parks officials worked out arrangements with the federal government even before a given project was completed. Sometimes, agencies such as the Army Corps of Engineers sought out tenants but found few takers if a lake was particularly isolated or hard to get to. In some instances, the federal government tried to run facilities at a given lake but found that the effort was not worth the expense and willingly sold, leased, or even gave recreational facilities to other entities, such as state parks authorities. Meanwhile, county and local bodies sometimes found, as did their colleagues who ran historical museums, that they had taken on greater responsibilities than they could handle. State parks authorities seemed perfect caretakers of private lakes that were too big for their current owners to manage.

For state parks officials, the arrangement was attractive as well. Although acquiring land-locked recreational sites could rouse the ire of cattle ranchers or wary federal agencies, many owners of these lakes were actually seeking out institutions to do the management for them. In addition, lakes usually proved to be instantly popular and well attended, making state parks at these sites profitable ventures. It was the rare historic or even scenic park that could compete with the attendance figures of a lake—especially if that lake was in the desert and accessible from urban centers. As a result, state park systems in the West have had a strong tendency toward lake-based recreation since the 1950s.[1]

Federal programs also played a major role in developing water-based recreation in the region. In 1958, Congress created the Outdoor Recreation Resources Review Commission (ORRRC) to look at the condition of outdoor recreation in the United States. The commission's 1962 report recommended that the federal government do more to stimulate the state-level recreational facilities. One outgrowth of this was the 1965 LWCF. Created with the support of Stewart Udall, the fund consisted in part of grant-in-aid programs to the states. State funds were to be channeled through the Department of Interior's Bureau of Outdoor Recreation.[2]

Just as New Deal programs promoted state parks in the 1930s, federal funding in the 1960s and 1970s again promoted state park development. Between 1955 and 1985, total acreage in state park systems in the continental United States tripled. Meanwhile, the interior West added significant numbers of state parks, many of them connected to lakes. For example, most of Wyoming's state parks were state-run recreational sites on BOR lakes. Even in the desert Southwest, lakes became important parts of the recreation landscape.

These lake-based recreational facilities became a common, and in some states prevailing, form of state park in the region. State parks were developing primarily into places for recreation, with preservation of natural, cultural, and even scenic resources secondary in importance.[3]

Table 4.1 Water-Oriented State Parks in the Southwest, circa 1987

State	Number of state parks	Number of state parks on or near places that offered boating
Arizona	21	7
Colorado	39	36
New Mexico	44	18
Utah	46	24

Sources: Young, *The State Parks of Arizona, The State Parks of New Mexico, The State Parks of Utah*; Kleinsorge, *Exploring Colorado State Parks*.

It is therefore ironic but not surprising that a desert state such as Arizona so intently catered to water-based recreation. Traditionally, outdoor recreation in Arizona implied hiking, camping, and hunting. Water-based recreation was confined to fishing along the banks of Arizona's small streams and rivers, stocked by the Arizona Game and Fish Department. From the 1930s on, however, federal projects, state government, and private enterprise made boating and water-skiing popular pastimes as well. For example, the number of boats in Arizona nearly tripled from 15,144 in 1962 to 43,078 in 1970.[4]

The demand for water-based recreation inundated Arizona's existing boating facilities. Initially designed as water storage for farms and cities, Arizona's man-made lakes were ill equipped to handle the deluge of boats that descended after World War II. Not even the Colorado River had enough landings to meet the demand. Boat landings and docking sites quickly became overcrowded. Ben Avery summarized the situation in a 1956 column about Canyon and Saguaro Lakes on the Salt River: "The conquest of these two lakes Saturdays by the family boating clan, the skiers and swimmers is just about complete. . . . The crowds around the landings are almost enough to discourage even the water sports fans. Both Saguaro and Canyon have little room for parking, but for weeks cars have been jammed into the available space like sardines."[5] The description clashed with the title of Avery's column, "Rod and Gun," which embodied the older notion of outdoor recreation that was quickly giving way to new forms. Lake-based activities dominated the Arizona recreation scene through the 1960s and 1970s. The demand for recreational spots that were "cool and wet" was central for a society where more than two-thirds of the population lived in deserts. It made sense, therefore, that in its early years the Arizona State Parks Board sought out and acquired parks related to water-based recreation.

Managing the Funds for Recreation

To meet the needs of boaters in the state, the Arizona legislature passed the SLIF in 1960. Money from the fund came primarily from taxes paid on motor fuel for boats. The funds were then apportioned to the county governments based on each county's percentage of watercraft registered in the state. The SLIF's founders assumed that around one hundred thousand dollars in funds from motor fuel taxes would accrue to the fund. The money was then to be used to develop boating facilities in each county, including boat ramps, parking lots, restrooms, roads, and trash bins.[6]

Arizona State Parks' staff administered the fund for a short time; however, that meant State Parks administered a fund to which it also applied for money. This conflict of interest was too glaring. The situation drew criticism even from Ben Avery. Avery argued against the idea, saying "I didn't want that, I wanted a separate agency to handle it because I knew that State Parks would be taking all the money for parks rather than lake improvements."[7]

A few years later, a similar debate emerged over the federal government's LWCF. The agency that administered the fund determined who received those moneys and developed the state outdoor recreation plan.[8] An obvious candidate for administering the fund was Game and Fish. A much older agency (its current form emerged in 1929), it had managed two of Arizona's most popular outdoor activities, hunting and fishing, for decades. By the mid-1960s, the agency had set up or managed nearly twenty man-made lakes and administered more than five hundred thousand dollars in federal moneys each year. With more than two hundred employees organized into six major divisions, the agency of Game and Fish was ten times the size of young Arizona State Parks.[9] Popular with individuals, including columnist Ben Avery, Game and Fish also enjoyed a considerable amount of visibility. Moreover, there had long been organized groups of hunters, fishermen, and wildlife enthusiasts, such as the Arizona Game Protective Association, that had supported these activities. Game and Fish had a natural constituency that Arizona State Parks did not.

Dennis McCarthy and the Arizona State Parks Board both worried that if Game and Fish received LWCF administration, the agency and its political influence would overwhelm the struggling parks agency. McCarthy's friend Ken Smithee of the Maricopa County Parks and Recreation Department was also concerned that Game and Fish might become too powerful. Together they approached the governor's office to ensure that LWCF administration did not go to Game and Fish alone.[10] The parks board argued that because its members were familiar with outdoor recreation activities, multiple-use agreements, and the conservation of natural resources, it should be placed in charge of the LWCF program. Not everyone agreed. Columnist Ben Avery quipped, "Before they [the parks board] merit the role of administrator of the Land and Water Conservation Fund Act, I think they should prove to the people of Arizona that they want to do something for the state, and, of course, I have to aim these remarks at the cattlemen who apparently control the board."[11] To deserve LWCF administration, the board had to prove that it could handle the responsibility.[12]

To strike a balance between the two agencies, Governor Paul Fannin created the Arizona Outdoor Recreation Coordinating Commission (AORCC) in 1963—well before the final bill that created the fund had passed. The body was a three-member committee with McCarthy; Wendell Swank, director of Game and Fish; and Kenneth Smithee. By having McCarthy and Smithee on the board, Game and Fish would be outnumbered two to one on nearly every decision, but this temporary body did not last beyond Governor Fannin's term.[13]

Governor Sam Goddard called for a new outdoor recreation coordinating commission, created by legislative statute, not executive order. The state legislature had explored a number of options regarding who would handle LWCF activities. One proposal, Senate Bill 82, called for a three-person committee similar to Fannin's, consisting of the State Parks director, the director of the Game and Fish Department, and the president of the County Board of Supervisors Association. The bill passed with widespread bipartisan support. Even Ken Smithee and Ben Avery endorsed the measure as a valid compromise between the parks board and Game and Fish. The new AORCC came into being. Arizona State Parks had representation on AORCC but shared that voice with Game and Fish. With its duties of outdoor planning and administering the federal LWCF grants-in-aid program, AORCC seemed a better agency to administer the SLIF. For nearly twenty years, this body influenced and shaped how outdoor recreation functioned in Arizona.[14]

Lyman Lake

The Arizona State Parks Board's first recreational site was Lyman Lake, along the Little Colorado River in eastern Arizona. In the late 1800s, a group of Latter-day Saints pioneers settled in the vicinity of a small Hispanic community along the river, Anglicizing the name of town from San Juan to St. Johns. The community formed an irrigation company and, under the leadership of Latter-day Saints Apostle Francis M. Lyman, built a dam along the Little Colorado. In 1915, this dam failed, sending torrents of water down the river. A small community at the base of the dam was totally wiped out. St. John's, with help from the state, built a replacement. Within ten years of its completion, however, Lyman Dam, named after the man who had overseen the construction of its predecessor, was unsafe and was in need of extensive repairs. The repairs took place in the 1930s and ever since, the dam has held, creating a lake behind it. By the 1950s, Lyman Lake, whose surface area covered about 1,500 acres, became the northernmost and largest of a series of artificial lakes that dotted the area.[15]

By 1960, the board was looking into a number of lake-based projects, including Painted Rocks Borrow Pit and Lyman Lake. Lyman had potential, although the level of the lake fluctuated dramatically, depending on water use downstream.

Lyman Lake State Park was Arizona State Parks' first lake-based recreational site. Promotion of the park's petroglyphs and ruins in later years made it as popular for archaeologists as for boaters.

The board of directors of the Lyman Water Company of St. Johns was immediately responsive to Dennis McCarthy's proposal that Arizona State Parks lease the surface area of the lake and about one hundred acres of shoreline for use as a park. By October 1960, the Arizona State Parks Board directed McCarthy to give the Lyman Lake project the highest priority. The proposal went so smoothly that within a few months, the twenty-five-year lease was sealed. Even before construction on the improvements began, the park opened to the public. The official dedication took place on July 1, 1961. Soon afterward, construction began on facilities at the lake, including a 330-foot-long boat ramp and adjacent parking area. The potential for visitors seemed clear when six thousand people visited the park even before all the facilities were completed. A few years later, the board expanded its holdings at the lake by acquiring a patent for sixty acres from the BLM.[16]

In the years since, the level of the reservoir has varied widely, depending on rain and snowfall upstream and the use of water downstream. In dry seasons, the water could get so low that boating was not feasible in many parts. During a particularly dry year in the early 1990s, there was no water in Lyman "Lake" at all.

Although an annoyance to boaters, the rising and falling water level has been a boon to archaeologists. Excavations in the 1980s and 1990s shifted the focus of Lyman Lake from being just a place to boat and fish to also being a site of archaeological significance. Arizona State Parks' staff developed a petroglyph trail along one of the central buttes of the park that showcased images from the Archaic (6000 B.C.E. to 300 C.E.) period as well as from later cultures. Although Homolovi Ruins State Park was the first state park to be dedicated exclusively to archaeological issues, Lyman Lake deserves to be remembered not just as Arizona's first recreation-based state park, but also as Arizona's oldest state park dedicated to the state's prehistoric past.[17]

Parks along the Colorado River

The central section of the Colorado River was remote, desolate, and undeveloped until the 1930s changed the fate of the river. The BOR, tapping into New Deal programs and money, began to construct several dams along the Colorado to store water for faucets in Los Angeles and fields in Phoenix. To the north, the most famous of these dams, now known as Hoover Dam, created the enormous Lake Mead. At the mid-point on the river between Lake Mead Dam and Yuma, the BOR constructed Parker Dam, primarily as a reservoir of water for the Metropolitan Water District that served Los Angeles. Completed in 1938, the dam backed up the Colorado River to form a reservoir called Lake Havasu.[18]

By the 1940s, the U.S. government brought limited development to Lake Havasu. In 1941, the U.S. Fish and Wildlife Service established the Lake Havasu National Wildlife Refuge to manage the habitat of the animals that lived along this stretch of the Colorado River. During World War II, the U.S. Army Air Corps set up a series of facilities, or "sites," along the river. Site Five, for example, was near Topock; Site Six was on a peninsula jutting into Lake Havasu called Pittsburg Point;[19] and Site Seven was at Planet Ranch near today's Buckskin Mountain State Park. After the war, a group of four veterans who had been at Site Six purchased part of the property from the federal government to create a small fishing resort.[20]

At first, Lake Havasu catered primarily to a handful of very determined fishermen who endured the long distances, harsh terrain, and lack of facilities to get to their fishing spots. In the years that followed, however, visitation jumped from 96,000 visitor days in 1950 to 566,000 visitor days in 1962.[21]

The National Park Service conducted a study of the Lower Colorado River in 1958 and concluded that something needed to be done to provide better visitor facilities at Lake Havasu. To meet this demand, the Fish and Wildlife Service established several facilities and concessions along the lake. One of these was Site Six, accessible at the time only from Topock to the north. Still, these facilities were not enough. The ever-growing numbers of visitors threatened the region's capacity for wildlife management.[22]

Demand for outdoor recreation facilities had reached such a level that in 1961, Secretary of the Interior Stewart Udall established a Lower Colorado River Land Use Advisory Committee primarily to identify areas for national, state, and local recreational areas and wildlife refuges. Representatives from federal, state, and local entities came together to plan the future of the region as a recreational site. Among the participants on the committee was State Parks Director Dennis McCarthy. The committee elected Arizona State Senator Harold G. Giss as chair. The committee pushed for the creation of the Lower Colorado River Land Use Office to help guide the planning process.

Soon afterward, Arizona State Parks and the Lower Colorado River Land Use Office looked at several areas to develop. The result was a prospectus of potential park sites that the board agreed to in principle in 1962. However, the state owned almost no land along the Colorado River. Nearly all of the land was in federal hands. To create parks, the board would have to either purchase land from the federal government or lease it. In 1964, a bill passed the state legislature to allow State Parks and Game and Fish to lease lands along the Colorado River for recreation and wildlife purposes.

That same year, the Lower Colorado River Land Use Advisory Committee published the *Lower Colorado River Land Use Plan.* The plan identified five state park sites: Buckskin Mountain, located at a meander in the Colorado just south of Parker Dam; Lake Havasu Recreation Area, located along the main body of Lake Havasu, including Site Six and Pittsburg Point; Fort Mohave—Colorado River State Recreation Area, south of Bullhead City; Ehrenberg—Colorado River Recreation Park, south of Ehrenberg; and Topock Needles Mountain Park, in the vicinity of Topock Gorge. The plan also proposed further study of the Bill Williams River Canyon between the wildlife refuge and the Alamo flood-control project.

Out of these different projects, only three ever developed into state parks: Buckskin Mountain, Lake Havasu, and Alamo Lake. Board minutes do not mention any major effort to acquire or develop the other potential park sites at that time.

The 1960s witnessed the first major development of recreation along the Colorado River. One result was Buckskin Mountain State Park, which has been especially popular among Californians.

Buckskin Mountain

When the *Lower Colorado River Land Use Plan* first came out, Arizona State Parks identified Buckskin Mountain as the top priority. Energy for the project came in part from the leaders of Parker, who were interested in marketing their community as an outdoor recreation site. The Arizona State Parks Board put forth a proposal for the 1964–1965 budget that included $102,000 for capital improvement and $16,900 for the operation and maintenance of the site. Meanwhile, the board worked out an arrangement with the SLD in which the department would lease a section of the Colorado River called Red Rock Point from the BLM. The SLD then agreed to sublease the land to the Arizona State Parks Board. However, details of the lease arrangements took another year to complete.

In late 1965 work began on developing Buckskin Mountain State Park. Original plans called for establishing an extensive concession area with a motel, gas station, and general store; however, the Lower Colorado River Land Use Office felt that the park was too small to contain all those activities. The board felt that the office was meddling too much in the affairs of state parks but conceded to a scaled-back concession area with only a general store and snack bar. Buckskin Mountain State Park opened to the public in October 1967. Over the years, the park has expanded in size and popularity. In 1981, for example, Arizona State Parks staff developed a small parcel a half-mile to the north, the River Island unit, to be a subunit of Buckskin Mountain.[23]

Lake Havasu

The activities involved in creating Buckskin Mountain State Park were low-key compared to those on upper Lake Havasu. Development of recreational facilities on this section of the river had been part of the Lower Colorado River Land Use Committee's report early on; however, the committee's participants weren't the only ones interested in Lake Havasu. Two California entrepreneurs, Robert P. McCulloch and his partner, C. V. Wood, Jr., also had plans for the area—and much more than just picnic tables and boat ramps. An engineer by profession, McCulloch had a savvy business sense and had developed several major corporations, such as McCulloch Corporation, McCulloch Oil, McCulloch Properties, McCulloch Aircraft, and McCulloch Chainsaw Company. C. V. Wood, Jr.,[24] was also an engineer by training but was especially adept at designing recreational areas. Wood was a major designer for Disneyland; Freedomland, U.S.A.; and Six Flags Over Texas. He was also behind the development that brought the Queen Mary to Long Beach. McCulloch and Wood had become friends and business partners in the late 1950s. Both had a flair for publicity, and together they designed profitable entities that embraced that flair.

In 1958, while flying over the Southwest in search of an inland test site for outboard motors, McCulloch came across the former Army Air Corps Site Six, at the time still run as a fishing resort. He was taken by the place. Three days after first seeing it, he purchased 3,530 acres of private land at Pittsburg Point for three hundred thousand dollars. He later acquired the remainder as a lease from the federal government. The planned site was going to be more than just a test facility. McCulloch and Wood set about developing a model city that eventually became Lake Havasu City. As one acquaintance remarked, "Havasu is McCulloch's baby, but Wood is the guy who spanked it and made it breathe." Construction on Lake Havasu City began in 1964.[25]

Although the Arizona State Parks Board opposed McCulloch's often unorthodox methods of land acquisition, they found McCulloch supportive of a park along Lake Havasu. The board was in the process of negotiating its lease with the federal government for land along Lake Havasu when McCulloch announced intentions to work with the board. He planned to develop several facilities at Pittsburg Point on land scheduled to become part of the state recreational area.

Created in the 1960s, Lake Havasu State Park was once one of the state's largest. Initially, the park was a state operation on land leased from the federal government. In the years that followed, development and land trades significantly reduced the park's acreage.

While relations between McCulloch and federal officials had been cordial, the developers felt that a state recreational area was more suited to the plans that they envisioned. After some months of McCulloch's convincing, the board agreed to push for an extended lease for the Lake Havasu property and to have McCulloch Properties as the sole concessionaire. In return, McCulloch agreed to spend eight hundred thousand dollars to develop the property initially and forty thousand dollars a year on annual improvements to the site.

During the next several months, negotiations took place between Arizona State Parks, the BLM, the Lower Colorado River Land Use Office, and McCulloch Properties. In February 1965, the Arizona State Parks Board entered into a fifty-year lease from the BOR for thirteen thousand acres. Lake Havasu State Park was born, but it took several more years to construct its boat ramps, campsites, and other facilities.[26]

In the years that followed, the concessionaire arrangement proved popular with Arizona State Parks' board and staff. It enabled the development of facilities at state parks through a mechanism whereby the private concessionaire would underwrite the costs in anticipation of making a profit. One such facility was in the very southern tip of Lake Havasu at a place called Cattail Cove. During the late 1960s and early 1970s, Arizona State Parks staff developed its Cattail Cove unit with the help of federal and state funds. One part of the unit was to include a trailer park and concession area. However, finding a concessionaire who had the financial resources to construct and operate such a facility was difficult. It was not until 1973 that the board established a new concessionaire facility at the site. This new concessionaire, Sand Point Campground and Marina, provided services to the lower part of the park and was particularly set up to cater to the needs of retired winter visitors, who stayed for several months. It was separate from the main part of Cattail Cove, which agency staff operated directly.[27]

The creation of Lake Havasu State Park coincided with the development of the adjacent community of Lake Havasu City. Part of the park was subleased to McCulloch for concession development, so the stories of the park and the community became intertwined. The state park became one of many lures that McCulloch used to promote the new town. The population grew rapidly, from 160 in 1964 to 2,400 in 1967. Success at Lake Havasu encouraged McCulloch Properties to develop a new community to the northeast of Phoenix called Fountain Hills.

Relations between McCulloch and Arizona State Parks were not always smooth. McCulloch often had different goals than did the board, such as over London Bridge. McCulloch and Wood were unabashed promoters for their investments. When Wood and McCulloch got word that London planned on selling its famed London Bridge to make way for a larger replacement, they jumped at the chance of bringing another feature to attract visitors to Lake Havasu City. McCulloch was undeterred by such details as there being no natural channel at Lake Havasu that warranted such a bridge. McCulloch and Wood came up with a solution: carve a channel through the neck of Pittsburg Point, make the point an island, and have the bridge span the channel. Not coincidentally, this new channel would be next to the downtown of Lake Havasu City.

McCulloch went to state and federal officials in January 1968 to outline his idea. Seeing compromise as the best course to follow, most of the Arizona State Parks Board, the Lower Colorado Land Use Office, and even Secretary of the Interior Stewart Udall approved the basic concept, albeit with reservations. However, the support was not unanimous. Board member Bert Fireman, an active member in the historic preservation community, was outraged at what struck him as a "Coney Island" venture. Fireman wondered aloud, "Does the State Parks Board actually have any voice or authority in this matter, or are we an impotent body with minor bureaucratic functions adroitly placed between the federal agencies and the public to serve as a buffer?"[28] Given the personalities involved, there was probably little the board could have done to oppose the project even if they wanted to. McCulloch purchased the bridge in April 1968. He then made arrangements to dismantle the bridge's stone exterior, ship it to the United States, and reconstruct it along the banks of the Colorado River at Lake Havasu City.

McCulloch and Wood settled on the idea of having the bridge itself on their own land. The channel would be carved through land that was part of Arizona State Parks' lease. McCulloch again went to the board to trade part of the property his company leased on Pittsburg Point in exchange for the neck of Pittsburg Point, for his new acquisition. Some board members felt that the bridge should be at least partly on state park land, as a feature of Lake Havasu State Park, and so had held off on relinquishing the land for the project until negotiations could be completed. McCulloch and Wood had different ideas. To encourage the board to comply, McCulloch invited them to a reception hosted in part by Governor Jack Williams. The reception celebrated the London Bridge being brought to America and included such dignitaries as the Lord Mayor of London. When members of the state parks board arrived, Governor Williams's assistant immediately called them aside. Board member Duane Miller recounted it this way: "He said 'you are to going to have to make the agreement now. Period. . . . You are going to have to make this arrangement because they have no right to go on and build this bridge, now. . . .' I didn't want to do it and finally it was forced upon us. And of course, in so doing, they got their bridge on their side of the land, too. Our conservation was ended quite quick."[29] In the pressure of the situation, the board had little choice but to give up yet another slice of Lake Havasu State Park.[30]

Lake Havasu State Park, in spite of the complicated negotiations required to set it up and operate it, quickly became the most popular state park in the system. In a few years it attracted nearly half of all visitors to Arizona's collection of state parks. The park was the largest in the system, extending several miles along the eastern edge of the lake. At its northern edge, the park started at Windsor Beach and extended down to the peninsula-turned-island of Pittsburg Point. Farther down the shore, just south of Lake Havasu City, was a separate unit of undeveloped desert called Aubrey Hills, a region known for its bighorn sheep. Because the only access was by boat, the interior of that unit was relatively undisturbed. South of Aubrey Hills lay the Cattail Cove facilities.

By the mid-1980s, much of Lake Havasu State Park did not look very park-like. Pittsburg Point was de facto a part of Lake Havasu City, with businesses and commercial establishments extending along the channel. To Arizona State Parks' board and staff, administering Lake Havasu State Park had become a series of never-ending contracts, subcontracts, concessionaires, and meetings over what to do with development. As board member Priscilla G. Robinson noted to Governor Bruce Babbitt: "I would conservatively estimate that one-fourth of the Board's time, and an important percentage of the planning staff's time, is taken up in dealing with the endless problems of the concession area."[31] Meanwhile, the park's land was increasing in value. During Bruce Babbitt's administration, these issues played an important role in the fate of Lake Havasu State Park and the site that would become Red Rock State Park.

The crux of the negotiations involved Pittsburg Point. In the resulting arrangement (detailed in the section on Red Rock State Park), the Department of the Interior ended its leasing arrangement with Arizona State Parks for Lake Havasu State Park. In return, the Arizona State Parks Board received title to the Windsor Beach unit of Lake Havasu State Park and the lands at Lower Oak Creek near Sedona. With this dramatic reconfiguration, Lake Havasu State Park was split in two. Cattail Cove and the adjacent Sand Point campground became a separate unit, which opened as its own park in July 1989. The Contact Point area and Aubrey Hills remained a part of Lake Havasu State Park along with Windsor Beach.[32]

The 1990s saw a second major change to Lake Havasu. The BLM received pressure from Secretary of the Interior Bruce Babbitt to get more involved in outdoor recreation matters and to develop more recreational facilities. In response, the BLM began to reestablish control over recreational areas it had earlier leased to other organizations. One of these was Lake Havasu, where the BLM had assumed management of federal lands from the BOR. After several years of negotiations, in 1995, the board gave up its leases on BLM land for a parcel of land that included Cattail Cove and Contact Point. By the end of the BLM transfer process, Lake Havasu State Park, once the largest in the system, consisted primarily of the Windsor Beach unit and Contact Point.[33]

Alamo Lake

While the Colorado River forms Arizona's western edge, the two main rivers of the state's western interior are the Bill Williams and the Gila, both prone to flooding. The 1944 Flood Control Act authorized the Army Corps of Engineers to construct a flood-control dam at Alamo Crossing, where the Bill Williams formed from the confluence of the Big Sandy and Santa Maria. It was also where the tiny community of Alamo stood. The purpose of the dam was to keep torrents of muddy water from entering the recently completed Lake Havasu. It was not until 1963, however, that the corps' Los Angeles district started construction, first on

Although many federal agencies were reluctant to part with their major sites, the U.S. Army Corps of Engineers sought out tenants to run recreational facilities at its projects. One of these was Alamo Lake, which became Alamo Lake State Park, on the Bill Williams River.

the administrative center for the project and then on a paved road to the site that extended north from the small farming community of Wenden. Construction of the 283-foot-high dam began in 1965 and took three years to complete.[34]

Although flood control was the primary objective of the project, Alamo was unique in that it was the first corps-built dam and reservoir in Arizona designed with recreation in mind from the outset. At Alamo Dam, the corps built a parking lot and picnic area on a bluff overlooking the construction site so that visitors could watch the work in progress. When completed, the resulting lake of five hundred surface acres extended three miles above the dam site and included picnic tables, a boat dock, and a swimming area. Surrounding the reservoir was the 17,243-acre Ocotillo Game Management Area, protecting the habitat for a variety of animals and birds. However, the corps was in the business of building dams, not recreation, so it worked with the state of Arizona to determine a suitable manager for the lake.

The Arizona State Parks Board was interested in the project early on. The board, in its first ten-year plan, included the creation of state parks in "Selected U.S. Corps of Engineers Flood Control Projects." Alamo was also listed as a potential state recreational area in the *Lower Colorado River Land Use Plan*. Even before construction of the dam itself began, the corps entered into negotiations with Arizona Game and Fish and the Arizona State Parks Board over final management of the site.

The site initially held promise. In 1966, Arizona State Parks staff conducted a feasibility study on the matter. By this time, Dennis McCarthy had changed his mind. He felt that since Game and Fish had such a large stake in the project, perhaps it was better for them to manage the site as a whole. With two state agencies both involved in lake-based recreation, but without clearly defined distinctions, sorting out who was the more appropriate manager for Alamo took time. During the next three years, Arizona State Parks and Game and Fish discussed the matter. The conclusion was that Game and Fish managed several lakes in the state but did not need to operate recreational facilities such as campgrounds. The solution lay with Game and Fish managing fishing at Alamo Lake but with State Parks staff managing the section of shoreline where the Corps of Engineers had built visitor facilities. McCarthy and the board reconsidered their position on Alamo and signed an agreement in April 1969. Within days of that agreement, the board signed a twenty-five-year lease with the Corps of Engineers to operate more than 4,892 acres as Alamo Lake State Park. The lease took effect on September 1, 1969, and the park opened to the public that November.[35]

Development at Alamo Lake State Park continued into the 1970s. State Parks established a concessionaire arrangement for a small store and snack bar operation. In 1977, the board amended its lease agreement with the corps to add an additional 760 acres to the park for additional recreational space. Alamo Lake has since developed into one of the region's major fishing lakes, drawing anglers primarily from Phoenix. Although Alamo Lake State Park is close to Parker and Lake Havasu City in terms of distance, there is no direct road to either of those communities. The only access to the park has been from the south, from the town of Wenden, which advertises itself as "the gateway to Alamo Lake."[36]

Roper Lake

Roper Lake State Park near Safford actually consists of two facilities located a few miles from each other. The larger one is Roper Lake, the smaller, Dankworth Ponds. Roper Lake began with a twentieth-century prospector named Winneford D. Roper. From the 1920s to the 1960s, Roper prospected for copper in the mountains around Safford. He had some success and in 1961 sold his claims to the Kennecott Copper Company and Phelps Dodge. In addition to prospecting, Roper

Local support for a recreational lake in Graham County resulted in the Arizona State Parks Board taking on a series of man-made lakes that became Roper Lake State Park.

loved fishing. During his time as a prospector, Roper had been chased off a prime fishing lake. He swore that would never happen to him again and decided to use the money from his claims to develop his own fishing and recreational lake south of Safford. Roper selected a site known for its natural hot springs and created a thirty-two–surface-acre lake with a small island in the center. (Visitors reached the island by ferry until the late 1970s, when a bridge was constructed.) The Ropers operated their facility for fewer than ten years. In 1969, Marie Roper died and Winneford sold his enterprise to the Arizona Department of Game and Fish.

Dankworth Ponds were twelve impoundments constructed as a privately owned fishing area known for its catfish. They got their name from their builder, Arnold Dankworth, who was also the owner of a local sawmill. Of these ponds, only one was large enough (ten to fifteen surface acres) to support any large-scale recreation. By the mid-1970s, Dankworth, too, was looking for another owner for his venture.[37]

Meanwhile, legislators from Graham County had been pushing for a park in the Safford area since the 1960s.[38] Graham County finally got its wish in 1972. That year, House Bill 2150, creating Dead Horse Ranch, was in the legislature. While in committee, two other projects got tacked onto the bill. One allocated $150,000 for the creation of a one hundred–surface acre, man-made lake to be constructed on BLM land fifteen miles outside of Safford and operated as a state park. The other involved a stretch of the Hassayampa River south of Wickenburg along U.S. 60. In effect, if State Parks wanted to have Dead Horse Ranch, it was also obligated to establish a park in Graham County and one south of Wickenburg. The Arizona State Parks Board knew about the Hassayampa project from Dennis McCarthy, but the Safford lake proposal took them by surprise. The board responded with alarm that this might start a trend of the legislature creating state parks without the board's approval. In fact, not long after this incident, the legislature did exactly that when it passed a bill creating Catalina State Park.[39]

In spite of the board's opposition, the passage of House Bill 2150 forced the agency to look into creating a park in Graham County. The agency did feasibility studies on a number of sites. Most were unsuitable for an artificial lake. One spot was so flat that the lake would have required a dam for almost its entire circumference. Dennis McCarthy concluded that while a lake-based park would be beneficial to the citizens of Safford, it was not financially feasible for State Parks to get involved in dam construction. He suggested that the existing plans were not drawn "based on sound engineering data such as hydrology and soils tests" and that the economic benefits would cover the costs of construction. Initially, the Dankworth Ponds seemed to have potential if they could be expanded into a single seventy-five to eighty–surface acre lake.[40]

Meanwhile, individuals from Arizona State Parks and Arizona Game and Fish started talking with each other on perhaps doing a joint project in the area. The Arizona State Parks Board was under pressure to acquire and manage more recreational sites. Meanwhile, Arizona Game and Fish staff was in the process of constructing several new lakes and was concerned about how to operate and manage the lakes once completed. By 1973, Game and Fish and State Parks were seriously looking at joint management of Roper Lake with the addition of Dankworth Ponds. The two were already discussing similar arrangements with two other lakes that Game and Fish was building: Leslie Canyon and Twin Peaks (neither of which became parks). Discussions between the two agencies over Roper continued during the next several months. State Parks proposed to the legislature that the large multipurpose lake originally proposed was not feasible but that the money allocated to the project be spent on the acquisition of Dankworth Ponds to supplement the arrangements being worked at Roper Lake.

As negotiations over the Roper Lake–Dankworth Ponds project continued, State Parks and Game and Fish differed over some issues. Most important, the board rejected Game and Fish's proposal that the Arizona State Parks Board simply lease Roper Lake. To the board, such an arrangement would give Game and Fish ultimate control over "their" park. Roper Lake was to be a partnership of equals, not a leasing arrangement. Eventually, the two sides worked out an arrangement similar to that proposed at Alamo Lake, whereby the board would acquire and manage the land and surface area of the lake while staff from Game and Fish would be mainly responsible for monitoring fishing activities at the site. In December 1974, the leadership of Arizona State Parks and Game and Fish agreed to the arrangement. Roper Lake officially opened as a state park in March 1975.[41]

Meanwhile in 1974, the legislature authorized State Parks to purchase Dankworth Ponds. For several years, the site was a small facility, separate from Roper Lake. In 1976, after discussion of various options for operating of the facility, the board approved an arrangement for Dankworth along the lines of Roper: Game and Fish managed the fishing at the ponds, but Arizona State Parks staff handled the recreational areas. After five years of the lakes being somewhat independent of each other, Arizona State Parks Board incorporated Dankworth Ponds into Roper Lake State Park. In the years since, agency staff has tried to develop the Dankworth site by including signs and trails that featured riparian habitat and the region's Native American heritage, including a partial reconstruction of a Native American village.[42]

Patagonia Lake

As a stream that ran year-round, Sonoita Creek had been a welcome relief in the Santa Rita Mountains of Santa Cruz County for decades. It was a natural oasis of trees and home to many species of birds and animals. The area's wildlife and potential for recreation caught the attention of the Nature Conservancy, which purchased 235 acres along Sonoita Creek in 1966. They purchased a popular picnic grounds named Blue Haven after the real estate firm of Ted Blue and Associates, which owned the property. Four years later, the conservancy went to Arizona State Parks to see if members of board and the agency were willing to work together on acquiring an additional three hundred acres for the grounds from Blue. Had it gone through, Sonoita Creek State Park would have been one of the first state-owned riparian areas. Negotiations dragged out for several years, however, and in 1972, the arrangement fell through. Yet that same year, the Arizona State Parks Board worked with Blue and Associates to acquire a site along Sonoita Creek: Patagonia Lake.[43]

In the 1960s, several local ranchers and business people, including the mayor of Patagonia, William J. Waggoner, proposed creating a recreational lake along

Patagonia Lake State Park began as a private recreation venture near Nogales. When managing the lake proved too great for its managers, Arizona State Parks stepped in. In recent years, adjacent land became part of the Sonoita Creek Natural Area.

the Sonoita. Although acres of riparian habitat would be submerged, these individuals also saw themselves as engaging in an "ecological experiment" to "stop pollution and destruction of resources right now," by providing a habitat for waterfowl and other animals as well as a place for humans to enjoy. In the mid-1960s, these individuals, lead by Waggoner, came together to form a nonprofit organization called the Patagonia Lake Recreation Association. Their plans were to dam the Sonoita and create a 260–surface acre lake to attract boaters and fishermen. They focused their attentions on a parcel called the Sonoita Creek Ranch and persuaded the owners to donate 80 percent of the land to the association to create the artificial lake. Meanwhile, they received a Farmer's Home Administration loan for $1.2 million to complete the project. Lake boosters even persuaded Arizona Senator Carl Hayden to support the project, making the senator one of its main spokesmen. They also arranged for Arizona Game and Fish to oversee the stocking and management of the lake's fish population.

Construction on the dam started in November 1967. Heavy machinery echoed through the once tranquil creek bottom to move earth into a 90-foot-high dam. By late 1968 the 260-acre lake, now named Patagonia Lake, extended more than two miles up the former river bottom. Work began on some of the additional facilities needed for visitors, such as boat ramps, docks, and rental facilities. Meanwhile, the association stocked the lake trout, bass, and catfish, in anticipation of making their venture a pay-to-fish lake. The association also built the lake's most distinctive man-made feature: a graceful footbridge over a cove near the main marina. In September 1970, the association officially dedicated Lake Patagonia, the largest lake in southern Arizona.[44]

Within a few years, however, the association found that managing a site was often harder than creating it. Being the only body of water in the area without boat-size or horsepower restrictions, Patagonia quickly attracted large numbers of visitors. The association simply could not keep up with the demands, especially regarding health and safety matters. The association hoped that a state agency could take over the management of Patagonia, just as Arizona State Parks was looking for more "cool and wet" park locations. In 1972, while working on the Sonoita Creek project, real estate agent Ted Blue brought the potential of Patagonia Lake to the attention of the Arizona State Parks Board. The board reacted quickly to the offer and began a feasibility study. Blue agreed to hold off on the sale of the land for one year so that the board could work out an arrangement to make the lake a state park. In the meantime, the board looked at several options for acquiring or exchanging lands to acquire the lake.[45]

The Patagonia Lake Project had the fortune of good timing. Individuals from Arizona State Parks and Arizona Game and Fish were starting work together on projects such as Roper Lake. In December 1973, the Arizona State Parks Board and Arizona Game and Fish Commission met jointly for the first time to discuss a cooperative venture regarding Patagonia. Game and Fish agreed to continue stocking the lake and to monitor fishing there. The Arizona State Parks Board would acquire the lake through assuming the FHA loan from the lake's construction and operate the recreational facilities on the shore.

To get the money for the purchase, the board successfully worked with the state legislature to get a bill passed authorizing repayment through the use of state park fees and revenues. This was the first time state park fees were used directly for the acquisition of a park. Prior to this, all state park fees went into the general fund, out of which Arizona State Parks received appropriations. House Bill 2295, which passed in May 1974, authorized the creation of Lake Patagonia State Park and enabled State Parks to use fees and charges to assume the Lake Patagonia Recreation Association's loan. It also provided for a land exchange between the State Land Department and Blue and Associates for lands adjacent to the lake. It took several months to clear up the legal issues surrounding the assumption of the loan. On April 1, 1975, the Arizona State Parks Board officially opened Patagonia

Painted Rocks State Park consisted of two sections: a petroglyph site and a boating and fishing lake along the Gila River. Although community support for the park was strong, Arizona State Parks had been reluctant to take on the responsibility of the lake portion, a concern that was confirmed when tests showed pesticide contamination of the water. The park closed in the late 1980s, and both parcels once again became the responsibilities of their federal owners.

Lake State Park. However, the land exchange portion of the arrangement came a few years later, after Blue and Associates sold the land to Conoco Oil Company.[46]

Painted Rocks

The park that was Painted Rocks consisted of two very different sites: one archaeological and the other, aquatic. Each site had its own separate story. The archaeological component preserved the history of the region's first inhabitants. Rivers such as the Gila were dotted with ruins and other signs of a Native American presence. One such site was Painted Rocks, located thirty miles west of Gila Bend. The Painted Rocks, a collection of boulders a few miles from the Gila River, represent one of the heaviest concentrations of petroglyphs in the Southwest.[47] Exactly who made the markings and why remains a mystery. The site was on the border between the Hohokam and Patayan peoples, and the petroglyphs bore features of both cultures. There were no ruins found nearby to verify who the makers were. With the markings' original meaning lost, early American settlers found the stones only decorative and took some of the smaller rocks to use as landscaping.[48]

Starting with a series of surveys done by the National Park Service in 1957, the federal government began a process to protect the petroglyph site. In 1963, the BLM, which owned Painted Rocks, fenced off the property and provided some security. Meanwhile, the Arizona State Parks Board had listed Painted Rocks (as well as the nearby Gatlin Ruin) in its first ten-year plan. In 1963, the board began the process of acquiring the site from the BLM. Initially, the prospect of developing Painted Rocks into a state park looked promising, and the board was even able to obtain funding for acquisition. The purchase had to be made before July 1, 1964, however, and the arrangement fell through because the BLM did not have the funds to complete an adequate survey in time. With a direct sale out of the question, the board looked into leasing the property. Meanwhile, the fate of Painted Rocks caught the attention of journalist Ben Avery, who spearheaded a move on the part of the Arizona Conservation Foundation to make a small but symbolic donation of fifty dollars to help with the acquisition of the site. The final agreement to lease the Painted Rocks site went through in March 1965. In 1972, the agency received the patent to an additional 110 acres. For its first ten years of existence, Painted Rocks State Park consisted only of the petroglyph site.[49]

The "lake" at Painted Rocks had a completely different story. Flood control on the Gila was as pressing a need as it was along the Bill Williams. As with

Alamo Lake, the corps' Los Angeles district proposed a flood-control dam near Gila Bend. Congress authorized the project in 1950. By the late 1950s, the corps was hard at work constructing a 174-foot-high, earth-fill dam across the Gila. Crews completed construction in late 1959.[50]

Unlike Alamo Dam, with its picnic tables overlooking the construction site, Painted Rocks had only temporary flood control as its main purpose. Painted Rocks Dam was also unique in that it did not create a permanent reservoir, or impoundment. The impoundment that formed could reach thousands of acres during a period of heavy rains but would last for only a few weeks. It was not reliable enough to be a permanent water-recreation site. In excavating material for the construction of the project, however, the corps created a large borrow pit in front of the dam site in the river bottom. This pit filled up with seepage from the aquifer and from periodic releases of water. When first constructed, the "lake" covered 150 acres and had a depth of twenty-eight feet in places.

As the borrow pit started filling in 1960, the community of Gila Bend looked to the dam as a recreational attraction. Dismayed over the Corps of Engineers' decision to simply close off the lake instead of developing it for recreation, locals began contacting Governor Paul Fannin. They also contacted public agencies, including Maricopa County Parks and Recreation Department and Arizona Game and Fish, to find a manager and developer of what the community had hoped would be a major tourist draw. Eventually Arizona Game and Fish agreed to manage the north side of the lake as a game refuge and to oversee recreation on the surface of the borrow pit. The board looked into the site and was initially interested in the possibilities there. The lake held promise. It was near the Painted Rocks petroglyph site, the recently excavated Gatlin Ruins, and a former Butterfield stage stop. In 1966, after looking at the matter, however, Arizona State Parks staff concluded the borrow pit would be more of a regional attraction than a state one and suggested that Maricopa County would be a better steward. Maricopa County was equally reluctant to take on the project.[51]

Neither the Corps of Engineers nor Gila Bend was willing to sit by and let what they considered a prime recreational spot go undeveloped. By 1971, the corps continued looking for a partner to help develop recreational facilities at the Painted Rocks Dam. Meanwhile, the corps spent thirty thousand dollars of its own money on facilities at Painted Rocks. The corps also hired two rangers to patrol the site. Happy with the way the Alamo Dam arrangement had worked out, the corps contacted Arizona State Parks.

Dennis McCarthy was receptive, noting once that "this makes a great deal of sense, since the Parks Board is already operating the Painted Rocks State Historic Park in the vicinity."[52] Developing the borrow pit cost about $150,000, with 50 percent of the money coming from federal matching funds. In 1973, McCarthy sought funding from the state legislature in 1974 or 1975 to support the project. By 1975, however, the situation had changed. The board was already involved in several major projects, including Catalina and the Dead Horse Ranch. The agency's staff was also in the middle of developing a new state parks plan. The Painted Rocks Project had to wait for at least five years until after the plan was completed.[53]

Meanwhile, the town of Gila Bend remained interested in having a park at the dam but did not have the money to run the facility itself. In December 1976, Mayor Willis Williams appeared before the board and encouraged them to consummate a lease with the Corps of Engineers. He pleaded that the corps "cannot justify expenditures without some Arizona interest in this site. I am here to try to get the State Parks Board to reconsider and remove Painted Rocks from the five year moratorium." He noted that there was a need for a lake in the vicinity. As it was, residents from Gila Bend, Ajo, and Buckeye had to drive a considerable distance to get to Saguaro Lake or Lake Pleasant. The board agreed to reconsider Painted Rocks' priority.[54]

Gila Bend wasn't the only supporter of the idea. Groups such as the Arizona Wildlife Federation and the Arizona Bass Federation pushed for the creation of a park at Painted Rocks. For the next few years, State Parks and the corps resumed discussions of the Painted Rocks project. The board wanted to acquire more water-based recreational sites but was unsure it could make the financial commitment to operate the facility, especially given its obligations to its new acquisitions of Boyce Thompson, Lost Dutchman, and Dead Horse Ranch, and with the ongoing efforts to establish Catalina State Park. Studies by staff with Arizona State Parks and Game and Fish found that the water quality at the lake was poor, with only Tilapia and a few other species of fish thriving. In spite of the corps' developments, there were still only limited facilities at the site.

By 1977, the Arizona State Parks Board indicated that it was not interested in further pursuing the matter until some of its other projects had been completed. The fear was that the legislature would approve Painted Rocks and, to fund it, take money away from other projects. Maricopa County was unwilling to participate in a cooperative venture on the matter. If Gila Bend wanted the park, the board concluded, the city could be the local sponsor for the Corps of Engineers. New State Parks Director Michael Ramnes reiterated McCarthy's view that "there were higher priorities such as Catalina, Patagonia Lake, Boyce Thompson, etc."[55]

Undaunted, Gila Bend's mayor went to the legislature. The local supporters of the park were able to persuade their legislators to launch a bill creating a state park at Painted Rocks borrow pit. The bill passed and received Governor Babbitt's signature in May 1978. The legislation appropriated $248,000 for Arizona State Parks to lease the borrow pit from the Army Corps of Engineers. Bowing to pressure from Gila Bend, the governor's office, and the legislature, State Parks finally agreed to conduct a feasibility study of the borrow pit and to lease the pit site from the corps. The Arizona State Parks Board opened the lake to the public in 1979. In spite of Painted Rocks' significant petroglyphs, the borrow pit became the park's main attraction. Only an hour from Phoenix, Painted Rocks Borrow Pit Lake proved to be a popular fishing and camping spot.[56]

Agriculture proved to be the park's undoing. In the 1950s and 1960s, agriculture in Arizona, like in the rest of the United States, made liberal use of pesticides, including DDT. As studies showed the danger of some of these chemicals, their use was curtailed. Arizona banned DDT in 1969 and its successor pesticide, Toxaphene, in 1982, but the damage was done. Through runoff, these and other chemicals found their way into the Gila River. Dams such as Painted Rocks made the problem worse by allowing the contaminated water to concentrate and get into the sediments. In the 1970s and 1980s, water testing by state and federal authorities detected rising levels of these chemicals at the park. In 1983, the Arizona Department of Health warned people not to consume fish from the lake. The Environmental Protection Agency noted that levels of contaminants were not high enough to be considered a health hazard, but they were close, and samples of fish taken from the lake showed traces of dioxin. A few years later, the Arizona Game and Fish Department issued a warning against eating fish from the Hassayampa and Gila Rivers, including from Painted Rocks State Park. In January 1989, in the face of rising concerns over the public safety at the borrow pit, the board closed the lake.

With the park's primary attraction off limits and the costs of cleanup at the site exorbitant, the board looked for new owners. The board attempted to transfer the site to the town of Gila Bend. When those plans fell through in 1990, the board returned the borrow pit to the U.S. Army Corps of Engineers and the Painted Rocks petroglyph site to its original owner, the BLM. With most of public's attention riveted on the Heritage Fund, Tonto Natural Bridge, and Kartchner Caverns, Painted Rocks slipped quietly from Arizona's roster of state parks.[57]

Finding a Place among the "Cool and Wet"

Although a number of lakes were listed on the early State Parks plans, there were few that developed beyond the initial discussion stages. The board had long looked into possibly managing the larger lakes on the Salt River, but board minutes report few additional developments.[58] As with cultural and recreational sites, the board received offers for water-based sites from county, city, and private ventures that wanted someone else to run the costly facilities. Some offers, such as Patagonia, developed into popular state parks. Others, however, were not so feasible. One of these was Nick Lause Park, on the Colorado River near Bullhead City. In 1970, the Mohave County Board of Supervisors wrote to Dennis McCarthy, suggesting that the state take over the management of the park. Mohave County simply did not have the funds to operate the facility. Over the next year, however, the county wavered between wanting Nick Lause to become a state park and simply wanting the state to assist the county in running it. After conducting a feasibility study, McCarthy concluded that the place was in poor condition, needed extensive maintenance, and had low attendance. The board decided not to pursue the matter further.[59]

Another venture that did not pan out was Lake Carl Pleasant, northwest of Phoenix. Maricopa County had leased lands from the SLD around the lake since 1960. In the early 1970s, Dennis McCarthy and the director of the Maricopa County park system, Thomas Wardell, had talked about either making the lake a state park or working on a cooperative arrangement. Some county officials suggested that if Lake Pleasant were made a state park, county funds could be used elsewhere. The question was whether staff with Arizona State Parks or Maricopa County would do the feasibility study on the matter. Ultimately, the two sides agreed to hire an independent consultant, Bivens and Associates, to do the study. The report that came back found that there were insufficient grounds for transferring the lake to Arizona State Parks. The costs of developing the lake were extensive, estimated at nearly a million dollars, yet there would be no significant change in the quality of the visitor experience.

By this time, however, the Arizona State Parks Board had become very interested in the idea. A cooperative arrangement among the City of Phoenix, Maricopa County, the BOR, and Arizona State Parks seemed possible. A growing number of voices in the county opposed the idea, however, and the Maricopa County Citizens Actions Committee had their parks and recreation subcommittee look into the matter. The subcommittee decided against turning Lake Pleasant over to the state (but did suggest making the San Tan Mountain Regional Park a state park). Even columnist Ben Avery had become disenchanted with the agency, suggesting that "it would be a shameful thing for the county board of supervisors to yield to any kind of pressure to transfer Lake Pleasant Regional Park to the state."[60] In November 1973, Maricopa County finally decided to retain control of the park, arguing that "the state had other and better things to do." The following month, the board also concluded that state park status for the lake was "no longer an issue."[61]

In the wake of the Lake Pleasant issue, the board and staff of Arizona State Parks felt several of Corps of Engineers and Salt River Project ventures near Phoenix had potential to be state parks. Arizona State Parks was learning that if it wanted to become involved in lake-based recreation, it was best to get involved early on in the planning stages. The Corps of Engineers was especially interested in working with the agency on three flood-control projects: Cave Buttes, Adobe, and New River. Maricopa County had taken the lead in developing recreational facilities in the area. Representatives from Arizona State Parks, the Corps of Engineers, Arizona Game and Fish, and the Maricopa County Parks met in 1975 to discuss a possible arrangement. There was a nagging question, however, of whether the projects would have permanent impoundments behind them. With that much uncertainty involved, the board was not willing to obligate itself to being the sponsor for recreational facilities at the sites. To date none of those three sites has been developed into a permanent lake.[62]

Of Partnerships and Lakes

Although lakes did not become as prominent in Arizona's state park system as they did in Colorado or Utah, Arizona's story nevertheless illustrates the reasons why state park systems of the late twentieth century have tended to have large numbers of recreational lakes in them. First, the lakes fit a need that other federal, state, and local agencies were not as enthusiastic to take on. Although people from Arizona State Parks encountered resistance from Maricopa County in the case of Lake Pleasant, local governments were more willing to turn over the responsibility of managing lakes to Arizona State Parks than other types of sites, as the next chapter explains. Meanwhile, smaller, private lakes could quickly outstrip the resources of the initial developers, prompting them to look to new owners as well.

Second, the growing cities of the West created needs for outdoor recreation that lakes could serve. Lakes were popular, not just with the public but with the legislators the public elected. In the case of Arizona, legislators pushed through endeavors such as Roper Lake and Painted Rocks borrow pit, in spite of objections on the part of the Arizona State Parks Board.

Finally, acquiring the land needed for such parks was relatively less contentious than for land-based parks. Creating parks in forests or other public lands often conflicted with the interests of other industries, such as cattle or forestry, or major federal agencies. In contrast to the resistance from the Forest Service and BLM in creating parks, the BOR and the Corps of Engineers were very willing to turn their sites over to someone else to run.

Lake-based recreation inherently involved partnerships. The builder of the reservoir, the owner of the land, and the manager of the completed facility were likely to be different entities. Larger lakes had to be constructed with federal help and were almost always on federal land, if for no other reason than that there was so little private land on which to have a lake. Only in the case of very small reservoirs could a private group or individual afford to construct a facility and run it. As the owners of Lyman, Roper, and Patagonia found out, running a lake, monitoring the public, and maintaining the facility and the dam could prove to be costly and difficult responsibilities. Government help, in this case through partnerships, was needed. In its early years the board found itself having to form partnerships with the Army Corps of Engineers or other federal agencies for lakes such as Alamo, Painted Rocks, and Lake Havasu.

Such partnerships were a mixed blessing. At Lake Havasu, for example, the activities of the Arizona State Parks Board were often subject to the interests of the real landowners—the federal government. It was partly for that reason that the board eventually sought to own rather than lease property along the river, even if that meant giving up large sections of leased federal land. Thus, the success of Arizona State Parks' board and staff in providing lake-based recreation has been, and will likely continue to be, an outgrowth of their ability to form partnerships with other local, state, and federal bodies. As the next chapter shows, such partnerships were not so easy to develop for land-based parks.

Chapter 4 Ambitions and Setbacks
The Natural Parks

The early park movements, both national and state, paid particular attention to the value of preserving scenic and natural places. Recreation was an important but secondary concern. Colonel Richard Lieber, a founder of Indiana's state park system and one of the best known state park advocates in the early twentieth century, once noted that he had no interest in parks should they "merely be to provide shallow amusement for bored and boring people. Folks so disposed should be referred to bingo or any other of the abounding inanities."[1] Although less pointed in their comments, other promoters of state parks agreed that spectacular spaces and important natural features were the key sites to acquire. Recreation was secondary. Rebecca Conard has noted, for example, that Iowa's 1917 State Park Act was set up primarily to preserve the state's natural and cultural locations, a goal that later got sidetracked by interest in recreation. Such attitudes made sense in the East and Midwest, where state parks preserved the Adirondacks in New York or forests in Maine. In these regions, state governments were the main public managers of natural resources, controlling large stretches of forest and beach. Likewise, along the Pacific Coast, with its miles of beaches and coastal mountains, many scenic and natural sites lent themselves to preservation as state parks, such as Big Basin in California.

In the interior West, however, with its vast federal lands, the situation was different. By the middle of the twentieth century, many of the prime places were already under federal stewardship. There were scenic national parks and monuments, such as Yellowstone, Mount Rainier, and the Grand Canyon. Other sites were leased to county governments or a variety of state agencies. State parks seemed unnecessary in a region with an attitude of "if it was worth saving, the federal government would have already done it." As one piece on Montana's state park system has noted "considering this vast (federal) resource base and the immense amount of land under public ownership, it is not hard to understand why the state and its residents relied heavily upon the federal government to provide recreation outside of cities and towns."[2] This attitude toward recreation mirrored similar sentiments for natural sites.

The dynamics that prevented the creation of state parks authorities in Arizona and Colorado until the 1950s and 1960s also prevented the acquisition of noteworthy scenic and natural places once those state park systems were created. According to Thomas Cox, for many years, "there existed but one real state park in the entire region—Heyburn State Park in northern Idaho."[3]

By the 1960s, things had changed. It seemed that state parks in places such as Arizona were perfectly poised to succeed. The Arizona State Parks Board emerged at the cusp of a major transformation in how U.S. society thought of land and resources. In the late 1950s and early 1960s, a number of figures in land policy, including Secretary of the Interior Stewart Udall, were redefining the traditional concepts of conservation policy, a movement sometimes called the "new conservation." These individuals argued that recreation and preserving wilderness needed to be fit into the uses of public lands. Meanwhile, the ORRRC suggested that grazing and other commodity-based industries were no longer the most beneficial use of the land and could stand to be curtailed or phased out entirely in certain areas. Recreation and wilderness had become acceptable uses. Such sentiments resulted in programs such as the LWCF of 1965 and the Wilderness Act of 1964. Even on the state level, the compromises over House Bill 72 were in large part to balance recreation and the tourist industry with those of ranchers and other industries.

In reality, Arizona's state parks board faced a number of challenges when it came to acquiring significant natural and scenic places. In the 1960s and 1970s the board tried to acquire several parcels that would have added substantial acreage and visibility to the system. However, the owners and managers of these sites, usually federal or state agencies, had no interest or incentive to turn over these places to the small and inexperienced Arizona State Parks Board. Even money from programs such as the LWCF was not always enough to persuade large federal agencies to let go of what some felt were prime state park sites.

Ironically, the mandate that federal agencies focus greater attention to developing outdoor recreation may have hindered the development of state parks by encouraging federal agencies to hold on to their own lands.

There were also challenges at the county and local government level. Counties had developed large parks of their own or had developed parcels that they leased from the federal government. Parks became valuable assets to developing the local economy. Counties had little incentive to turn over their properties, especially with growing numbers of grants programs to fund development of local recreational sites.

For the state, acquiring the handful of major privately owned sites depended on the willingness of the owner to sell at reasonable prices. Sometimes the existing owners changed their minds, forcing all involved to start over. Even getting parks created with state land could prove complicated.

Meanwhile, the requirement that parks over 160 acres had to be approved by the legislature made acquiring any major site a political event. Parks that had support of a key senator or representative stood a much greater chance of being created than ones that did not have a political benefactor. Endeavors on the parts of local leaders and sympathetic legislators forced the board to wrestle with a number of small projects that diluted efforts to acquire more important places. After two decades of trying to acquire significant natural and scenic parks, Arizona State Parks had only a handful of major sites to show for its efforts. Some, such as Catalina, were the result of a decade of struggle and negotiation.

The late 1960s and 1970s also witnessed the development of the environmental movement from the activities of isolated thinkers to broader public awareness. Books such as Rachel Carson's *Silent Spring* and the writings of Edward Abbey pointed out that development and growth damage the environment. Overpopulation, urban sprawl, pollution, deforestation, and loss of animal species and habitat became national issues. Timber, water, wildlife, and plants, once thought of as individual resources, gained new identities as integrated parts of whole ecosystems. There was also concern that whole systems would be upset, which, if allowed to continue, could threaten human society and human health as well.

Alarmed by these changes, growing numbers of people joined groups such as the Sierra Club and the Wilderness Society. In addition, there were citizens groups and environmental coalitions geared to specific issues, from preserving greenbelt space around cities to limiting pesticide use. The once radical notion of setting aside areas to remain undeveloped as wilderness or natural areas became almost quaint compared to the activism of Greenpeace.

Historians such as Samuel Hays have pointed out the irony that such groups had their greatest strength among urbanites. City dwellers saw in nature the antithesis of the development they saw around them. People in cities visited wilderness (itself a largely urban concept) for recreation and renewal and were not apt to see it as a source of livelihood.

The American West was a major participant in this shift, and in some ways led it. By the 1970s, the West had become home to millions of people, most of whom were urban. These new westerners had become accustomed to visiting parks, lakes, campgrounds, and trails on a regular basis. They had also become numerous enough to challenge the traditional industries in state politics. The old constituencies of cattle, timber, and mining no longer held the hegemony they once did. In the states of the Pacific Coast, the environmental movement was especially strong. In the interior West, conservationist sentiments still held out, but things were changing there as well. Environmental groups emerged to challenge traditional uses of land. Agencies such as Arizona State Parks found themselves catching up with the shift in attitude and tactics.[4]

During this time, the board consisted largely of appointees from two Republican governors, Paul Fannin and Jack Williams. Prominent members included Sedona rancher Duane Miller, park professional A. C. Williams, developer Ralph Burgbacher, and history advocate Bert Fireman. Ricki Rarick remained on the board until 1980. Although the legislature was by this time dominated by Republicans, the partisan ties did not help the parks board. Arizona's legislature was reluctant to allocate money for state parks, and the board did little to lobby for more funding until the mid-1970s. Some, including Duane Miller, understood that if the board was to get its funding passed, it had to show that it did not pad its budgets. Therefore, the board kept its operating budget low and developed a reputation for submitting budgets whose figures did not contain a lot of additional expenses. Yet Arizona State Parks also languished as a fairly small presence in state budget discussions. As Doug Cerf of the legislature's joint budget council remarked, "It has been my observation that State Parks has suffered in budget hearings due to a lack of credibility for the past several years."[5]

The board was caught in a vicious cycle. Its budgets were frequently underfinanced because the agency lacked credibility and visibility. Without the financing, however, the board had almost no means to improve its situation. Getting adequate financing and support for the existing state park system was tough enough, but asking for additional funds to expand the system was even more difficult. Each move to create a new state park required financial assistance, as did any effort to develop the site. It was far easier to get the legislature to create a park than to get it to fund the staffing and improvements to develop it. It was not surprising, therefore, that board members were reluctant to go before the legislature more than absolutely necessary and were wary of programs and park sites that entailed additional responsibilities.[6]

The same could not be said of Dennis McCarthy, who remained as director of State Parks until 1976. From the very beginning, McCarthy had seen the board as serving an important role in providing outdoor recreation to the state. To him, the state parks were the primary but not the only means to achieve this goal. In 1958, for example, he lamented at the California Pacific Southwest Recreation Association Conference regarding outdoor recreation planning:

> In most simple terms, I would see that an already prepared 'state outdoor recreation master plan,' or one even under way, would be a most logical procedure, particularly since ours is a brand new agency. No such plan of the scope and character of your California effort even exists or is even proposed. ... Unfortunately, my agency is not equipped, or even empowered to develop such a plan.[7]

Often it was McCarthy and his staff who guided and steered many of the policy changes in the 1960s and 1970s. By the early 1970s, however, relations between McCarthy and the board became strained. Disagreements over policy and concerns over McCarthy's performance worsened over the years. Disillusioned, the overworked McCarthy began to neglect his duties, landing him into further trouble, and in early 1976, the board fired Arizona's first state parks director.

Replacing him was Michael Ramnes, whose military background brought a more disciplined, structured, and even regimented approach to state parks.[8] The change in tone was apparent even in Arizona State Parks' annual reports. Under McCarthy, the reports were narrative, with discussions about potential park project and recent happenings. Under Ramnes, the reports were spreadsheets of numbers and statistics, with no narrative at all. McCarthy was theoretical and philosophical about his job. Ramnes valued state parks as well but also understood the machinery of state bureaucracy and the techniques needed to get things done. McCarthy brought concepts; Ramnes, procedures. Both, however, struggled to create state parks, especially ones that protected scenery and natural resources.

The Ones that Did Not Make It

Arizona State Parks' story is filled with sites that the agency tried to establish as parks but could not. The board had looked into acquiring a forest of Joshua trees since 1957, when citizens from nearby Wickenburg first suggested that a nearby stand would be a good state park. The most promising site belonged to a local rancher and businessman, J. Wayland Barnett, who leased land from the state and from the BLM for grazing purposes. The proposal initially looked promising, and Joshua Tree State Park even appeared in some very early state parks annual reports in the early 1960s. In April 1963, however, things changed when Barnett faced financial troubles that prevented a clear transfer of the lease.[9]

The board and staff of Arizona State Parks also had an interest in developing caves as state parks. For example, soon after coming on board, State Parks Director Dennis McCarthy pursued acquiring Colossal Cave, at the time on state land leased to Pima County. Pima County, however, was not at all interested in turning over Colossal Cave to the state. State Parks pushed the matter to the point of straining relations with the county, before finally having to back off in 1966. Then, in 1967, the owners of Coconino Caverns, later called Grand Canyon Caverns, looked into selling the property to Arizona State Parks. However, the owners decided not to go ahead with the sale and leased the site to the Fred Harvey Company. About five years later, the owners returned to the board, suggesting a sale would be possible, but by this time, the agency was involved in a number of other issues, and the board voted to table any further action on the caverns.[10]

In several instances, the Arizona State Parks Board actively sought to create state parks at various locations, only to be rebuffed by the sites' existing managers. Among these locations were USFS sites, including Sabino Canyon, in the Santa Catalinas, and Horsethief Basin, a site administered by the City of Phoenix. The board had expressed an interest in Sabino Canyon since 1957, with Tucson-based board member Ricki Rarick especially interested in the matter. Shortly after Dennis McCarthy made his first inquiries about acquiring the property, however, the Forest Service flatly rejected the offer. Negotiations over the property resumed a few years later but did not change the situation.

Likewise, as early as 1958, the board requested that McCarthy look into acquiring Horsethief Basin. A report from the National Park Service on the feasibility of the site stated that construction in the area limited the basin's potential as a state park. The Forest Service again responded that it wanted to keep its responsibility for the site. In 1964, the board officially withdrew its interest in pursuing the matter. The USFS maintained that because of legal difficulties over land transfers, it was practically impossible for the Arizona State Parks Board to acquire the property.

Relations with the BLM did not go much better. One of the largest park projects was that of Aravaipa Canyon in the Galiuro Mountains of Pinal County. Featured in the first ten-year plan, Aravaipa became one of the board's top priorities in the 1960s. Ambitious goals from that time anticipated a park in Aravaipa open as early as 1969. Part of the canyon was privately held, yet a significant portion was part of the jurisdiction of the BLM, with Arizona Game and Fish handling its management. The Department of the Interior designated Aravaipa Canyon Primitive Area in 1969 as a BLM project. The notion of a state park with considerable provisions for public access seemed to be at odds with federal concerns about limiting development in the area.

The state owned a number of parcels of land in the canyon, and State Land Commissioner Andrew Bettwy considered trading several blocks of state land with federal holdings to create a large contiguous parcel that included a state park; however, the head of the BLM's local office, Joseph Fallini (who, ironically, later became State Land Commissioner), was cool to the notion of a federal-state land exchange for Aravaipa, especially given its recent classification as a wilderness area. The federal government reasserted its intent to maintain control of its part of the canyon. Meanwhile, the environmental organization Defenders of Wildlife had managed to acquire a major part of the private land in the region. With other, more pressing issues emerging, the board had little choice but to acquiesce on Aravaipa.[11]

In the 1960s and 1970s, the board looked into a number of other sites, including Cluff Ranch in Graham County, Baboquivari Peak in Pima County, and the Crater Range south of Gila Bend. The board usually decided not to acquire a property either because they concluded it primarily served local needs instead of statewide ones or because acquiring the land seemed to be too costly or difficult to take on. A successful state park program required landowners, both public and private, who were willing to part with their land or at least give up the administration of it.[12]

Tonto Natural Bridge, Part I

Perhaps the best-known venture that did not develop (at first) was Tonto Natural Bridge. Located near Payson, Tonto Natural Bridge was a prime park site. Tonto is the largest natural travertine bridge in the world, and the surrounding canyon

Tonto Natural Bridge had been one of Arizona State Parks' top priorities since the 1950s. Legal issues involving land ownership, however, delayed the acquisition of what was Tonto Natural Bridge State Park until the 1980s.

possesses a stunning beauty. Tourists have visited the bridge for more than a century. In the 1920s, the owners expanded their resort to include a two-story hotel and several tourist cabins. In 1948, the family of Glen Randall purchased the site and made some minor modifications. By the late 1950s and early 1960s, some began to wonder what the fate of the bridge would be if it became the property of less conscientious stewards than the Randalls. One article in *Arizona Highways* commented that "it comes as a surprise to many that, like Meteor Crater, Tonto Natural Bridge is privately owned and not a national monument or park."[13] Tonto Natural Bridge had been considered a potential state park, however, since the report of the Arizona Development Board in 1955. It also appeared in the early plans of the Arizona State Parks Board.[14]

When Glen Randall died in 1967, and the possibility of acquiring the site from the estate seemed likely, the Arizona State Parks Board made Tonto its number one priority. The family was amenable to the idea and suggested the state purchase the property for $250,000. In 1968, a bill creating and funding the park appeared in the legislature. The legislature was not enthusiastic about what they felt was a hefty price tag, however, and the bill died in the House Appropriations Committee.[15] Undaunted, Arizona State Parks, the Randalls, and other supporters worked to get a bill passed the following year, but the state and the Randalls soon disagreed about the value of the property. By now, the Randalls had increased their price to between $300,000 and $450,000. Both sides struggled to find an acceptable figure.

In 1970, the Randall family shocked Arizona State Parks when they announced that they had sold Tonto to a Flagstaff firm called North Star Development. The board and the staff of Arizona State Parks had to start over. As with the Randalls, the purchase price remained an issue. When North Star turned down a state offer of three hundred thousand dollars, state parks looked to create a land trade with state trust lands. By 1972, the proposal for a land trade seemed promising.[16]

Just when it seemed that Tonto Natural Bridge would become a state park, however, a lawsuit erupted among the North Star partners over who actually owned the 160-acre parcel that contained the bridge. The hopes of Arizona State Parks acquiring Tonto Natural Bridge had to wait until the legal ownership could be sorted out, a battle that raged for twelve years. By 1976, the board had to temporarily forgo the acquisition of what would have been one of its most popular state parks.[17]

Dead Horse Ranch was the legacy of Calvin Ireys, who wanted his cattle ranch to become a park for the benefit of his adopted state. Today it is part of the Verde River Greenway, a collection of public and private lands working together to protect a stretch of one of Arizona's most scenic rivers.

Dead Horse Ranch

The Arizona State Parks Board established its first land-based recreational park at Dead Horse Ranch along the Verde River. In 1950, a former Minnesotan, Calvin "Cap" Ireys, had purchased the ranch to make a new start in life. The Ireys family named their acquisition "Dead Horse Ranch" after encountering on the property the carcass of a horse the prior owner had just put down. In the Arizona cattle business, however, Ireys's three hundred head of cattle proved too small to make a profitable ranch, and by 1970, Calvin was ready to sell.

Although only small-scale ranchers, the Ireys had become friends with many of the other cattle families in the area, including that of Duane Miller in Sedona. When Calvin Ireys wanted to sell, he approached Duane Miller, chair of the Arizona State Parks Board, with the proposal of selling the property to the state to be used as a state park. Ireys saw making the ranch into a park as a way of giving something back to the community. A handshake between Ireys and Miller sealed the arrangement. Ireys's only stipulation was that the park retain the name of Dead Horse Ranch. Ireys's children, however, were quite upset. They had wanted the ranch to stay in the family. Their father objected, noting that the children were each so different that they would likely not make good neighbors and the ranch would end up ruining their relationship with each other.[18]

Miller and Dennis McCarthy presented Ireys's proposal to the board in late 1971. By December, the board harnessed the support of State Senator Boyd Tenney and others to draft a bill to go before the 1972 legislative session. This bill authorized the creation of the park and allocated eighty-five thousand dollars toward the purchase of the property, with money from the LWCF making up the rest of the purchase price.[19] It was the first major appropriation that the legislature made for land acquisition for a state park (other parks had been donations, leases, or land trades). The final cost of the 280-acre park was $125,000, an amount far less than what Ireys had originally paid for the ranch. While going through the legislative process, two riders were attached to the bill: one for a park on the Hassayampa River (never completed)[20] and the other for a recreational lake in Graham County (a project that resulted in the creation of Roper Lake State Park).[21]

Development of the park began soon afterward. One of the most pressing issues involved access. The most direct way to get to the ranch was to cross the Verde River at Fifth Street in the town of Cottonwood. When the owners of the lands adjacent to the ranch refused to sell to Arizona State Parks, the board entered into a condemnation procedure to acquire the properties. The condemnation was only the first hurdle for the entrance area. A few years later, when the Verde River washed out the main route into the park (not once, but twice), the state followed local advice and constructed a wet water crossing, allowing vehicles to ford the river. Later, State Parks built a large and imposing bridge to allow motor homes to cross.

On June 1, 1977, Dead Horse Ranch State Park opened. The local chamber of commerce was pleased, feeling that the park was a "recreational plum." Speaking at the event, State Senator Boyd Tenney praised the work of Duane Miller in getting the park created. Duane Miller could also be justifiably pleased with the fact that three of Arizona's state parks, Jerome, Fort Verde, and Dead Horse Ranch, now lay in his back yard, the Verde Valley. Even before the park opened, board member Ricki Rarick had called the Dead Horse Ranch, "the best park we have."[22]

Even so, the development at the site proved to be more intensive than Calvin Ireys had expected. With motor homes, a massive bridge, and entrance fees for everyone, locals and visitors alike, Ireys was dismayed that his gift to the community was not turning out as he had hoped. In later years, when he decided to sell an additional parcel to State Parks to expand Dead Horse Ranch, Ireys charged

Boyce Thompson Southwestern Arboretum began as a research facility to study the productive uses of desert plants. In the years that followed, the University of Arizona and Arizona State Parks joined efforts to manage this popular attraction on the route between Phoenix and Globe.

full price for the land, making as much on a fairly small parcel as he did on selling the original ranch holdings.[23]

Boyce Thompson Southwestern Arboretum

William Boyce Thompson matched a ruthless passion for empire building with an equally strong sense of philanthropy. During the late nineteenth and early twentieth centuries, his Magma Copper Mine in Superior produced wealth beyond all his expectations. Yet Superior meant more to Boyce Thompson than just riches. He was taken with the sheer cliffs of Apache Leap and the vast stretches of desert. In particular, Boyce Thompson stood in awe of the large, rocky, haunting block of a mesa called Picket Post. At the base of that rock, he built an estate along Queen Creek called Picket Post House.

While representing the American Red Cross in Russia during World War I, now Lieutenant Colonel Boyce Thompson became acutely aware of the issues of famine and the need for food production, transforming him from a mining entrepreneur into a passionate supporter of plant research. In 1920, he established an institute for the study of plants in New York, with a focus on how they can be used to make human life better. Soon afterward, he transformed his estate near Superior into the Boyce Thompson Southwestern Arboretum. On April 6, 1929, a public ceremony officially dedicated this unique site. A few months later, however, William Boyce Thompson died, leaving behind an institution that he hoped would be "a mecca for those interested in the study of desert plants."[24]

In the years that followed, the arboretum became well known to botanists and tourists alike. It was a regular feature in *Arizona Highways,* which continued to recount the legend of the mine owner who became a lover of plants during World War I.[25] Yet by the 1950s, the glowing *Arizona Highways* pieces overlooked the reality of the situation—that the arboretum was an institution in decline. Boyce Thompson died before having a chance to adequately endow the arboretum, and his estate was put into turmoil with the onset of the Depression. Developed out of the passion of one person, the arboretum did not have a large cadre of local supporters who could continue managing and funding the operation. Perhaps symbolically, Boyce Thompson's beloved Picket Post House had been sold in 1946 to a new owner and later suffered from a fire that destroyed almost half of the structure.

By the 1960s, help came in the form of the University of Arizona's Dr. E. Lendell Cockrum. He suggested that the university look into the Boyce Thompson Arboretum as a potential biological field station. In the negotiations that followed, the University of Arizona and the Boyce Thompson Southwestern Arboretum board agreed to a joint operation between the university and the arboretum foundation. Formed in 1965, the new arrangement created an advisory board to oversee the management of the site with two members from the arboretum foundation and three from the University of Arizona. Day-to-day administration came from a director, the first of whom happened to be Dr. Cockrum.[26]

Cockrum quickly realized that the arboretum might benefit if another party got involved to share the work: the Arizona State Parks Board. After seeing an article in the *Arizona Daily Star* about the Arizona State Parks Board being able to access the federal LWCF, Cockrum contacted the board about working more closely together. In August 1965, Cockrum and State Parks Director Dennis McCarthy met in Phoenix to discuss a possible arrangement. The promising talks of 1965, however, did not continue as the board looked to other parks as higher priorities.[27]

The early 1970s were a time of budgetary belt tightening among many segments of the state government, including the universities and state parks. The University of Arizona even considered getting out of the arrangement with the arboretum altogether. A now worried arboretum board went back to Arizona State Parks to see what had happened to the earlier proposals of a partnership. When the arboretum board threatened to pull out of discussions if nothing happened soon, the board directed Dennis McCarthy to resume negotiations. Over the next several years, the three sides discussed ways to work together on the facility.[28]

In March 1976, the University of Arizona, Boyce Thompson Southwestern Arboretum, and Arizona State Parks Board signed an agreement to become partners. In this arrangement, management of the arboretum rested with an advisory committee consisting of representatives of all three agencies. Arizona State Parks' staff ran the facilities that catered to the general public. Given its financial constraints, State Parks agreed to the arrangement provided the other two parties paid the full operating expenses of the facility for the first year of operation. Meanwhile, the University of Arizona maintained the research facilities at the site.[29] The arboretum maintained ownership of the land and general oversight. The arrangement transformed the arboretum into a state park that reopened to the public in a ceremony held on October 1978, with Governor Babbitt in attendance.[30]

Lost Dutchman

The Superstition Mountains have attracted visitors for more than a century, the most famous of whom was Jacob Walz, the Lost Dutchman, whose fabled mine continues to draw the curious to the mountains.[31] In the twentieth century, searching for the mine had become a popular pastime for nearby Phoenix. By the 1940s, a road called the Apache Trail was a highway for tourists from Phoenix to get away into the mountains and to fish in the reservoirs created by the dams along the Salt River. The natural beauty of the region was a factor in both its preservation and its development.

By the late 1960s and early 1970s, the BLM launched a program to develop more of its lands for outdoor recreation. In 1968, as part of that program, the BLM developed 320 acres adjacent to the USFS-run Superstition Mountains in the Tonto National Forest. Known as the Lost Dutchman Recreation Site, the location had day-use units, ramadas, and restrooms. However, there was no BLM staff at the site, which was primarily a picnic area. The only protection was a gate that the BLM opened in the morning and closed at night.

Beginning as a Bureau of Land Management facility, Lost Dutchman State Park provided public access to the dramatic landforms that the U.S. Forest Service administered.

The site attracted more than just picnickers. The lack of supervision at the recreational area attracted squatters to the campground and farther into the Superstition Wilderness Area. By the middle of the 1970s, more than two hundred families squatted in the desert below the Superstition Mountains. Some of them had been homeless for a long time, and others were seasonal workers or new arrivals living out in the wilderness until they found a job and a place to live. Some of them were hippies, or those who wanted to live as cheaply as possible by taking advantage of the open land. Some of them were prospectors searching for the Lost Dutchman Mine. There were no easy solutions. For the BLM, the solution was to transfer the Lost Dutchman Recreation Site to another agency that could patrol it more frequently. Lost Dutchman proved to be more trouble than it was worth.[32]

Coincidentally, Charles Eatherly at Arizona State Parks was friends with some of the BLM staff members and talked with them about the future of the campground. In 1976, Eatherly presented to the Arizona State Parks Board the idea of a making Lost Dutchman a state park. Although the site was small, the board was warm to the idea. Board member Ralph Burgbacher considered Lost Dutchman "a valuable piece of land," with great potential for visitors because it was so close to the Phoenix metropolitan area. The original plans were for State

Parks to purchase the campground from the federal government for $2.50 an acre, or $800. Then a change in policy from Washington, D.C., allowed the BLM to give away land, provided it was for recreational purposes. Arizona State Parks could have Lost Dutchman at no cost.

Because the site was over 160 acres, however, a bill had to go before the state legislature authorizing the transfer. In the spring of 1977, Senate Bill 1287 appeared before the legislature to accept the 320-acre site and to provide almost seventy thousand dollars for the operation and development of the facility. The bill passed, and the official transfer took place on September 1, 1977, with an official opening ceremony in December.[33] The park quickly proved popular to Phoenix residents, who came out to enjoy the scenery and to search for hidden gold in spite of reminders that the site is Lost Dutchman State Park and contains no features that would make it "Lost Dutchman State *Historic* Park."[34]

Catalina

The years after World War II witnessed a tremendous growth in Tucson's population. By the 1960s, developers began planning and building subdivisions in the foothills north of town, along Highway 89. One by one, access points to the mountains fell to the bulldozer and the tract home. The city's once accessible foothills seemed threatened in a sea of suburban development. Then, in the early 1970s, opponents to growth found a place to make a stand against the paving over of the foothills: a former ranch, sandwiched between Highway 89 and the Coronado National Forest, called Rancho Romero. If developed, locals soon learned, Rancho Romero would become a planned community of seventeen thousand. It was the brainchild of John Ratliff, a professor of English at Arizona State University who gradually replaced his teaching load with a successful career as a land developer.

When local conservationists found out about the project in late 1972, they were horrified at what they saw as a rape of the desert. They were also concerned about the impact of development on the bighorn sheep that lived in the foothills above the small Canada del Oro. The following year, a coalition of environmental, hunting, and recreational groups organized to stop the development and to turn the place into a public park. Participants included the Tucson Natural History Club, the Tucson Mountains Action Committee, the Southern Arizona Hiking Club, the Arizona Big Horn Council, the Defenders of Wildlife, and the University of Arizona Wildlife Society. This Rancho Romero Coalition came together partly through the help of an organization called the Southern Arizona Environmental Council (SAEC). The SAEC was a forum for a wide assortment of

Catalina State Park began when Tucson citizens mobilized to protect a stretch of the Santa Catalina foothills from development. A bewildering patchwork of land ownership made establishing the park a ten-year effort. The Santa Catalinas also contain Sabino Canyon, a site that Arizona State Parks had tried unsuccessfully to acquire from the federal government.

groups, ranging from civic organizations and environmental groups to the Coronado National Forest and Saguaro National Monument, and had support from County Supervisor Ron Asta and State Representative Charles King.

Through the SAEC, these groups and individuals worked together on a variety of environmental issues, such as clean air, open space, and water pollution. By the time the matter reached the county board of supervisors, pleas to "Save Rancho Romero" resounded in letters to the local papers. The public outcry against the development helped persuade the supervisors to unanimously vote against the development in September 1973.[35]

In response, County Supervisor Asta had encouraged Pima County to set up an Oracle Road Greenbelt Committee (ORGC) consisting of local, county, state, and federal representatives. Its purpose was to find ways to preserve undeveloped land around the city. Members included political leaders such as Morris K. Udall, Charles King, the superintendent of Coronado National Forest, the mayor of Tucson, and representatives from groups such as the Defenders of Wildlife and the Citizens Committee Against Rancho Romero. Although reluctant to have the site as a state park, the Arizona State Parks Board made its presence felt on the new committee through the presence of Dennis McCarthy, Deputy Director Wallace Vegors, and board member Ricki Rarick. The committee also included Betsy Rieke, a member of the planning and zoning commission, who became a state parks board member years later.

By the time ORGC began planning for Rancho Romero, the project expanded to include a nearly twelve thousand–acre area of desert, foothills, and riparian habitat along the Canada del Oro, from the edge of urban development north into part of Pinal County, near the town of Catalina. To the east lay the Coronado National Forest; to the west, Highway 89. This larger area consisted of 2,865 acres of state land and a bewildering array of private holdings.

Stung by the county's decision against Rancho Romero, Ratliff reconsidered his development in favor of either compensation of $7 million or a land trade with the state. In the expanded area under consideration, however, there was another major player: Lloyd W. Golder III, a rancher who owned a large parcel in the northern section of the park as well as grazing rights on some of the state land. These lands were the southern part of a large ranch that extended into Pinal County. The new park would effectively cut off his ranch house from the rest of the ranch as well as sharply limit his grazing area. He, too, would have to be compensated, preferably through a land exchange. In addition, Golder had subdivided part of his property and sold parcels to more than eighteen other owners, each of whom also had to be compensated. Both Golder and Ratliff were willing to temporarily hold off development of their parcels so that supporters for the park could come up with arrangements for compensation.

Another obstacle proved to be the Arizona State Parks Board. State Parks Director Dennis McCarthy was warm to the idea of creating a park at Rancho Romero, as was State Land Commissioner Andrew Bettwy. The rest of the Arizona State Parks Board were not as enthusiastic. When park supporters went to the board in late 1973, the response was downright cold. Tucsonan Ricki Rarick suggested that Sabino Canyon would be a better state park. Duane Miller, angered at the prospect of being railroaded into taking on a state park at Rancho Romero, was even more forceful when he instructed Dennis McCarthy that "we were not interested in Rancho Romero as a park." Even so, the board instructed Dennis McCarthy to complete a feasibility study on the matter. McCarthy's study concluded that Rancho Romero did qualify as a state park, but the board was still not convinced. After a heated debate, the board voted 4–2 against the Rancho Romero project.[36]

Undaunted, the park's supporters went ahead with their plans throughout

1974. The ORGC managed to get $4.5 million in bonds passed in a county election so that Pima County could purchase certain parcels at Rancho Romero (representing about a third of the land acquisition necessary) and then engage in a land trade with the state.[37] Meanwhile, Representative Charles King worked with the state legislature to pass a bill (House Bill 2280) establishing the park, by now named Catalina State Park, at the Rancho Romero site.

The bill had widespread support except from the organization expected to run the park: the Arizona State Parks Board, which passed a resolution against House Bill 2280 in March. The board argued that that the success of the county bond issue implied that perhaps the site should be run by the county. In spite of the board's opposition, the bill passed the legislature and became law on May 1. Now the board officially had no choice but to work for the creation of Catalina State Park.[38]

The bill authorizing the park was only the first step of a very complicated process. The state legislature had to appropriate funds to acquire certain parcels. Land trades were promising ideas, but Bettwy, a de facto member of the State Parks Board, knew that these trades were difficult to implement. To handle the complex arrangements of acquiring the land, the state established a committee consisting of Governor Raul Castro, Bettwy, and Attorney General Bruce Babbitt. In the spring of 1975, the acquisition process began when Pima County purchased roughly 2,600 acres of Rancho Romero property from Ratliff and from Golder.

The land trades for the remaining Rancho Romero parcels quickly soured with debates between Ratliff and the county over zoning issues for his Rancho Vistoso development, located across Highway 89 from Rancho Romero. Meanwhile, Ratliff waited for Arizona State Parks to indicate what its intentions were regarding the acquisition of the remaining Rancho Romero parcels. He warned that if the board did not act soon in acquiring his property, he might have no choice but to look to other options to develop the land.[39]

Many in the community blamed Catalina's slow development on Arizona State Parks Board's reluctance to act. As a newspaper editorial quipped: "The board may feel that if its members wait long enough, everyone will forget about the park and then they can go about their business of doing as little as possible."[40] The issue came to a head at a State Parks Board meeting in Tucson in December 1975, which seventy-five local citizens attended, including Betsy Rieke, then a spokesperson for the Rancho Romero Coalition. Board member Duane Miller again argued that Catalina should be a county park and that it would be difficult for the board to get funding from the legislature to complete the project. "I appreciate all the work that the people have done," he noted. "I am not saying it should not be a park, but you do realize that . . . if it was a County Park, you would have much more control." Dennis McCarthy, by contrast, believed that Catalina would be large enough to be of interest and significance to the state, even though it was adjacent to a major metropolitan area and most of its visitors would likely come from the local area. McCarthy supported the idea of Catalina being a state park from the outset. Board member A. C. Williams, tired of the impasse and controversy, moved that the board delineate most of the Rancho Romero property as part of Catalina State Park. The board passed the motion 6–1 and thereby allowed work to begin on acquiring the Ratliff property.[41]

Momentum gradually picked up, in part because the supporters for the park reorganized. In January 1977, the Catalina State Park Planning Committee formed to coordinate the support of eighteen different organizations, including the Rancho Romeo Coalition (which soon afterward renamed itself the Catalina State Park Coalition), the SAEC, several state and county agencies, and the local chapters of the Audubon Society and the Sierra Club. Another source of support came from a new organization called Southwest Environmental Service (SES), an organization interested in promoting an array of environmental issues. The director of the SES, Priscilla Robinson, became one of the leading advocates for the park, working closely with Betsy Rieke on this and other local environmental matters. Meanwhile, Bruce Babbitt, who became governor in 1978, began pushing for the creation of Catalina State Park. As attorney general, Babbitt was familiar with the complicated negotiations involved. In 1980, he appointed Priscilla Robinson to the Arizona State Parks Board, guaranteeing the park's promoters a voice in board meetings.

Together these individuals ensured a continued source of energy behind the development of the park. By 1978, their main focus was getting the legislature to pass an appropriation of $982,000 for the purchase of the 285-acre Golder holdings. This was the first major state financial commitment to the park. Temporarily held up by a political controversy between Governor Bruce Babbitt and the senate president, the bill finally passed in May. However, the legislation stipulated that the purchase could not go through until all the state land trades were completed, a task that remained a major hurdle to overcome.[42]

Slowly, the logjam broke. Ratliff and the county finally agreed on the zoning classification of Rancho Vistoso. Soon afterward, the SLD and Ratliff agreed to a land exchange whereby Ratliff exchanged 1,889 acres of his holdings for 2,379 of state land. Meanwhile, the land trade between the state and Pima County finally succeeded in February 1981, with Pima County exchanging the 2,655-

acre Catalina parcel for 4,754 acres of state trust land in the Tucson Mountains. Negotiations between the state and Lloyd Golder finally broke down, however, when Golder could not provide clear title to the properties he held. The board gave up on trying to purchase Golder's property as well as buy out his leases on state land, eliminating the northern half of the park as originally planned. A bill passed the state legislature that reallocated the $982,000 that would have gone for the Golder lands toward the development of the existing park. Negotiations on the smaller parcels varied in their success.

In August 1981, the Arizona State Parks Board agreed to a twenty-five-year lease of the now 5,500-acre parcel from the SLD. Initial rental fee was for $35,333 but would go up as the value of the land changed. By the early 1980s, development of the park facilities began and continued for the next year and a half. After more than ten years of action and activism, Catalina State Park officially opened on May 25, 1983.[43]

The 1983 opening was not the end of the story, however. Development in the area rapidly raised the value of the land on which Catalina sat. Obligated by law to utilize state land for the highest economic value to the state, the SLD had to continually raise the leasing rate to the Arizona State Parks Board. By 1987, the annual lease for the park had almost tripled from the 1983 amount. Soon, the board would likely not be able to afford the rent on the property.[44]

A solution appeared in the form of the Santa Rita Land Exchange Project, a federal-state land trade that involved several parcels, of which Catalina State Park was only one facet.[45] Under the arrangement, the land of Catalina State Park went to the Forest Service as part of the Coronado National Forest. The Forest Service could lease the land to state parks at a much lower rate. The plan had the support of Arizona State Parks, the SLD, SES,[46] the SAEC, and the Sierra Cub. The state of Arizona agreed to the exchange in May 1988, but it took several more years of work before all of the transfers went through, in 1991. Today, most of Catalina State Park is technically USFS land that Arizona State Parks manages, although State Parks does own nineteen acres of the park.[47]

Enthusiasm and Resistance

In November 1961, Secretary of the Interior Stewart Udall noted that "Arizona has the weakest park system in the nation and this is a great concern to me."[48] He blamed both an unresponsive parks board and equally stubborn state legislature, noting, "In my home state of Arizona, I can't even talk to the park people. The Legislature has deprived them of the power to acquire land the state needs."[49]

Udall felt that the board and the agency lacked vision and was unwilling to push for a major acquisition. Defenders of the board countered that the agency was being realistic in a state whose government faced constant budget constraints and whose legislature was notorious for not funding projects.

Both sides had valid points. Arizona's legislature was reluctant to allocate money for state parks, and the board did little to lobby for more funding. Moreover, once the flash of establishing or acquiring a new state park had died down, the mundane but essential work of developing the site or even acquiring the land just could not capture the attention of the legislature or the general public.

There were other, perhaps even more significant obstacles to creating state parks in Arizona. One was that the Arizona State Parks Board existed in a state in which most of the land was already under the administration of another agency, in particular the BLM and its rival, the USFS. Because of the territorial relationship of these two agencies, the Arizona State Parks Board was not able to acquire any major pieces of property, such as Aravaipa or Sabino Canyon. In addition, Arizona had a number of parcels administered by state agencies that predated Arizona State Parks, most notably Arizona Game and Fish. Even county-level organizations had already staked their claims. This meant that the main option lay with small, privately owned sites or parcels that the other agencies did not want to administer. The Arizona State Parks Board sometimes worried that their agency might become the dumping ground for sites that other organizations did not want. A frustrated Duane Miller once wondered, "Are we going to be the Park system for the State of Arizona or all the cities or counties . . . ?"[50] Meanwhile, the failure of the board to acquire such places as Horsethief Basin and Colossal Cave showed the limits in what it could do. Even when private owners were supportive, legal complications, especially over the price of the lands, proved to be formidable obstacles. In many ways, the board had to act according to the wishes of its legislative founders: accepting small parcels from interested donors or sellers so that the state would not have to take large tracts of land out of "productive" use. Where there was public support for a park, however, as in the case of Catalina, a complicated and drawn-out battle could be successful—even when the Arizona State Parks Board was not supportive of the measure.

Catalina represented a new approach to state park creation in Arizona. Earlier parks emerged out of the negotiations of a handful of interested community leaders, such as Edna Landin, or with negotiations among agencies, as with the Colorado River parks. Catalina, along with a few other 1970s park endeavors such as Painted Rocks, represented a more public and statewide approach. Park supporters harnessed the press to create public demands for making a place a state park. Public sentiments inspired local and state politicians to get involved. Although parks still included the development of recreational facilities, the dynamics were akin to those of the growing environmental movement, where organizations went to the public to promote a particular cause. The creation of parks had become public events. These were the techniques that came to characterize many subsequent park projects, particularly those taking place during the administration of Governor Bruce Babbitt.

Chapter 5 **The Babbitt Era**
Creative Approaches

The late 1970s and the 1980s were a turbulent time for park issues on all levels. President Ronald Reagan and his secretary of the interior, James Watt, became infamous for cutting back many of the federal programs that had emerged in the 1960s and 1970s relating to environmental, cultural, and recreational issues. As historian Roderick Nash summarized the situation from the environmentalist perspective, "Turning back the conservation clock at least a century, Watt set out to liberate American business and technology from the restraints of proenvironmentalist policy."[1] Reagan and Watt did not act alone. They tapped into widespread frustration with the federal government, and as a remedy, proposed cutting back on federal programs, including those that favored environmental issues, outdoor recreation, and historic preservation. These sentiments clashed with an environmental movement and historic-preservation movement that had moved from the radical fringe of society to being mainstream.

State-level clashes were just as volatile as the national discussion. At one end of the spectrum were supporters of the Sagebrush Rebellion, who were fed up with federal land policies that they saw as forcing them out of business. Instead, they advocated turning over vast stretches of federal land in the West to the states, with the implication that the state governments might be more open to business, corporate, and commercial uses of the land. Between 1979 and 1982, "sagebrush legislation" appeared in every western state. In Arizona, supporters

Bruce Babbitt served as governor from 1978 to 1987. He harnessed public sentiment to support park projects, tapping into a growing urban, pro-environment constituency.

of sagebrush legislation passed a bill in the state legislature in 1980 (and overriding the governor's veto) demanding that large sections of federal land be turned over to the state. It took a popular referendum in 1982 to overturn the law.

At the other end of the spectrum were a host of citizens groups and activists who supported very different concepts in land stewardship. By now aspects of the environmental and historic preservation movements had been around for over ten, and in some cases twenty, years. A new generation of activists and politicians had come of age, including people such as Governor Bruce Babbitt, an outspoken critic of the Sagebrush Rebellion, who developed a reputation for his work on environmental, recreational, and cultural issues during his term from 1978–1987.[2]

Babbitt emerged on the scene just as western politics was changing. Where rural-oriented state legislatures in the West were still business and industry focused, western governors started developing roles as shapers of policy, sometimes around environmental issues. By the 1970s, a number of increasingly visible and active governors, such as Richard Lamm of Colorado, challenged the hegemony of state legislatures in guiding western politics. Personality rather than party became a feature of governors' effectiveness. Media campaigns often geared to urban voters became standard features of politics. Whether the issue was the environment or race or energy, these governors could direct and guide policy on certain issues—but their influence seldom lasted beyond their terms of office.

The son of a northern Arizona ranching family, Bruce Babbitt was exposed to Arizona's cultural and natural heritage from an early age. His father had helped found the Arizona Wildlife Federation and the Arizona Game Protective Association. The elder Babbitt regularly took his son hiking and out to explore local ruins. Bruce Babbitt's interest in environmental issues continued. In college, Babbitt received a B.A. in geology and an M.S. in geophysics, even doing graduate fieldwork in the Andes Mountains. He went for a law degree but never lost his interest in the natural environment and Arizona's historic and prehistoric pasts. These interests placed him on a course that ultimately led to becoming secretary of the interior in the 1990s.[3]

By the time he started his political career, Babbitt had developed a perspective very different from his cattle-industry relatives. He found a sympathetic constituency among a growing segment of urban voters interested in environmental issues and outdoor recreation. This was the "new environmental West" that historian Samuel Hays has described. By the 1970s the populations of many western states were urban and embraced a different ethic than those who worked in timber, cattle, or mining. These new westerners tended to be more open to the environmentalist approach that emerged in the 1960s and 1970s. They focused on issues such as pollution, loss of habitat, preservation of wilderness, endangered species, erosion, and water shortages. They saw the region's natural areas under threat from development and overuse, although ironically, their own suburban lifestyle contributed to those problems. Their attitudes were reinforced by the energy crisis of the 1970s and the environmental stance of the Carter administration. Looking back on the Sagebrush Rebellion in Arizona, Babbitt was pleased to have worked with the coalition of "hunters, fishermen, bird-watchers, hikers, backpackers—all of us interested in preserving Arizona's natural environment. . . ."[4] This was a core group that he could count on. He courted state and national groups on these issues, taking part in a variety of causes from the work of the Nature Conservancy to participating in the meeting at Montecito, California, that resulted in the founding of the National Council on Public History. When Babbitt became attorney general of Arizona, he was an activist and openly liberal Democrat, and did little to hide that reputation. It was an odd fit in a state known for its populist-conservative nature, a state that produced another prominent figure in the late twentieth century: Barry Goldwater.

Babbitt was also a skilled politician. Like Goldwater, the Babbitt name carried weight in Arizona politics. In addition, Babbitt understood the role that media could play in harnessing and shaping public opinion on a given issue. Conservative politician Jim Kolbe once noted, "He's a natural at dealing with the press."[5] As governor, Babbitt made sure to be on good relations with the media, cultivating an informal, approachable persona. He also understood the importance of creating an image, in this case, of being an environmentalist and supporter of historic and cultural preservation issues. This image would be one of Babbitt's key assets, although some critics have questioned how deep his commitments actually were. To some, the reputation as an idealist masked a more calculating and shrewd reality. Babbitt was a determined individual who was willing to make compromises and work out arrangements to make sure his pet projects happened. On many issues, he used his image and media connections to mobilize public opinion to pressure and even bypass the resistance of the legislature.

Babbitt represented a new type of governor for Arizona: visible, active, assertive, dynamic, and driven enough to make sure his goals took place. This approach naturally made enemies. Cattle interests had little sympathy for someone, even a native son, who seemed so determined to ignore or even oppose their interests. Babbitt did not seem, at least in public, to be especially concerned. As Arizona's youngest governor, Babbitt had bigger ambitions, even running for the presidency in 1986. Although governor, national constituencies were probably never far from his mind.[6]

Arizona State Parks and its many activities became a natural outlet for Babbitt's interests. Here was an agency that dealt with the environment, with historical issues, and with archaeology all at once. In addition, park endeavors helped establish and reinforce his reputation as an activist on the environmental and historical fronts. Babbitt's patronage made the late 1970s and the 1980s a time of growth and expansion for Arizona State Parks—at a time when state park systems elsewhere in the interior West struggled under budget crises. When he became governor following the death of Wesley Bolin in 1978, Babbitt inherited one of the smallest state park systems in the country. A *New York Times* article lamented that "despite Arizona's size and reputation as a top attraction for vacationers, parks lag far behind the state's neighbors in both number and size. Nationally, only Delaware, a fraction of the size of Arizona, has fewer state parks."[7] In 1985, Arizona had twenty-one state parks compared to Utah's forty-six and New Mexico's thirty-nine. Arizona's situation was relatively consistent with other states with high percentages of federal land, such as Nevada, which in 1985 had twenty-one state parks, or Idaho, which had twenty-six.[8]

Acquiring new sites had not been a top priority for the members of the Arizona State Parks Board, who felt their main responsibilities were to develop what they already had. For example, Arizona State Parks' 1980 regular plan in the Statewide Comprehensive Outdoor Recreation Plan (SCORP) focused on developing existing park projects rather than expanding the system. In contrast to the long lists of potential parks found in earlier plans, this document listed only three sites as having high priority for acquisition: Tonto Natural Bridge; Baboquivari, a site already partly in the hands of the Nature Conservancy; and Woodland Reservoir, owned by the USFS. The plan was intended to provide a defense against what the report called "white elephant parks."[9]

Bruce Babbitt had more ambitious goals. Soon after becoming governor, he set out to change what he felt was an embarrassing reputation for the state. First, he appointed a number of individuals to the State Parks Board who had backgrounds in parks, outdoor recreation, and related issues. Priscilla G. Robinson was executive director of the SES in Tucson and a major player in the creation of Catalina State Park. Gwen Robinson was very active in the development of state parks in Yuma and became an important catalyst behind the Yuma Crossing Project. She eventually left the board to take a full-time position developing Yuma Crossing. Other board members included Joni Bosh of Phoenix, who had been involved in the activities between the Arizona State Parks Board and the City of Phoenix Parks and Recreation Department; and William G. Roe, an activist with the Nature Conservancy and a friend of Babbitt's, who served for a number of years with the AORCC before arriving on the State Parks Board.[10]

Babbitt also worked to create a more activist SLD. The governor first appointed Joseph Fallini, the retired head of the BLM in Arizona, as state land commissioner. Earlier in his career, Fallini had gained many years of experience with state parks, although some of his work involved resisting board attempts for land acquisition, such as with Aravaipa. Fallini served only a few years as commissioner, succeeded by his second-in-command, Robert K. Lane, in 1982. When Lane came on board, he brought with him creative approaches to acquiring land for state parks, especially through land exchanges. Such exchanges enabled the Arizona SLD to get around the restrictions of the 1910 Enabling Act, which dictated that state lands had to be used only for profit-generating ventures, not for exchanges.[11]

Babbitt frequently worked on park issues through his Office of Economic Planning and Development (OEPAD), headed by Larry Landry. Through this office the governor worked on planning issues such as land use, parks, outdoor recreation, and archaeology. In 1983, Babbitt even appointed OEPAD legislative liaison Donna Schober,[12] who was already working on archaeology issues, to be SHPO.[13]

The Arizona State Parks Board acquired an even greater role in outdoor recreation when budget constraints forced the merger of the staff and duties of the AORCC into that of the Arizona State Parks Board. AORCC received limited state money to operate and helped fund itself through an administrative surcharge taken from the total cost of each project. Reagan-era budget cutbacks meant less money to fund AORCC's operations. By 1982, AORCC had to receive some state funding if it was to survive, and Babbitt's solution was to place the body under an existing state agency—Arizona State Parks. The news broke when State Parks Director Michael Ramnes announced at the end of a board meeting that from then on, the board would handle the budget of AORCC. The stunned board wondered why they had not been consulted on this issue. The reason was that the decision had just come from Babbitt's office, without Babbitt consulting the board first. In the months that followed, AORCC gradually became a part of State Parks, a process completed in 1984. AORCC continued to exist as an advisory body to the board, and its staff were merged into Arizona State Parks.[14]

Task Forces

Task forces and advisory groups[15] were a hallmark of the Babbitt administration. Each body contained a number of individuals who examined a certain issue and formulated recommendations for future policies. Babbitt created these bodies for a host of topics, including recreation on federal lands, historic preservation, bicycling, and scenic roads. The task forces usually lasted only about a year, but their suggestions guided policy for long afterward.

One of the first task forces was related to historic preservation. At the request of the Heritage Foundation and in the wake of his visit to the destruction at Homolovi Ruins near Winslow, Governor Babbitt convened a Task Force on Historic Preservation in 1980 to develop a comprehensive program for historic preservation in Arizona. In December 1981, the task force submitted its final report and concluded that more needed to be done to improve historic preservation in the state. The direct result of this task force's recommendations was the 1982 State Historic Preservation Act. Although the act's main purpose was simply to clarify issues, members of the historic preservation community, including the Heritage Foundation, praised the act as being a step in the right direction.[16]

Perhaps the most critical task force for Arizona's state parks concerned parks and recreation. Created in June 1981, its goal was to plan state's provisions for outdoor recreation in the wake of declining federal support. This task force had an unusual assortment of members. Robert K. Swanson, president and chief officer of the Del Webb Corporation was chair. The twenty-one-member group included Secretary of the Interior Stewart Udall; Sam Ramirez of the Arizona State Parks Board; Frances Werner, an active member in wildlife-related organizations as well as in the Arizona Fish and Game Commission; a representative of the Hopi tribe; and philanthropist Robert Herberger, who was especially known for his support of the fine arts. Support came from the Arizona State Parks Board, AORCC, OEPAD, Phoenix Parks and Recreation Department, and the Game and Fish Department. In the months that followed, the task force held town hall meetings, met with various constituencies, and discussed matters among themselves. They also incorporated other studies, such as an ongoing survey of water-based recreation that Governor Babbitt had commissioned through AORCC. The task force released its findings in a report in early 1982.

The task force concluded that the main purpose of these parks was for recreation, with preservation as an important but not primary concern. The report defined a state park as "an intensive recreational site of regional or statewide significance available for public use." Rather than simply outlining places that might make good state parks, as earlier plans had done, this plan suggested that the board look for types of parks to develop. Recommendations were for the board to place water-based recreation as the highest priority for development of sites along the Colorado, Rio Salado, and Santa Cruz Rivers.[17]

In contrast to the low priority earlier governors gave to park issues, Babbitt's active involvement in several projects helped him expand the number of parks considerably. The creation of state parks at Homolovi Ruins,[18] Red Rock, Slide Rock, Oracle, and the Verde River Greenway involved a wide array of techniques, from partnerships with federal agencies to creative institutions for fundraising. Each instance, however, had Babbitt as the main force behind its development.

Homolovi Ruins

Archaeological sites had been part of Arizona State Parks' mission since the beginning. Of the sites listed in the first five- and ten-year plans, nearly twenty were directly related to Native American ruins or petroglyph sites. There is little evidence, however, that the board did much to seek out and acquire these places. Painted Rocks, acquired in the late 1960s, was the only park specifically intended to preserve a Native American site, but even that mission changed when the board accepted a lease at the nearby reservoir; Painted Rocks became better known for fishing than for petroglyphs. The board leased the Adamsville site during the 1970s but did not develop visitor facilities there.

One of the first major state park sites to preserve archaeological ruins centered on a collection of settlements along the Little Colorado River known collectively by their Hopi name: Homol'ovi, or "place of the little hills." The largest of these settlements was a collection of four villages, now known as Homol'ovi I, II, III, and IV. I and II were on the east bank of the river, III and IV, on the west. The Homol'ovi communities were part of a string of settlements, with the nearest neighbors being Sakwavayu, better known as Chevelon Creek; an additional site on Cottonwood Creek known in Hopi as Sohoptsok'vi; and a site to the southwest called Nuvakwewtaqa in Hopi but known to Anglos as Chavez Pass. Although pit houses in the region date back to 600 C.E., the largest and latest structures date between the thirteenth and fifteenth centuries, depending on the site. At their height, they were among the largest communities in the region. Homol'ovi II, the largest of the pueblos, may have had as many as 1,200 rooms. According to tradition, a period of drought and flooding along the Little Colorado forced the residents to leave to the three mesas of the Hopi homeland.

Although the homes and public spaces fell into ruin, the Hopi still considered these places living parts of the Hopi world and community. They called these ancient southwesterners Hisatsinom, or "ancient ones." To the Hopi, the ruins are more than just history—they are an integral part of their sacred genealogy. These sites are integral parts of religious practice as well as memorials to the actions and accomplishments of their ancestors. Ruins are not simply abandoned property, as later Europeans would see it. Certain clans have responsibilities for shrines and other sacred places. Even the pottery fragments on the ground are sacred.[19]

This was not the view of later settlers of Arizona. By the late 1970s, the vandalism at the site was devastating, with the ruins pocked with more than seventy craters from looting. *Arizona Highways* once lamented that Homol'ovi II "resembles a combat zone." Destruction ranged from small holes to trenches dug by backhoes.[20]

Homol'ovi was not alone. Pot-hunting had become an epidemic in the Southwest. Only a handful of ruins received protection as parks and monuments. SHPO Shareen Lerner once suggested there might be as many as one hundred thousand ruins and sites in Arizona, most of which were nearly defenseless because of loopholes in antiquities laws. Homol'ovi, however, was able to make some very powerful friends. The SLD, the archaeological community, private landowners, and federal agencies all became interested in Homol'ovi at roughly the same

Vandalism at what became Homolovi Ruins State Park fueled a concern for archaeological stewardship in Arizona. The park emerged out of a cooperative effort among the state, federal agencies, local leaders, and private landowners.

time. The Museum of Northern Arizona (MNA) conducted surveys of the site starting in 1978. Through the MNA, the BLM commissioned archaeologist Charles Adams to survey Homol'ovi I. Adams's 1980 report noted that although the ruins were not as dramatic as those of other sites in the Southwest (for the most part, the ruins were buried and relatively little was visible from the surface), their significance was tremendous. Because of oral tradition and archaeological evidence, the site was one of the few ruins in the Southwest directly attributable to modern peoples at all, let alone with clan designations.

The MNA launched a similar study of Homol'ovi II, published in 1982 by the State Historic Preservation Office. Meanwhile, the looting in the region also caught the attention of a rancher named Michael O'Haco, who owned the land on which Homol'ovi IV sat, and the SLD, which owned the land containing the Homol'ovi II and III sites.[21]

In September 1980, Governor Bruce Babbitt took a tour of Homol'ovi II. Appalled by what he saw, Babbitt vowed to protect the site and pushed for greater protection of archaeological resources throughout Arizona. Along with his visit to Lower Oak Creek later that year, this was a turning point for state parks in

Arizona. At Babbitt's request, the SLD commissioned two feasibility studies to determine whether and how a state park could be set up at Homol'ovi. These reports all suggested that finding a suitable manager was important.

Meanwhile, Fred Plog, an archaeologist at Arizona State University and member of the Hopi Research and Development Company, went out to get the Hopi perspective on the issue. As part of the process, Hopi leaders were taken to a few of the ruins to learn about the extent of the damage. Although the Hopi considered excavations as desecrating sites, they also realized that archaeology was going to be central to convincing the larger, non-Hopi world of the value of protecting these places. What the Hopi wanted most of all was to keep Homol'ovi a living place, and like the archaeologists, they wanted to stop pot-hunting. They also saw Homol'ovi as a tourist draw—drawing tourists away from other, more fragile sites. That said, the Hopi were also concerned that contemporary archaeologists, like a number of their predecessors and colleagues, would want to claim credit for "discovering" the site and then give it a non-Hopi name. These talks were the beginnings of dialogue to balance the ceremonial needs of the Hopi and the research needs of archaeologists.[22]

The community of Winslow, meanwhile, expressed an interest in developing Homol'ovi as a park to stimulate tourism. In 1978, the city had approached the Arizona State Parks Board about possibly establishing a state park at the nearby ruins of Brigham City, a community of Latter-day Saints who sometimes used materials from the more ancient ruins to construct their own buildings. Winslow needed the economic boost that a regional park could provide and went to the state because, as Mayor Dick Bates freely admitted, "the State has more money than the County or the City." The creation of a major archaeological park just outside of town and right off the highway had the potential to be a tourist draw, encouraging people to stay, shop, and eat in the area. Among the local supporters was Lou Ceballos of the Winslow Chamber of Commerce, who was a tireless promoter of the endeavor in the local community. Working with the archaeologists, the state, the landowners, and the Hopi, Ceballos helped bring Winslow into the process.[23]

The consensus of these different groups and interests was that Homol'ovi and the neighboring sites should be preserved as an archaeological park of regional significance. Neither the federal government, limited by Reagan administration cutbacks, nor city or county governments were feasible managers of such a park. Arizona State Parks became the manager of choice for Homol'ovi. Babbitt threw his support solidly behind the endeavor, aware that such a park would not only preserve archaeological resources, but also be a politically appealing endeavor for the northern part of Arizona and the Hopi community.

In June 1983, an advisory group called the Homolovi Management Board (HMB) formed to guide the development of the park. With State Land Commissioner Bob Lane as chair, the board included representatives from the City of Winslow; private property owners, such as the New Mexico and Arizona Land Company and Michael O'Haco; the USFS, Arizona Game and Fish, and the BLM. Accompanying the HMB was a planning committee, chaired by SHPO Donna Schober, and consisting of the representatives from the Hopi Tribe, Arizona State Museum, Arizona State Parks, the City of Winslow, the USFS, the BLM, Arizona Game and Fish, and OEPAD. This organization provided a forum for the different groups interested in Homol'ovi to work together. Through this team effort, the park that resulted became a model for cooperative ventures among agencies, communities, professional archaeologists, politicians, and grass-roots activists.[24]

Homol'ovi still faced two major challenges: getting the legislature to authorize the creation of a park and then getting them to fund the acquisition of the property. Land trades were possible but had the potential of becoming a drawn-out and messy process, as Catalina State Park had been. Fortunately, the issue coincided with a wave of publicity about the need to expand Arizona's tiny state park system. A December 1985 article in the *New York Times* noted that Babbitt was doing a lot to improve the state park situation in Arizona. Arizona had to play catch-up, however, because the system began so late compared to other states.[25]

Even *Arizona Highways* got into the act when, in January 1986, it published a feature story on the Arizona state park system. Echoing the sentiments of the *New York Times* article, this piece noted that in contrast to Arizona's twenty-one state parks, "to the west, neighboring California administers some 280 state parks. To the north, Utah maintains thirty-eight. To the east New Mexico supports state park lands thrice the acreage of the Arizona state parks system."[26] As always, *Arizona Highways* tried to keep an upbeat tone to the article by then stating that efforts were being made to accelerate the acquisition and funding of state parks. The article clearly supported the efforts of Governor Babbitt. It was not by chance that the magazine devoted several pages to the possible state park sites, including Tonto Natural Bridge, Lower Oak Creek (the future Red Rock State Park), Homolovi Ruins, Hualapai Mountain, and Yuma Crossing—all projects that Babbitt and members on the Arizona State Parks Board were actively working on. This campaign coincided with the launching of House Bill 2498, which proposed creating a state park at Homol'ovi, including Sakwavayu/Chevelon Ruins and Sohoptsok'vi/Cottonwood Creek. Nuvakwewtaqa was too far away to be a feasible part of the Homol'ovi endeavor.[27]

The bill also had provisions for creating parks at three other locations. Two sites were archaeological in significance: the ruins of the presidio at Quiburi (pronounced KEE-bur-ee) and the Cerro Prieto—Pan Quemado site. Board member Cabot Sedgwick first proposed what he called the Quiburi Presidio to Governor Babbitt in 1980, suggesting that the site's owner, Tenneco Corporation, might be a willing donor. The Quiburi site included the ruins of an ancient Sobaipuri village and the site of the Presidio of Santa Cruz de Terrante. Cerro Prieto and Pan Quemado were both Hohokam sites located not far from Picacho Peak. In 1985, a developer proposed creating a firearms-based resort nearby, complete with shooting ranges and a seven thousand–square foot Arizona Museum of Military History and Firearms. In response, concerned archaeologists and the AHS went to Governor Babbitt about creating a state park at the sites and acquiring adjacent private land to create a buffer from future development. The bill also called for a park at Empire Ranch. The *Arizona Daily Star* had endorsed the idea of Quiburi and the Empire Ranch becoming state parks, noting that "the state is fortunate to have a governor who appreciates the value of preserving and enhancing sites where the first Arizonans struggled to survive in a rugged environment."[28]

This multifaceted bill authorized the Arizona State Parks Board to acquire and establish these four sites as state parks and allocated $890,000 to fund the process. The Homol'ovi sites were clearly the main focus of the legislation. Even archaeologists who promoted the bill agreed that the other sites served to an extent as bargaining chips—to be sacrificed to protect the Homolovi Ruins should the legislature have some reservations on the matter. In the end, the bill's supporters won out—without even having to give up a single site. The bill passed the legislature, and in May 1986, Babbitt signed it into law at the Homolovi Ruins themselves.[29]

While the three other sites made it through the legislative process, they did not end up becoming state parks. Funding and support went almost exclusively toward the development at Homol'ovi. In March of 1986, the BLM, H. B. Bell Investments of Phoenix, and Tenneco worked out a land exchange to acquire the thirty-seven thousand–acre parcel that included the Presidio of Santa Cruz de Terrante. The parcel became the San Pedro National Conservation Area in 1988. That same year, the BLM acquired the Empire Ranch, which became part of the Empire-Cienega Resource Conservation Area. In 1997, the Empire Ranch Foundation formed to work with the BLM in restoring and protecting the site. In 1999, President Clinton, at the urging of Secretary of the Interior Bruce Babbitt, established the Ironwood National Monument, which contained the Cerro Prieto and Pan Quemado sites.[30]

After Homol'ovi was authorized as a park, the next step was to acquire the land. The SLD exchanged 157 acres of state land for the 160-acre Homol'ovi IV site, with the understanding that the ruins would have a protective fence around them but the O'Haco's cattle still had open access to the rest of the parcel. In 1987, the BLM granted eighty acres containing the Homol'ovi I site to the Arizona State Parks Board. Not long afterward, the board leased almost three thousand acres from the SLD that included Homol'ovi II, III, and IV. John Thompson, whose grazing lease was on the land, agreed to the arrangement provided he would have lifetime grazing rights on the property, with those rights terminating at his death. Other leases and acquisitions followed, including a section of rock art near Homol'ovi II.[31]

Meanwhile, the park's development took place in consultation with Hopi elders. For example, the elders occasionally recommended places where roads should go or not go, so as to divert visitors away from shrines and other sacred places in the park. Fourteen years after vandalism at the site first prompted archaeologists and concerned citizens to protect the ruins, Homolovi Ruins State Park opened to the public on May 27, 1993. It reflected an attempt to balance a variety of needs—tourism, archaeology, sacred sites, and ranching—into one park. Although a long and complicated process, the creation of Homolovi showed what several different interests and organizations could do when they worked together.[32]

Red Rock

Bruce Babbitt was directly responsible for the creation of two parks in the Sedona region. The first was Red Rock State Park, the site of a ranch created after World War II. In a story not unlike that of McCulloch's "discovery" of Site Six, Jack Frye, once President of TWA Airlines, and his wife Helen, were flying over northern Arizona when Helen instantly fell in love with Sedona. Soon afterward, they purchased seven hundred acres of farmland along Lower Oak Creek and called their getaway the Old Smoke Trail Ranch. In its early years, the ranch hosted parties and gatherings. Among the visitors was a young Bruce Babbitt, who often vacationed in Oak Creek Canyon with his family. A few years later, Helen Frye, a believer in reincarnation and spirits, met a religious leader named Paul Twitchell and soon became a follower of Twitchell's religious organization, called Eckankar. With Frye's help, Eckankar purchased 286 acres from Frye in 1976 and began plans to develop a commune and retreat center. However, Eckankar found that it did not have the funds to develop the retreat center as planned and considered selling the ranch even before Helen Frye's death in 1979.[33]

Then Bruce Babbitt literally hiked into the picture. Babbitt once told the story this way:

> On a November morning in 1980 we set out to hike along Lower Oak Creek. . . . As we splashed through cold water and pushed through the undergrowth, I saw expensive new houses crowded up to the streambanks, subdivisions stretching across the fields and fences plastered with "NO TRESPASSING" signs. The stream of my childhood, an accessible, free-flowing waterway dense with blackberries, grapevines, cottonwood, sycamore and alder, bordered by open fields stretching back to thousand foot sandstone rims was disappearing. The unique red rock country, the setting for "Broken Arrow" and a hundred other westerns, was being transformed before my eyes into land of hamburger and taco stands, time sharing condominiums, and subdivisions.[34]

Then, as the hiking party attempted to go through the orchard of the former Frye estate, they got chased off. "Almost immediately," Babbitt recalled, "a caretaker appeared out of the orchard and gave us a firm message, 'Mrs. Frye is no longer the owner, this is private property, and you must leave immediately.'"[35] Bruce Babbitt realized that unless something was done, there might soon be no public access to Oak Creek. He later called the event "that moment that marked a new beginning for the Arizona state parks system." Along with his visit to the ruins of Homol'ovi two months earlier, this visit inspired Babbitt to launch a six-year campaign to expand and strengthen the responsibilities of Arizona State Parks.

Babbitt noticed that the Old Smoke Trail Ranch was one of the last large parcels along the creek that wasn't developed and still had riparian areas in good condition. The former ranch would make a good state park, he thought, but there were challenges. Getting the legislature to fund the $5 million price tag in a recession year was unrealistic. Meanwhile, the site was still relatively undeveloped, and a lot of work would need to be done to improve the roads and public access. The access road went past a number of homes, and the county was interested in having whoever developed the ranch pave the road for the benefit of the other residents (which had been a major sticking point with Eckankar).

Babbitt turned to Bob Lane, at the time still an official with the SLD, for ideas about possible land trades. Soon afterward, Lane came back with an unusual idea, involving, ironically, the Anamax Mining Company. At the time, Anamax

To become a reality, Red Rock State Park required a complex set of land exchanges. In the arrangement, the state acquired land at Red Rock and returned land at Lake Havasu State Park to the federal government.

was leasing nearly four thousand acres of state land south of Tucson as a place to dump tailings and wanted to acquire the property outright. Within six months, Babbitt, Eckankar, and Anamax put together a complicated two-stage arrangement that would get Anamax its land, help the state acquire the Smoke Trail Ranch, and provide additional income to the Eckankar organization. First, Anamax would purchase the ranch from Eckankar. Then, Anamax and the State of Arizona would swap the Oak Creek Canyon land for the parcel in southern Arizona.

One challenge was convincing Eckankar that selling their land to a mining company was a good thing. Babbitt had to promise the group that the land, once in state hands, would not be sold off but would be specifically set aside to become a park. Babbitt and sympathetic legislators, with the help of Arizona State Parks' board and staff, drafted a bill authorizing the land trade, which passed in April 1981. Because of bureaucratic delays, however, the negotiations that should have been finalized at the beginning of the year took several months longer to complete. Finally, at a formal ceremony at the site, Anamax purchased the ranch for more than $5 million. Anamax then immediately traded the 286-acre site for more than 3,940 acres in Pima County.[36]

In November 1981, the agency's board and staff unveiled its proposed development of the former Frye ranch, which generally received a favorable response from the community. The land belonged to the SLD, not ASPB, however, so the board had to formally establish Lower Oak Creek as a park either through a lease from the SLD or by acquiring the land through purchase or a land trade. Persuading the legislature to come up with the money to do either would be a challenge, especially with the legislature just passing the bill creating Slide Rock and Yuma Crossing. Meanwhile, the Homolovi Ruins project was also proving to be a major undertaking, and by 1985, it would require legislative support for the following legislative session.[37]

The solution lay in a second land transfer. Just as complicated as the 1981 arrangement, this endeavor had a new set of characters. At its heart was Pittsburg Point, a part of Lake Havasu State Park that Arizona State Parks managed as a lease initially from the BOR and later, the BLM. The BLM, meanwhile, required the use of state land to complete its part of the Central Arizona Project.

At a meeting in September 1985, individuals from Arizona State Parks, the SLD, and the BLM came together to work out a land trade. The Land Department would give the BLM the Lower Oak Creek parcel and the state trust lands for completion of the Central Arizona Project. In return, the BLM would terminate its lease with Arizona State Parks at Lake Havasu and transfer several holdings, including Pittsburg Point, to the SLD, who would then work out an arrangement with the City of Lake Havasu. As compensation for the end of the Pittsburg Point lease, the ASPB would receive the Lower Oak Creek parcel from the BLM. All parties agreed to the land transfers in November 1985.

Now owners of the Lower Oak Creek site, Arizona State Parks staff could begin to develop it into a park. After several more years of work, Red Rock State Park opened in October 1991. It represented a different approach to recreational parks: the focus was on light use of the land, with environmental education a key activity. There was no swimming or fishing in the creek. Moreover, archaeologists identified more than thirty Native American sites within the park's boundaries, making the park significant from an archaeological perspective as well. It took ten years and two land trades, but the public could finally be guaranteed access to this section of Lower Oak Creek without encountering "no trespassing" signs.[38]

Slide Rock

The second Babbitt-era park in Sedona was farther upstream on Oak Creek at a natural water slide along the smooth rocks of the creek. It had long been a popular spot for Arizonans such as Babbitt, who went there as a teenager. Technically, Slide Rock, like much of the land surrounding the canyon, belonged to the USFS, but the best access was from the south, from a flat section of the canyon bottom that belonged to the Pendley family. The Pendleys had operated an orchard along Oak Creek for much of the twentieth century. In the 1930s, the Pendleys even constructed a series of small tourist cabins along the creek to take advantage of the ever-increasing flow of visitors. Yet Oak Creek Canyon was changing. Crowds increased, placing greater stress on the almost nonexistent parking. The banks along Oak Creek became littered with trash. Shoddily constructed septic systems from summer cabins, waste from cattle and wildlife, and the crowds using the creek contributed to an elevation of unhealthy bacteria in the water.

By the late 1970s, the crowds and overuse, along with the challenges of making the orchards financially feasible, convinced the Pendley family that it was time to sell the ranch. The question was to whom. In 1982, Bruce Babbitt approached the Pendley family about acquiring their homestead as a park. As Babbitt recalled: "I asked, 'would you consider selling it to the state for a park?' The response from Tom Pendley was unequivocal—'I would never, ever sell my property to the government!'"[39] Tom Pendley and his family had found the federal government, and the Forest Service in particular, to be at best awkward neighbors to live with. However, there was a long relationship between the Babbitts and the Pendleys (Bruce Babbitt's grandfather prevented foreclosure on the Pendley homestead during the Depression). This prompted Tom to at least talk to the governor. Even though this was an election year, Babbitt devoted considerable energy to finding a way to acquire the Pendley property, even spending the election day itself at the site.[40]

In talking with his planning director, Larry Landry, Babbitt suggested that a way to get around the Pendley's reluctance to sell to the government would be to create a private sector foundation to support state parks. Since the early 1970s, the Arizona State Parks Board had been considering the concept of an intermediary organization to acquire parcels on its behalf.[41] The Parks and Recreation Task Force also recommended creating a supporting institution for state parks. The time seemed right to establish a foundation, and the Pendley property would be a good test case.

Babbitt created the Arizona Parklands Foundation in late 1982. The organization's founding membership included persons involved with Arizona State Parks, such as board member Duane Miller. Robert K. Swanson, a Del Webb executive who chaired the Task Force on Parks and Recreation, served as president. Philanthropist G. Robert "Bob" Herberger was vice-president, and Larry Landry

Although the slide itself is on federal land, Slide Rock State Park provides visitor access and facilities. To acquire the land for the park, Bruce Babbitt and his staff set up the nonprofit Arizona Parklands Foundation.

was secretary-treasurer. The foundation served as a nonprofit corporation to purchase property and receive gifts of property for state parks. All land acquired by the foundation would be donated to the Arizona State Parks Board as a gift, bypassing the limitations of House Bill 72.[42]

In 1984, the Arizona Parklands Foundation launched an ambitious Arizona State Parks Expansion Program. Rather than acquire sites on an ad hoc basis, the foundation's report listed several sites it believed should be acquired or developed as state parks. Among the proposals was that an act go before the legislature authorizing the creation of fourteen parks:

Bull Pen Ranch. A private parcel on West Clear Creek
Davis Camp. Along the Colorado River
Empire Ranch. A former ranch near Sonoita, owned by Anamax Mining Corporation
Homol'ovi. Hopi Ruins near Winslow
Hualapai Mountain. Former CCC and WPA park operated by Mohave County
Lehner Mammoth Kill Site. A Clovis-point site near the Mexican border
Lower Oak Creek. The future Red Rock State Park
Pendley property. The future Slide Rock State Park
Picket Post House. The summer home of Colonel Boyce Thompson, overlooking his arboretum
Quiburi. The ruins of a Sobaipuri village and the Spanish presidio on the San Pedro River
Thomas Canyon (Baboquivari). Owned by the Nature Conservancy
Tonto Natural Bridge. A privately owned parcel near Payson
Walnut Grove. Located on the Hassayampa
Yuma Crossing. The former quartermaster depot in Yuma

Together, these locations would add six thousand acres to the state park system, involve $7 million in donated land value, and require $22 million in development costs (not counting $9 million for road access). In addition, the foundation proposed cultural centers for Native American and Spanish culture. It also suggested plans be made for future state parks at Box Canyon on the Hassayampa, Castle Hot Springs, the Gatlin site, Muleshoe Ranch, Casa Malpais, Arivaca Lake, and a place along the San Francisco River near Clifton.[43]

Through this foundation, Babbitt seemed to have found a way to make properties, such as that at Slide Rock, into state parks while bypassing the restrictions of the state legislature and the Pendleys' own resistance to selling to the government. Babbitt even recalled that Swanson had been selected as foundation president in part because he had a reputation as a successful businessman to appeal to Tom Pendley. The idea worked. Negotiations over the property lasted almost two years, but eventually the foundation and the Pendleys agreed on a purchase price for the homestead: $3.6 million.[44]

Babbitt's more pressing problem was getting funding to purchase the Pendley homestead. Even with its major corporate sponsors, the foundation simply could not collect the millions of dollars in donations needed to fund the endeavor. Babbitt also mused that "the Arizona legislature was not at all interested in spending money for park proposals by the Governor." What Babbitt needed was a loan—a big loan—to the foundation that the legislature could reimburse. In considering their options, Babbitt and his staff looked to an industry that specialized in making loans—banks.

One of the issues that Governor Babbitt had to contend with during his administration was interstate banking. The major financial institutions in Arizona were very interested in getting the interstate banking provision passed in the state. One morning in late 1984, as Babbitt recalled, "Larry and I arranged a morning coffee at my office with the CEOs to the major banks to discuss legislation to open Arizona to interstate banking." The meeting was straightforward at first. Then, "after assuring them that I supported the concept and would work with them, we turned the discussion to the Pendley property and asked them to come together on a loan to the Park Foundation." Stunned by the sudden change in the discussion, the banks were reluctant to fund the venture. "Naturally they wondered how the loan would be repaid, to which I replied 'you can help us lobby the legislature to fund a purchase from the Park Foundation to create a new state park.'" Babbitt and his staff forged a connection between the interstate banking issues and Slide Rock. In return for state support of the interstate banking provision, several major banks agreed to float a loan to the Arizona Parklands Foundation, with the understanding that the foundation would pay back the loan once the legislature appropriated the money. The banks agreed to the arrangement. Not long afterward, the Arizona Parklands Foundation purchased the Pendley homestead for $3.6 million, and a bill authorizing the creation and funding of Slide Rock State Park appeared the legislature in early 1985.

In his January 1985 speech to the 37th legislature, Babbitt talked at length about the need to improve state parks in Arizona. He concluded that if figures were broken down per person, "we spend less on parks than we would for a hamburger." He noted that other western states had eight times as much land in their park systems. Nationwide, only Rhode Island had less acreage, and only Delaware had fewer state parks. He then noted that several sites would help address this deficiency if they became state parks, the Pendley property being one example. Other projects included Lower Oak Creek, Homol'ovi, and sites along the San Pedro River. The legislature was persuaded. The bill for Slide Rock passed while a seemingly unrelated issue, interstate banking, also became a reality for Arizonans. On June 21, 1985, the former Pendley homestead became Slide Rock State Park. A few weeks later, the board officially purchased forty-three acres from the Parklands Foundation for $3,756,000.[45]

As in earlier days, the actual Slide Rock remained in the possession of the USFS. What state parks acquired was the access to the site, resulting in a symbiotic relationship. Although there was potential at the park for interpreting the agricultural history of the Sedona area, the park's main attraction was, of course, the creek and Slide Rock itself. The USFS gained a partner who was willing to take on the daily responsibility of handling access, crowds, and even cleanup of Slide Rock. In October 1987, the park officially opened to the public.[46]

The bill did not cover just the Pendley property site. It had two other major additions. The first was the creation of a state parks fund. Through the fund, money could be set aside for specific park projects. If enough money could be placed in the fund from gifts, donations, and appropriations, land and developments for state parks could be financed without having to go before the legislature for each project. It was the start of a modest degree of financial independence for the agency.

The bill also authorized the Arizona State Parks Board to acquire and develop a new state park at Oracle (a last-minute addition) and several other sites outlined in the foundation's 1984 report: Yuma Crossing, Hualapai Mountain in Mohave County, Davis Camp near Bullhead City, and Picket Post House at Boyce Thompson Arboretum. Mohave County decided to retain control of Hualapai Mountain and Davis Camp, however, and the Picket Post House plans fell through when the owners refused to sell at the appraised value. Of these ventures, only Oracle and Yuma Crossing (to be discussed in the following chapter) went on to become state parks, both of which proved more complicated than the optimism of 1985 had predicted.[47]

Oracle

The Kannally Ranch was a local institution for the community of Oracle, located north of Tucson. In 1976, the last surviving sibling of the original family, Lucille, died and stipulated two things in her will. The first was that all family artifacts, papers, records, photos, and even furniture be burned. The second was that the family ranch house and remaining land be turned over to the Defenders of Wildlife as a nature preserve to become Oracle Wildlife Refuge.[48] In the words of a rancher who grazed his cattle on the Kannally's ranch, "She was afraid it would end up a political football and get kicked around and end up something else. It was to be a wildlife refuge, not people-oriented." However, the programs and leasing of the facility never brought in the type of revenue needed to run the operation. When Lucille Kannally's modest endowment to support the ranch ran out in the mid-1980s, the Defenders looked for another owner and approached the Arizona State Parks Board.[49]

Unlike neighboring Catalina State Park, Oracle was a relatively easy sell. The board's changing composition made it more responsive to park acquisitions in general. Also, unlike Catalina's cacophony of different claims, Oracle was a single parcel with a very willing seller. At nearly four thousand acres, the park would be one of the largest in the system. Arizona State Parks included Oracle in the Slide Rock Bill. In May 1985, the legislation creating Slide Rock State Park also established Oracle State Park, although no money was specifically allocated for the project. So confident was Babbitt of Oracle's potential that he officially dedicated Oracle State Park on October 25, 1985—before the Defenders of Wildlife had even formally relinquished ownership. The following month the Defenders sold Oracle to the foundation for ten dollars. The foundation then turned the site over to Arizona State Parks. The acquisition of Oracle was quick and clean, the very antithesis of Catalina's torturous story.

The Arizona Parklands Foundation immediately set about developing a plan for the site. The foundation proposed an expansive education center, featuring retreat accommodations, campgrounds, and picnic sites, with the Kannally ranch house as the centerpiece of the complex. In some of the adjacent arroyos, there would be small hidden gardens, including an equestrian staging area, a sensory-sound garden with wind sculptures, and an astronomy garden with laser shows. Meanwhile, philanthropist Bob Herberger offered five hundred thousand dollars for the development of Oracle if the Tucson business community could match it. Del Webb Corporation donated twenty-five thousand dollars toward the match. The Arizona Parklands Foundation projected that $15 million was needed to fully develop the facility. Members of the foundation felt they were on the way to developing another major state park and were sure the community would be pleased with their hard work.[50]

Then came the dedication ceremony. Oracle residents were appalled by the master plan that the foundation unveiled to them—at an event to which half the

Oracle State Park originated in 1985 when the Arizona Parklands Foundation acquired the Kannally Ranch from the Defenders of Wildlife. Subsequent development sought to balance the interests of the local community, nearby supporters, prominent benefactors, and state officials, each with its own goals for the site.

town did not even receive invitations. To many locals, the proposed center looked like a Disneyland-type development financed by outside investors. As Herberger spoke, one girl approached the podium saying, "Leave the land alone. Leave us alone." Herberger's comments about wanting a people-oriented park seemed to clash with the community's ideals of making it a wildlife refuge. As one Oracle resident noted, "I don't think people object to the refuge being opened. It's the way it's going to be opened. If you're going to have extensive building, there's not going to be any wildlife." Board member William Roe, himself a member of Defenders of Wildlife, believed that much of the response was an overreaction because a vast majority of the park would be in its natural state. Yet, Babbitt, the Arizona Parklands Foundation, and staff and board from Arizona State Parks had to back off on the development and reconsider their plans for Oracle.[51]

The ambitious plans of the proposed Oracle State Park never got beyond the dedication ceremony. By 1990, after several years of public meetings, the staff and board of Arizona State Parks unveiled their more modest plans for the Oracle Center for Environmental Education. Yet even this plan did not satisfy everyone.

A park that the citizens of Oracle once hoped would be an asset to their community has remained a source of contention between them and the Arizona State Parks Board.[52]

By now, the buildings and facilities of Kannally Ranch needed considerable maintenance. In 1994, work on restoring the buildings began. While Tucson architects and contractors did much of the heavy restoration work, the project also benefited from a small and determined collection of volunteers who helped restore some of the woodwork and interior artwork. Ironically, the volunteers who showed up tended not to be from Oracle but from a newly built retirement subdivision to the south called Saddlebrooke. In 1996, these volunteers formed an organization called the Friends of Oracle State Park (FOSP) to support the completion and operation of the park and to raise money toward that goal. Theirs was the first incorporated support organization for state parks. FOSP also helped with the park's limited environmental programs. Although the Kannally buildings were restored, a road built, and even ramadas put in, the park required a decent—and expensive—water system before it could open. It also needed a ranger station. At the time of this writing, the park is open mainly to schools and other groups, who can set up specialized tours and programs at the site for limited numbers.[53]

Verde River Greenway

One of the major issues of the emerging environmental movement involved riparian habitat. Concerns over the protection of rivers and the ecosystems they supported led to the passage of the National Wild and Scenic Rivers Act of 1968. In the 1970s, state and local groups also became interested in protecting and preserving riparian resources. Riparian issues emerged even in a desert state such as Arizona. By the time Babbitt became governor, 90 percent of the riparian areas in Arizona were gone, either through development or through flooding from dam construction. One spot that survived was along the Verde River near Dead Horse Ranch State Park. Interest in protecting this stretch of the Verde began in the 1970s, when several people and organizations in the Cottonwood area began looking into ways of saving the river. In 1979, people representing the City of Clarkdale, the Yavapai-Apache Tribal Council, Yavapai County, Arizona Game and Fish, Dead Horse Ranch State Park, Tuzigoot National Monument, and several Forest Service ranger districts came together to form an organization called the Verde Valley Recreation Resource Information Group (VVRRIG). Concerned with providing outdoor recreation in the area, the group's members began working together to coordinate the many different recreational interests in the region.

One of VVRRIG's main activities was to commission the University of Arizona's cooperative extension service to study the recreational resources along this section of the Verde River (also called Cottonwood Reach). Published in 1979, the report suggested that something needed to be done to preserve the natural and cultural heritage of Cottonwood Reach as well as to develop the recreational potential of the area for the new residents and increasing number of visitors. Stretching from Sycamore Canyon to the north down to Camp Verde in the south, the reach contained large stretches of riparian habitat, places for outdoor recreation, and some striking features, such as Tavasci March and Tuzigoot National Monument. Wise planning and development would be essential, and the study proposed that the community establish a network of habitat preserves and recreational areas to ensure the region's character and natural features would last.[54]

The natural and recreational value of the Verde River was undisputed. VVRRIG and the Verde Valley Chamber of Commerce commissioned additional studies, this time looking more closely at the nature of tourism in the area. One study, published in 1981, went so far as to say in its introduction that "the Verde Valley may well contain the greatest density of different types of vacation or recreational experiences of any similarly sized area in Arizona."[55] That same year, the USFS published a study on whether a seventy-eight–mile stretch of the Verde River should be included in the National Wild and Scenic Rivers System. The study recommended that a nearly forty-mile segment below Camp Verde be included.[56]

Governor Bruce Babbitt added his support to the efforts to protect the Verde. As he later recalled, "I've walked or flown over every inch of this area.... This is the best cottonwood bottom land anywhere in Arizona."[57] Thus Babbitt and the local community became alarmed when they learned of plans to create a gravel operation near Tuzigoot. In 1984, Babbitt and his supporters proposed a "greenway," a six-mile stretch of the Verde from Tuzigoot National Monument to below Dead Horse Ranch State Park. The project served an odd dichotomy, providing both public access to the river and protecting the habitat along its banks from further development.

In late 1985, Bruce Babbitt, Bob Lane, and the state director of the Nature Conservancy, Dan Campbell, began to quietly contact landowners along the Verde about their willingness to sell their land to the state to create the greenway. Not long afterward, Babbitt and his allies in the legislature proposed a bill that would establish a Verde River Protection Fund and provided an appropriation of $2 million for the acquisition of lands along the Verde. This was in the middle of the publicity campaign on behalf of state parks, mostly surrounding the creation of Homolovi Ruins and Red Rock State Parks. The hope was that the Verde River Project could ride the wave of public support.[58]

Although the so-called Verde River Protection Fund Bill did not pass, a similar piece of legislation that used most of the same language did. House Bill 2510 was a dramatic departure from earlier state parks legislation. Until this time, legislative approval for acquisition extended only to specific sites that were to become parks, with defined boundaries and costs. This legislation gave the board permission to acquire whatever parcels and easements they determined important to make the greenway possible—provided the board worked with the cooperation of the SLD. Everyone involved, including Bruce Babbitt, admitted that $2 million would not begin to cover the cost of acquiring all of the land in question, but it was a start.[59]

Setting up the legislation that created the greenway was the easy part. The hard part was the acquisition of the land. Babbitt created yet another task force, this time to save this stretch of the Verde. Tapping into the growing cooperative nature of the various recreation- and nature-oriented bodies in the state, this group included representatives from Arizona State Parks, the SLD, the governor's office, the Nature Conservancy, and Game and Fish. The task force initially identified thirty-five different parcels along the river, varying in size, importance, and cost. Each parcel had to be surveyed, appraised, and negotiated. To facilitate the process and maintain amicable relations with the community, negotiations would take place only with willing sellers. No coercion or condemnation would take place to acquire property. Through this process, the board acquired 293 acres with the original appropriation from the legislature. Meanwhile, public support for the project also resulted in the donation of $250,000 worth of additional property.[60]

In 1988, the Verde River Greenway Ad Hoc Advisory Committee formed to help staff from Arizona State Parks foster dialogue with the community over the development of the greenway. The committee included members of Arizona Game and Fish; the USFS; the towns of Cottonwood, Camp Verde, and Clarkdale; the local chamber of commerce; Yavapai County; and other interested groups and individuals. At its first meeting, the committee recommended that the Arizona State Parks Board extend the scope of the greenway to include a thirty-six–mile stretch of the river from north of Clarkdale to south of Camp Verde. In July 1988, the board accepted that task. By 1998, 410 acres of riparian areas had been acquired, not counting Dead Horse Ranch. The Verde River Greenway represented the first of what would become a series of state-managed riparian areas that later included Sonoita Creek and San Rafael Ranch.[61]

The End of an Era

After Babbitt's nearly ten years in office, those with Arizona State Parks found that things changed almost overnight when he left. In 1987, Governor Evan Mecham suggested eliminating $10 million from Arizona State Parks, leaving the agency to operate on less than three hundred thousand dollars. Mecham's special assistant, Sam Steiger, once said, "We think we have a responsibility to existing parks and new park opportunities. But we can't be classed as aggressively seeking new park opportunities."[62] The impetus for state park development no longer came from the executive office.[63]

An additional blow to the agency came in June 1988, when the Arizona Supreme Court ruled that state and federal land exchanges were unconstitutional. In the case of *Deer Valley School District v. State Land Department*, the court said that state trust lands could only be disposed of through public auction.[64] A proposition placed on the ballot in 1990 to authorize land exchanges failed to pass. In 1991, the state did allow one last major land exchange: the Santa Rita exchange, which included the arrangement with the Forest Service regarding Catalina State Park. Ever since, the board and staff of Arizona State Parks have had to work without one of the key tools Babbitt and his administration had used to create parks such as Red Rock.[65]

The Babbitt legacy showed the importance of having a major supporter behind state parks. It also illustrated the challenges in getting parks established in the interior West. Babbitt's enthusiasm for parks alone was not enough. He had to use media and public opinion to bypass the limitations and obstacles to state park development, such as lack of funds, hegemony of federal land ownership, and legal restrictions on Arizona State Parks and the SLD. Like the Catalina project, each of Babbitt's major parks—Homolovi Ruins, Red Rock, Slide Rock, Oracle, and the Verde River Greenway—required complicated land exchanges. Not one was a simple donation to the State Parks Board. None was an outright purchase from the state's general fund. To help preserve access to the immensely popular Slide Rock, Babbitt set up the Arizona Parklands Foundation as a means to acquire land and bypass some of the restrictions that plagued earlier state park efforts. The Arizona Parklands Foundation was a good idea, but the approach it used in Sedona did not work out as well in Oracle, with its very different community dynamics. Once Oracle State Park was created, the staff and leadership of Arizona State Parks found themselves having to create community support for the park, which never fully developed. Ironically, the strongest support for the park came from volunteers who did not even live in the town of Oracle. Red Rock required two land exchanges, involving an array of federal, state, local, and private entities. Homolovi Ruins was a mosaic of parcels, some privately owned, some state-owned, and some owned by the federal government but administered through a number of different agencies. In spite of the emergence of the "new environmental West," state park advocates still had to overcome formidable obstacles in the creation of state parks.

These parks were legacies of an activist governor who could marshal resources to support what he felt were valuable projects, which may prove to be their greatest weakness. They came about because Babbitt thought they were important. Most were in the Flagstaff area, suggesting that they were the products of a local boy who continued to support his home region once in office. Only Slide Rock started out as a popular recreational spot, but critics may wonder whether the complicated arrangement with the banks and the Pendleys was worth the effort, especially given that the Slide has been closed periodically because of water contamination. Homol'ovi was known among archaeologists, but the low attendance in recent years suggests that the traveling public did not accord it the same status as a Wupatki or a Casa Grande. Perhaps it was a victim of the attitude that "if it were worth saving, the National Park Service would already have done it." Even so, Homolovi Ruins State Park did focus public attention on the dangers of pot-hunting. It also enabled Babbitt to connect politically with the Native American community and the Winslow area.

Oracle and Red Rock, in spite of their official environmental focus, have had their own issues. Oracle was created at least in part to showcase the efforts of the Arizona Parklands Foundation, a well-intentioned move that misread the desires of the local community. Red Rock has proven to be popular, although there is some irony in the fact that Babbitt and Arizona State Parks dismantled Lake Havasu State Park to create it. This, plus the fact that as Secretary of the Interior he ended up preserving some sites under federal auspices, suggests that Babbitt's primary goal was to set aside sites, regardless of what agency or level of government was needed to do it. Places may have become state parks not because they merited being state (as opposed to national or local) parks but because the Arizona State Parks Board was the most viable institution at hand to an activist governor.

It was ironic, then, that after all of Babbitt's work, a state auditor general's report of 1987 found a number of weaknesses in the state park system and the agency that ran it. It echoed the fact that Arizona ranked forty-ninth in the nation in the number of state parks. In addition, the audit concluded that several sites were not large or significant enough to merit being state parks. The auditors suggested that the small state park system stemmed in part from the agency's unwillingness to develop and expand the system, noting, "Generally, SPB [the State Parks Board] has operated within the public interest by operating and maintaining the state parks system. However, SPB needs to adopt a more aggressive acquisition and development program if the system is to keep pace with population demands. . . . Further, until recently, SPB has made limited efforts to acquire sites for ensuring the conservation of the state's scenic and natural resources."[66] The report made several recommendations, including acquiring more parks, finding better ways to fund park acquisition and maintenance, and engaging in more long-range planning. At the time, most of the Babbitt-era parks had yet to open, and this may account for some of the tone. It also showed, however, that in spite of Babbitt's successes, many of the key issues that faced Arizona's state park movement in the 1950s remained in place.

Chapter 6 **New Directions and Old Challenges**
Redefining the State Park

In 1992, State Parks Director Kenneth E. Travous described Arizona State Parks as "a steady ship in rough seas," where "the waves were a result of hard economic times, decreasing budgets, increasing visitation, consistent demands and political turmoil. . . . At the same time, though, our ship has gotten bigger. Program dollars for needed facilities, budget flexibility, and some new staff in key areas have allowed us to take on some daunting tasks."[1] Such attitudes were a far cry from those of a few years earlier, when the end of the Babbitt administration seemed to signal an end to state park development in Arizona, and when the Arizona State Parks Board continued to get criticism for its small holdings. Once its main champion left office, the agency faced the possibility of handling its responsibilities alone, just as it had started acquiring some of its most impressive sites.

Yet the late 1980s and early 1990s witnessed a dramatic increase, both in quantity and quality, in Arizona's offering of state parks. This was a period when several of the "Babbitt Parks"—Red Rock, Slide Rock, Homolovi Ruins, and Yuma Crossing—came on line. Thus, the board was already moving in the direction of acquiring major sites when it brought on Kartchner Caverns and Tonto Natural Bridge. Meanwhile, the board worked in connection with a host of other agencies to establish the facility at Fool Hollow. Cooperative arrangements became commonplace, even if not all ventures worked smoothly, as the case of Yuma Crossing

Director Ken Travous, shown here at Tonto Natural Bridge, has guided Arizona State Parks since the 1980s, overseeing the acquisition of some of its largest and most significant sites.

demonstrated. Meanwhile, the creation of the Heritage Fund dramatically improved the funding situation for Arizona State Parks, resulting in acquisitions such as Sonoita Creek State Natural Area, San Rafael Ranch, and Spur Cross Ranch.

As state parks director, Ken Travous guided the agency through these years. Travous brought and maintained an energy that enabled Arizona State Parks to tackle a number of major issues, even when legislatures and governors treated state parks with benign neglect. He came to the agency as assistant to Director Don Charpio. Don Charpio had been state parks director in Tennessee and came in 1986 as a replacement for Michael Ramnes. Charpio served less than two years as Arizona's state parks director, resigning over differences of opinion with the board. Then, after a nationwide search, the Arizona State Parks Board hired Travous, who began in April 1987. He began just months after Babbitt left office.

Travous and other park professionals of his generation realized that parks could not be taken for granted as benign features on the landscape. Rather, overuse could destroy the very qualities that once inspired a park's creation. In musing about the role of a park in protecting something such as an endangered plant, he once quipped, "The last thing you want to do if you want to protect that plant is to draw its [the public's] attention. Have people come and look at it, trample it, pick it up, and look at it by the roots and all of a sudden you've killed the very thing you tried to protect."[2] He recognized that conservation was inherently part of the mission of Arizona State Parks, but preservation was not always feasible for an agency that needed visitor attendance to be viable. Park creation and management involved the paradox of making things available to the public while protecting it at the same time.

This balance became increasingly difficult when visitors engaged in more intensive forms of recreation throughout the interior West, which had become the nation's playground. Lakes where previous generations sauntered in small boats now resonated with the roar of jet skis. Swimming was relegated to small, protected basins so that boats could have full run of the lakes. Hikers had to share trails with mountain bikers and even people on motorized off-road vehicles. Camping was more likely to involve a motor home with full hookups than a tent and portable stove. Moreover, population growth in the West resulted in greater numbers at recreational sites. For example, most of the visitors to the Colorado River parks came from California, many of whom drove from Los Angeles with their personal watercraft in tow.

Another feature of the next generation of park professionals was the acceptance of partnerships rather than rivalries among agencies. Travous observed that "in the final analysis, people don't know and don't care who is running the land, who's managing it." In fact, "They don't care one bit whether it's the Forest Service that runs it or the BLM or the National Park Service or State Parks or the county parks. All the badges look the same to them. . . . You know, they don't need to learn us. We need to learn them." Prior officials might have worried about acquiring a site from an agency so that another would run it. Travous was not as concerned. Members of the public "don't care. Why should we care? As long as we're providing the service, or somebody is, then it doesn't matter to us."[3] Ownership of the land, management of it, and the funding for the facilities on it might each come from three different agencies—or a combination thereof. In an era of scarce resources but greater demands, it made sense for agencies to pool resources to accomplish goals.

Although the energy for state parks in the 1980s came from Babbitt's office, the agency's energy in the 1990s rested in the director and staff, who had become more savvy about getting support for parks projects. State Parks now had legislative liaisons and public relations staff. Events were carefully planned to have maximum effect and to gain visibility. No longer were parks simply museums that communities donated to the state. Each park effort was complex, usually involving several partners. Arrangements defied earlier concepts of park development.

Kartchner Caverns

The Kartchner Caverns issue took the staff and board of Arizona State Parks completely by surprise. In 1984, a resident from Tucson named Randy Tufts approached Charles Eatherly, who was then in charge of planning for potential state park sites. Tufts explained that he knew of a site that he was sure would make a perfect state park. However, he could not tell Eatherly what the site was. Initially hesitant, Eatherly went to southern Arizona to investigate the claims and encountered what has become one of Arizona's major state-level attractions: Kartchner Caverns.

The cave's most amazing quality was its condition. Within the cave's four main rooms and countless smaller spaces were formations such as the fifty-eight-foot column called Kubla Khan, one of the world's longest soda straw formations (twenty-one feet long), and dainty, intricate formations so delicate they would

Kartchner Caverns was once a closely guarded secret among a handful of spelunkers. It took years of careful planning to get the site protected as Kartchner Caverns State Park without revealing its existence and location to potential trespassers and vandals.

shatter if disturbed by so much as a human breath. It was what geologists called a living cave, where water in the rock still trickles down to create formations.

For thousands of years Kartchner had not had a large opening to the outside. Thus, the air in the cave remained at a near constant 99 percent humidity, providing the perfect incubator for the formations inside. The lack of an opening also protected the cave in another way—making it unknown to humans. Thus, the cave was undisturbed and safe—until 1974.[4]

Gary Tenen and Randy Tufts were friends at the University of Arizona who shared a passion for spelunking. Tufts had looked for caves in the area since the 1960s. When exploring around the Whetstone Mountains near Benson, he had come across a small sinkhole in a rather unassuming hummock on the eastern slope of the mountains. Initially this sinkhole seemed to lead nowhere. Then, in November 1974, Tufts happened to be in the vicinity of the sinkhole with his partner Gary Tenen when they felt and smelled moisture coming from a cleft in the rock. Investigating further, they noticed a small opening that led to a cave. Upon opening the hole big enough to get through, Tenen and Tufts scrambled inside and, in a story like the discovery of King Tut's Tomb, found a nearly pristine cave. During the next two years, Tenen and Tufts carefully explored the caverns, which they initially named Xanadu,[5] mapping out a series of rooms and formations.

As amazing as they were, however, the caverns soon posed an ethical dilemma. Xanadu was close to Highway 90 and easily accessible to the public—and to vandals. The cave was on private land, and if the word got out, there would be nothing to stop people from coming in and destroying the very qualities that made the cave so precious. Like their colleagues in archaeology, these cavers knew that sometimes the best things had to be hidden to prevent them from being destroyed. As Tufts once explained, "The cave is defenseless. . . . It has to have people who will love it, who will protect it, who will argue on its behalf."[6] So Tenen and Tufts kept the cave a secret except to a small group of confidants—not even telling the National Speleological Society about their find. Yet, secrecy would not protect the cave forever, especially after leaks in even their small circle resulted in unwelcome visitors. Reluctantly, Tenen and Tufts approached the Kartchner family, who owned the land containing Xanadu, in hopes that they could do something to protect the cave and restrict access. The best form of protection, ironically, seemed to be making the cave a park. If done right, the public could enjoy the cave under controlled circumstances without damaging the resource in the process. The Kartchner family's patriarch, James, was immediately supportive of the idea and proved to be an essential ally in the process until his death in the mid-1980s. The Kartchners became caretakers of the cave and, like the posses of the previous century, occasionally patrolled the area on horseback with sidearms to deter potential intruders. It was soon apparent, however, that developing the cave would be beyond the financial resources of the Kartchners.

The cave's supporters went to Representative Morris K. Udall to have the site turned into a federal park. When those plans did not work out, Tenen, Tufts, and the Kartchners approached individuals from Arizona State Parks in December 1984, resulting in Eatherly's visit the following month. Soon afterward, Tenen and Tufts invited Governor Bruce Babbitt to visit the cave, creating a new entryway (called the Babbitt Hole) for his visit. Babbitt, in addition to being a lawyer, also had a background in geology and visited the cave in April 1985 with his two sons. He was immediately committed to making the cave a state park and brought in William Roe of the Nature Conservancy (and later a member of the State Parks Board) to begin negotiations to acquire the land. As Babbitt's administration wound down, however, so did hopes for making the cave a state park. Eventually, the resignation of Michael Ramnes and then Don Charpio as state parks director made the possibility of a state park seem even more remote. The cave's supporters began to look for another manager for the site. Officials from the National Park Service and the BLM went out to see the cave but were cool to the idea of taking it on as a responsibility. The situation was becoming critical. With each organization and group brought into the process, the secrecy that protected the cave diminished.

In 1987, the cave's supporters again looked to state parks, this time with William Roe on the board and Ken Travous as the new state parks director. Travous quickly became one of the park's key supporters. On his first visit to the cave, he was astounded at a landscape that had been unchanged for fifty thousand years. On reflection, however, the enormity and challenge of the task ahead was numbing. He later wondered, "How do you get people close enough to the formations so that they can fully appreciate their beauty but at the same time not so close that a curious hand will damage them?"[7]

Before development could happen, the land that contained the caverns had to be acquired. The best hope for acquiring the land seemed to be an arrangement whereby the Nature Conservancy would buy an option on the caverns that would then be acquired by the state. This required the passage of a bill in the legislature to create a park and authorize state funds for the purchase. The cave was still relatively secret, but its supporters had to work out a fine compromise between keeping it from the public's attention and informing legislators enough to support the matter.

Meanwhile, Travous and the Arizona State Parks Board had to come up with a way to get the legislature to fund the park without giving away the cave's secret in the text of a legislative bill. The plan that emerged was to graft the legislation onto a bill that allowed the entrance fees from state parks to go into a special account for park acquisition and development. By creating this fund, Arizona State Parks could channel its entrance fees into a fund that could pay for the purchase of the caverns.

By the beginning of 1988, things looked good for Kartchner Caverns. The Nature Conservancy went ahead and bought an option on the caverns from the Kartchner family. Then, in April 1988, the legislature passed the bill creating the acquisition and development fund. Only on April 27, the day of the vote, did the legislators who were in the know push through the last-minute change in the text of the bill that gave the necessary authorization for the Arizona State Parks Board to acquire and establish the James and Lois Kartchner Caverns State Park. The secret was finally out.

This legislation was a double victory for Arizona State Parks. It authorized the creation of what had the potential to become Arizona's most spectacular state park, the one that would have the greatest name recognition and likely be the most popular attraction in the system. Perhaps even more significant, however, was that this legislation gave the board an unprecedented control over its own financial destiny, allowing it to use some of its own money to fund new state parks. The board now had an incentive to acquire and develop major sites in the state. The first beneficiary would be Kartchner Caverns.

The same day that the legislature passed Senate Bill 1188, creating the fund, both television and print media let loose with the announcement that Arizona had a new state park. Ken Travous persuaded local television stations and the newspapers to hold off on their stories about the caverns until the day the legislature voted on the bill, creating an immediate public sensation. That way, the cave's location would remain a secret should the legislation bog down or fail. With the passage of the bill, however, the board could now go public about what it hoped would be its star attraction. In September 1988, the Arizona State Parks Board purchased the cave from the Kartchner family. Agency staff made preparations for opening the cave to the public, anticipating an opening date of 1992.[8]

In the exuberance of 1988, it seemed that thirteen years of secrecy and hard work were over. In reality, the work had just begun. Developing the park proved to be a challenge so great that it almost threatened the very existence of the agency tasked with developing it. Provisions had to be made to protect the cave's fragile mineral and geologic features from the outdoors and from contact with thousands of tourists. Staff with Arizona State Parks worked closely with the caving community to come up with a plan that would both protect the cave and make it accessible to the public. The challenge was daunting. The visitors who made the park a possibility also posed a constant threat to the cave's delicate balance, both from the outside air that came with them and from their own breath. The light that enabled people to see the formations also encouraged the growth of algae. Overuse and careless development were constant threats. Kartchner was *not* going to be another Carlsbad Caverns, with snack bars and gift shops in the cave itself. Visitors would come inside in small groups and be strictly confined to carefully placed pathways. The main entrance would be a 1,100-foot tunnel leading down to an airlock to prevent the desert air from drying out the cave.

The real challenge was in building these facilities. As with any construction project, there were unforeseen, time-consuming, and costly obstacles. The biggest at Kartchner was the entrance. In 1994, excavations for the main entrance began. When workers were within one hundred feet from the cave wall, the construction team discovered that the surrounding rock was fractured with fissures and loose material. As it neared the caverns, the entrance tunnel would have to be more like that of a mineshaft: braced and supported to prevent cave-ins. However, unlike a mining operation, blasting and excavation had to be done in such as way as to ensure the cave itself was not damaged. The mining contractor in charge of the digging estimated that the last one hundred feet of the tunnel was as difficult to complete as the previous one thousand. Inside and out, nearly fifty workers toiled in shifts around the clock to construct pathways, wheelchair ramps, lighting, and handrails. They had to do their jobs with the same care and discipline that the spelunkers shared, working while confined to a narrow workspace of trails and paths. One misplaced tool could destroy a formation thousands of years old. There was no construction equipment inside the cave—all debris had to be carried out by bucket. Outside, the surrounding land, which had many natural amenities in its own right, yielded to the construction of several miles of trails. Meanwhile, the twenty-three thousand–square foot, state-of-the-art visitor's center, telling the story of the cave and its discovery, was the largest structure Arizona State Parks ever built.

Developing Kartchner proved far more costly—and laborious—than anyone had imagined. The entrance tunnel, figured at eight hundred dollars per square foot, wound up costing nine thousand dollars per square foot in areas near the cave itself. Tentative opening dates for the park got pushed back, revised, and delayed. The board had to ask the legislature for more money—the cavern development was more than even the acquisition and development fund could handle. During the 1990s, Kartchner required so much money to develop that members of the agency decided to defer development and maintenance at other sites. Although State Parks was still able to open Tonto Natural Bridge and a revamped Yuma Crossing, many other park projects had to wait. There were few remaining places in the budget that could be cut out.[9]

In fact, so much money went toward the necessary construction that State Parks had to scramble to find money for the grand opening celebrations. With the opening of the caverns tentatively set for November 1997, a group of the cave's supporters came together in April of that year to form the Friends of Kartchner Caverns, supported by a consultant that the board hired. Based on a similar "friends" group established at Oracle State Park, this organization's purpose was to raise funds for the opening celebrations and for promotional activities for the park. They set up a fund through the Arizona Community Foundation and began getting ready for the park's opening. With construction delays, however, the opening date kept getting pushed back further and further. Arizona State Parks' staff soon learned never to promise the opening date of a park.[10]

By late 1998, the legislature was fed up with the constant delays and threatened to close down the agency if Kartchner Caverns was not opened soon. Finally, after ten years of pushing, struggle, and cost overruns, Kartchner Caverns opened to the public on November 12, 1999, with a price tag of $28.4 million for its creation. It was by far the most expensive state park in Arizona. Individuals with Arizona State Parks as well as Tenen, Tufts, the Kartchners, and the Friends of Kartchner Caverns, hoped that the park's popularity would soon make up for the difficulties. Initial attendance figures seemed to play that out: Reservations to visit the caverns during its first months of operation sold out almost overnight. More people visited Kartchner in December 1999 than visited the rest of Arizona's state parks put together. It remains to be seen whether even the extensive precautions will be enough to both preserve the cave and make it accessible. For now at least, the caverns have dramatically changed the nature of Arizona's collection of state parks.[11]

A few years after the bill establishing Kartchner passed, Ken Travous had a conversation with his deputy about Kartchner Caverns. The deputy remarked, "You know, it used to be, when we got here, Travous, we were kind of the doormat." But after the acquisition of Kartchner, the deputy concluded, "Now, we're winning our share of games on the road. And if you come to our home court, we'll clean your clock." Travous agreed. "You know," he once mused, "we started saying, 'by gosh, we can do this right.' And so that was the retrospective. It made us a lot more confident of what we could do. Of what the possibilities were."[12] The Arizona State Parks Board started taking a more proactive approach to acquiring and managing parks. Acquiring major sites such as Tonto and Kartchner gave the agency more legitimacy as well. It was no longer the collection of "catfish farms, ponds, and boat docks" imposed on the agency by powerful politicians. Instead, Arizona State Parks had become an important player in providing recreation and in preserving natural, scenic, and cultural sites.

Tonto Natural Bridge, Part II

Tonto Natural Bridge took the longest of any Arizona state park to be created. Its story as a park went back to the very origins of the agency and remained a nearly constant issue for the next thirty years. While the Arizona State Parks Board contended with various park proposals, the board held onto the dream of Tonto Natural Bridge with an unusually strong tenacity because the site had so much potential. In the late 1960s and early 1970s, several attempts to create a state park at the bridge had appeared, each time to be defeated by lack of finances, lack of legislative support, and eventually legal issues over land ownership.

In the 1980s, a renewed effort to establish a state park at Tonto commenced. In 1985, land ownership issues finally cleared themselves up when Clifford Wolfswinkel's Southwest Properties acquired title to the property, settling the ownership dispute. Soon afterward, more than $360,000 worth of improvements went into fixing up the now aging facilities, and the lodge was placed on the National Register of Historic Places. After Clifford Wolfswinkel died in 1988, his family and representatives of Arizona State Parks embarked on a renewed attempt to transfer the site. In 1990, the legislature approved a lease-purchase agreement for $3.2 million. As with a person buying a house, the state made payments (annually instead of monthly), with money coming from entrance fees. The Arizona State Parks Board dedicated the bridge as a state park in June 1991.[13]

Fool Hollow

The Mogollon Rim and the White Mountains contain several lakes, including Fool Hollow, outside the community of Show Low. The site got its name from the taunts a farmer named Thomas Adair received when he proposed an agricultural

Fool Hollow Lake Recreation Area is called a recreation area and not a state park because of the arrangement among Arizona State Parks, the U.S. Forest Service, Arizona Game and Fish, and a host of other groups. This cooperation enabled Fool Hollow to become one of the nicest campgrounds in the region.

settlement in a small valley along what is now Show Low Creek. People said only a fool would want to farm in such a rocky little hollow. Perhaps Adair's critics were right. The community never expanded beyond a few buildings, and by the middle of the twentieth century, it was abandoned.

Then, in 1956, Fool Hollow changed for one reason: copper. The Phelps Dodge company needed more water for its mining activities in southern Arizona. To obtain those rights from the state, the company purchased property at Fool Hollow and traded the land to the state in exchange for water rights. In the process, the state authorized Arizona Game and Fish to build a dam on the site, creating the 149-surface-acre Fool Hollow Lake. Not only did Phelps Dodge get its water, the community of Show Low got another amenity for its residents and tourists. The waters covered every trace of Adair. Arizona's newest lake was mostly on the land of the Apache-Sitgreaves National Forests[14] but Game and Fish managed the dam, spillway, and water rights for fishing and waterfowl habitat.

For the next thirty years, Fool Hollow was relatively undeveloped as a recreational site. Until the construction of a boat ramp in 1987, boaters at the lake had to use what one report euphemistically called "innovative launching techniques." Meanwhile, the lake began to attract a rough crowd, and long-term visitors reported increasing problems with loud parties, littering, and vandalism of the limited facilities that were there.

Meanwhile the USFS found itself faced with growing demands for outdoor recreation that exceeded existing facilities. The USFS had a large amount of land but limited staff to manage and patrol ever-popular recreational sites and limited funds to build new ones. This need prompted the USFS to see other agencies in the area as partners toward solutions. The question was where to expand. Pressure from the City of Show Low and other interested parties made Fool Hollow a promising possibility.[15]

The decision of the USFS and Show Low to do more at Fool Hollow coincided with efforts of Arizona State Parks and Arizona Game and Fish in working together. By the mid-1980s, both agencies had new leadership and were interested in developing closer ties with each other. In 1987, a joint meeting between the Arizona State Parks Board and the Arizona Game and Fish Commission came about in part to work on the upcoming SCORP and also to "establish an ongoing relationship between the Board and the Commission which can identify problems and develop solutions, [and] stimulate cooperation which will lead to joint ventures, projects and programs."[16] The agencies had worked together on ventures such as Roper Lake, Alamo Lake, and Lake Havasu and were looking for more projects when the matter of Fool Hollow came up. Game and Fish found that it did not have the staff to adequately maintain its holdings. Meanwhile, the Arizona State Parks Board was increasingly under pressure to have more facilities in the mountains. The need to do something about Fool Hollow was the perfect opportunity to start building these connections.[17]

In June 1989, the USFS staff at the Apache-Sitgreaves National Forests called together a meeting of their staff with representatives from Game and Fish, Arizona State Parks, the City of Show Low, Arizona Public Service, and the local firm of McCarty Construction Company to discuss Fool Hollow. Using a partnership in California's Los Padres National Forest as a model, the group began to work on a partnership. Development of the lake would cut down on vandalism and other problems by increasing public visitation, providing better facilities, and involving more active management. It would also help staff from the USFS, Arizona State Parks, and Game and Fish in accomplishing their objectives, which was to provide more "cool and wet" water-based recreation in the mountains for the ever-burgeoning populations of Phoenix and Tucson. However, not everyone was in total agreement about the idea. Some in the USFS, for example, resisted the notion of sharing responsibilities with Arizona State Parks officials. Others wanted the whole lake to go to State Parks and have the USFS out of the matter entirely.[18]

Over the next several years, the different sides worked on plans to further develop the lake and to manage it effectively. The arrangement that emerged was complicated. The USFS still owned most of the land and provided education and interpretive staff. Arizona State Parks' staff provided most of the administration of Fool Hollow, including supervision, fiscal management, and annual planning. Game and Fish was responsible for monitoring fishing and boating, for enforcing relevant laws for those activities, and for maintaining the dam and spillway. Show Low provided support for maintenance and sanitation as well as administration of certain SLIF funds used to develop the project. Arizona Public Service provided electrical service design, and McCarty Construction assisted with the water systems involved. Various partners also contributed financially to the project because each agency could apply for grants and funds—effectively quadrupling the potential for bringing in money to develop the site.[19] The partners formalized their arrangement when they signed a memorandum of understanding in 1991. Although staff with Arizona State Parks officially took over the management of Fool Hollow in July 1992, it took an act of the state legislature in 1994 to finally permit the board to manage Fool Hollow on a permanent basis.[20]

Construction at Fool Hollow began in 1991. New camping areas emerged as well as facilities for boaters, fishermen, and picnickers. The facilities installed were some of the finest in a public campground, leading some to refer to Fool Hollow as the "Hyatt Regency of campgrounds." There were also provisions for undeveloped areas for the benefit of wildlife. Even the construction of roads proved to be a challenge. With Show Low growing around the lake, the partners had to design an entryway that did not allow too much traffic on adjacent city streets. The amount of work put into Fool Hollow was striking given that Arizona State Parks' staff was at the time deferring other developments to concentrate its efforts on getting Kartchner Caverns ready. From the perspective of the Apache-Sitgreaves National Forests, Fool Hollow was the Kartchner Caverns–like project that forced staff to put activities at other locations on hold.

Although some work remained to be done, the Memorial Day weekend of 1994 featured the opening of the Fool Hollow Lake Recreation Area.[21] Within four months of opening, more than forty thousand people visited the lake. Fool Hollow, in spite of its funny name, proved to be a success story of partnership among several agencies whose relationships in the past have been rocky, but who were able to overcome those differences to rehabilitate a popular lake in eastern Arizona.[22]

Yuma Crossing

Not all local-federal-state partnerships had the same amount of success as Fool Hollow. Overly optimistic plans could strain even the most supportive arrangements, as was the case with Yuma Crossing State Park. Yuma Crossing was originally the site of the U.S. Army's quartermaster depot, which housed supplies on their way upriver to posts in Arizona and Nevada. The depot served military installations in the Southwest until its closure in 1883. By the 1970s, a handful of structures remained. The BOR owned the warehouse and reservoir as a base for several nearby reclamation projects. The bureau also owned the corral building but let the Yuma County Water Users Association use it. In 1956, the City of Yuma applied for, and received, control of the quartermaster's residence, also known as the Old Customs House, as a historical monument. By the mid-1960s, the building was still basically a storage unit, with windows boarded up and a barbed-wire fence around the property. In 1967, the city allowed a local women's philanthropic group, the Assistance League of Yuma, to operate a museum in the building as one of their charitable projects.[23]

The office of the depot quartermaster, which the Arizona State Parks Board

Yuma Crossing State Historic Park is at the site of an army depot on the Yuma River in the 1850s. It took two decades to consolidate federal, state, and local holdings into what some hoped would become "the Williamsburg of the West."

had acquired from the U.S. Boundary Commission in 1969, functioned as a satellite of Yuma Territorial Prison State Historic Park. By itself, the quartermaster depot office was not enough to be a viable state park. With the City of Yuma interested in a park along the river, however, and with federal and state officials open to relocating the Yuma Water Users' offices, the possibility of a larger complex at the site held promise.[24]

In 1974, the Yuma City–County Bicentennial Commission promoted the idea of a park along the Colorado River, making it an official bicentennial project. President of the endeavor was a local businessman, Joe Atmar, with Gwen Robinson as treasurer. They envisioned a large city park along the Colorado River to enhance Yuma's downtown. When the commission disbanded in 1976, the city took up the park idea. Mayor Ersel Byrd created a Yuma Colorado River Greenbelt Committee to look into the matter. Again, Joe Atmar and Gwen Robinson served on the committee. The result was a proposed two hundred–acre greenbelt park along the Colorado, from Yuma Territorial Prison at its eastern edge to Joe Henry Park at the western. Along the way, the greenbelt included the historic waterfront, including the quartermaster depot and Customs House. In general, the project had the support of the city and others in the community; however, in 1980, voters rejected a $625,000 bond issue to start construction.

With the defeat of the bond issue, Yumans still interested in the park idea organized the Yuma Crossing Park Council, Inc. Among the group's main founders were Gwen Robinson, Joe Atmar, and Barry Patterson, an architect who was also chair of the city planning and zoning commission. To Patterson, the site "has the potential of being one of the finest parks in the Southwest" and could "spur redevelopment and rehabilitation of the entire north end of the city as well as beautify the 'gateway to Arizona.'"[25] Yet the City of Yuma did not have the financial resources to work on the project. In early August 1981, the city proposed turning a substantial part of its land along the Colorado River over to Arizona State Parks. This would free up city resources to focus on recreational parks in the city.

For the board, the prospect of acquiring a state park through donation, with little cost of acquisition to the state, was tempting. Moreover, Governor Bruce Babbitt appointed Yuma Crossing Council President Gwen Robinson to the Arizona State Parks Board. The board agreed to go ahead with the arrangement with the city in late 1981. Sadly, Joe Atmar, one of the founders of the Yuma Crossing idea, died that same year, and the movement lost one of its main promoters. It was up to people such as Patterson and Robinson to help make Yuma Crossing a reality.[26]

Work on developing the park began rapidly. The city began the process by passing a resolution in 1981 to donate the customs house and 175 acres to the state. That same year, the Arizona State Parks Board acquired the depot's reservoir from the BOR. Arizona Senator Dennis DiConcini sponsored legislation in Congress to have the BOR relocate the Yuma County Water Users Association. Babbitt did not get as directly involved with Yuma Crossing as with some of his other projects, but his Arizona Parklands Foundation did recommend the site be a state park. In October 1982, Governor Bruce Babbitt hosted a press conference at the Yuma Territorial Prison announcing state money for designing the facility. After several years of further negotiations, on May 9, 1985, the Arizona State Parks Board, the City of Yuma, and the Yuma Crossing Park Council signed an agreement at the territorial prison creating the historic portion of the Yuma Crossing Park. Meanwhile, the legislature also allocated $171,400 for the restoration of the depot quartermaster office and the adjacent reservoir.[27]

The City of Yuma hired Gwen Robinson to be the Yuma Crossing Park coordinator. She presided over the Yuma Crossing Park Resource Panel, which consisted of two representatives from each of the signing parties, to carry out the master plan. In order to prevent there being a conflict of interest between her work on the board and her work as coordinator, Robinson could not vote on matters related to Yuma Crossing when they came before the Arizona State Parks Board.

During this time, the Phoenix-based firm of architect Gerald A. Doyle and Associates created a master plan for the historic section of the park. Doyle had been the architect behind the restoration of the Arizona State Capitol and Phoenix's Heritage Square and knew how to design historic spaces, but Yuma Crossing was ambitious even by Doyle's standards. The park included the land stretching from the prison to the quartermaster depot. There was also a small site on the Quechan lands, accessible from Yuma by a ferryboat. Central to the park's interpretation were camps with living history characters depicting the lives of Spanish explorers, mountain men, American soldiers, townspeople, convicts, immigrants, rivermen, boundary surveyors, and the Quechan people. In addition to the living history exhibits, the proposed park would have a reconstructed Southern Pacific hotel and depot. There was even to be a replica of a Colorado River steamboat. The architects hoped that this $8.5 million facility would be a major tourist attraction, requiring visitors to stay at least two days to see and do everything thoroughly. An article in *Arizona Highways* celebrated Yuma Crossing as "the Williamsburg of the West."[28] A market analysis funded by the City of Yuma projected that Yuma Crossing would eventually bring in 420,000 visitors a year and create more than 1,100 new jobs.[29]

In 1986, a new player in the development of the park emerged: the Yuma Crossing Foundation. It was incorporated as a nonprofit corporation with the goal to make the master plan a reality. It had a seven-member board, appointed by the Yuma Crossing Resource Panel, that included State Senator Jones Osborn; Susan DiConcini, the wife of Senator Dennis DiConcini; and State Parks Board members Gwen Robinson and Duane Miller. With its powerful connections, the foundation seemed well suited to tap into state and local funding resources to make the park work. The foundation also hired an executive director: John Patterson. Patterson had worked with living history sites such as Conner Prairie in Indiana, Old Sturbridge Village in Massachusetts, and the New Salem Historic Site in Illinois.

Gradually, restoration of the buildings on the Yuma Crossing site began to take place. The first of the restoration projects began in October 1986 on the office of the depot quartermaster, which opened to the public in October of the following year.[30] The board acquired the commanding officers' quarters and kitchen from the City of Yuma in January 1987. In May 1988, the board began leasing the corral buildings and warehouse from BOR. Meanwhile, the AHS's Yuma branch announced its intentions to build a replica the 149-foot twin-stack steamer Mohave II, the largest steamboat to sail on the Colorado. However, little came of the new Mohave II endeavor—the first of many setbacks for the park.[31]

To further coordinate the development of Yuma Crossing, the City of Yuma, the Arizona State Parks Board, the Yuma Crossing Park Council, and the Yuma Crossing Foundation entered into a quadripartite agreement in 1988. The foundation agreed to take on the landscaping, further land acquisition, and operations and maintenance of the park. The Yuma Crossing Park Council, by contrast, was to monitor the development of the park and serve as the liaison between the foundation and Arizona State Parks. In 1990, the Yuma Crossing Foundation applied for and received a contract to operate the depot for Arizona State Parks as a concessionaire.[32]

Implementing the impressive plans of 1984 soon proved a lot more difficult and time consuming than anyone had imagined. Visitorship at the incomplete park remained low. The average visitor paid three dollars to get in but costs averaged fifteen dollars per person to keep the park open. After five years of fundraising and other activities, the foundation had raised only a tiny fraction of the amount needed to implement the master plan. In response, the foundation looked to the city for help. In 1993, the following year, the voters of Yuma extended a 2 percent hospitality tax on motels, restaurants, and bars, with four hundred thousand dollars of the income going to Yuma Crossing to promote more rapid expansion. However, growth at the park continued to creep along.[33]

By 1996, Yumans had had enough. They had waited more than twenty years for the Yuma Crossing Park to come into being, and only a small part of the proposed park was operating. Visitors saw costumed staff on site but no reenactors' camps. There was no restored Southern Pacific hotel, no riverfront expanse from the prison to the depot, and no riverboat. Even Barry Patterson, president of the Yuma Crossing Park Council, concluded that "at this juncture it is necessary to take a different avenue to keep the concept alive."[34] In April 1996, the foundation and the city announced the end of the 1992 arrangement. On June 30, the museum closed, the Yuma Crossing Foundation dissolved, and the grand plans of the 1980s came to an end.[35]

On July 1, 1996, Yuma Crossing became the sole responsibility of the Arizona State Parks Board. The following month, the City of Yuma and the Arizona State Parks Board entered into an agreement in which State Parks operated the facility with $150,000 in financial support from the city. The City of Yuma and State Parks took an additional year to fix up the site, expand the parking lot, and continue the restoration work. In early 1997, the BOR designated the corral building, storehouse, and watchman's house as surplus property, enabling the board to acquire the property it had been leasing from the federal government. Thanks to the $1 million redevelopment completed by the City of Yuma, with assistance of Arizona State Parks staff, Arizona State Parks reopened the new Yuma Crossing State Historic Park on September 27, 1997.[36]

Financial Struggles

Finances had always been a critical issue for the Arizona State Parks Board, but the late 1980s and early 1990s brought things to a head. Benevolent landowners were seldom donating sites to the state as simply a good gesture for all to enjoy. The days of the local community donating their historic museum to the board were fading. The best sites had to be purchased or acquired through trade and involved parcels of land whose values regularly reached into the millions of dollars. Even though lobbying efforts at the state legislature were increasingly effective and the agency could now use entrance fees to pay for acquisition and development, funding remained one of the board's biggest obstacles.[37]

In spite of the challenges involved, creating state parks was relatively easy compared to obtaining funds to develop and operate them. New parks were popular and made good press, as Bruce Babbitt understood very well. Announcing a new park with bold headlines and color photos supported the image that Arizona's state government was interested in protecting the environment. In an increasingly urban state, where environmental issues played well to the majority of voters (now concentrated in urban areas and often searching for new forms of outdoor recreation), getting popular support behind a park was always a good political move. However, it was harder to get the same level of political and public support for such mundane things as building rest rooms, paving roads, and paying staff—as if parks developed by themselves. Thousands and even millions of additional dollars might go into developing a site into a state park, whether big attractions, such as Kartchner, or smaller sites, such as Yuma Crossing. After all, the legislature authorized the creation of parks at Quiburi and Cerro Prieto, but the follow-up support to make these parks a reality never, in fact, came about.

Parks needed regular maintenance and staffing, even if visitation levels were low. Some parks simply drew more visitors than others, with lake-based recreation drawing the most and historic sites usually drawing the least. Yet disposing of costly parks with low visitation was politically dangerous. In its history, the board had disposed of only one state park, Painted Rocks, and that was because of health concerns.

A visible example of this challenge took place in early 1991, when Arizona State Parks faced severe cutbacks in its operating budget. The legislature proposed cutting the agency's budget by a hefty $668,000. In response, Ken Travous announced that his agency did not have enough money to operate on and thus proposed, as a cost-cutting measure, closing seven parks with the lowest attendance: Riordan, Tubac, Lyman Lake, Fort Verde, Dead Horse Ranch, Roper Lake, and Buckskin Mountain. Howls of protest erupted from the communities adjacent to these parks. Almost immediately, members of Arizona State Parks and the office of Governor Fife Symington were inundated with calls, letters, and petitions from school children to mayors. By the middle of the year, funding was restored and the governor's office and individuals with Arizona State Parks worked on other ways to cut expenses. No parks were closed, but Travous's announcement showed that there was indeed strong public support for keeping parks open. It also showed that closing a park would prove a difficult endeavor. Throughout the early 1990s, threats of closure remained, and the parks with low attendance were top on the list.[38]

The Heritage Fund

These challenges were not unique to Arizona. Around the United States, pressures to create more state parks frequently clashed with state legislatures worried about how to balance their budgets. Simply funding existing state park systems, let alone expanding them, was difficult for many states to achieve. As Phyllis Myers, a researcher on state parks, observed, "Many states experienced sharp declines in spending for parks in the early 1980s. These cutbacks were propelled to a large extent by cutbacks in federal LWCF (Land and Water Conservation Fund) grants. At the same time, downturns in state economies and increased competition for state funding revealed the weakness, in many states, of constituency support for state parks."[39] State parks from Minnesota to Connecticut to Pennsylvania faced severe funding problems during the 1980s. By 1990, federal grants made up 1 percent of state park expenses nationwide.

States tried a number of different solutions to fund park development and operation. For many, raising entrance fees was a standard approach. Others, such as Tennessee, looked to the development of lodges, gift shops, and resort-type facilities in their parks. Still others looked to corporate sponsorship to fund state parks. State or local bonds financed state park systems from Alaska to New York, and Hawai'i to Alabama.

The use of lottery money was another technique states used to supplement meager finances for state parks. By 1985, five states had established such funds.[40] Arizona was also willing to consider this move, having created a state lottery in the 1980s. A poll conducted by the auditor general's office found that 87 percent of the respondents favored using a portion of lottery money to aid state parks.[41]

Early in 1990, a movement emerged to designate some of Arizona's lottery money for parks, recreation, and heritage-management purposes. This pool of designated lottery money gained the name Arizona Heritage Fund. From this fund, Arizona State Parks and the Arizona Game and Fish Department would each receive $10 million per year. A broad coalition of individuals and organizations called the Arizona Heritage Alliance officially led the movement. Coordinator for the alliance was Eva Patten, a lobbyist for the Nature Conservancy who had been a director for the Governor's Commission on Arizona's Environment back in the 1970s. At its first organizational meeting, the Arizona Heritage Alliance immediately embarked on a campaign to drum up popular support for the Heritage Fund, which appeared as an initiative on the November 1990 ballot as Proposition 200.[42]

The campaign to create the Heritage Fund was very popular. A poll conducted late in 1990 by the Nature Conservancy found that 78 percent of the respondents supported the Heritage Fund. The secretary of state's office tallied more than 130,000 signatures to place the measure on the ballot, although the proposal needed only 86,699. By July 1990, the Arizona Heritage Alliance contained more than eighty recreational, environmental, wildlife, historic preservation, and archaeological groups. Both political candidates for governor in 1990, Terry Goddard and Fife Symington, supported Proposition 200, and the movement's leaders included the unlikely combination of Barry Goldwater, Bruce Babbitt, and Morris Udall.[43]

Only a handful of individuals dared criticize the proposal. A few opponents in the state legislature argued that tinkering with the lottery money set a dangerous precedent that threatened the lottery funding intended for the education of Arizona's children. Chairman of the Senate Finance Committee, Doug Todd, and the Arizona Tax Research Association felt that diverting money that would otherwise go to the general fund would leave the state legislature scrambling to make up the difference, probably through raising taxes.[44]

With such a broad array of support, Proposition 200 passed the November ballot by more than a two-to-one margin, in an election where most other propositions were defeated. Yet even that percentage was not enough to fully protect the Heritage Fund. In Arizona, the state legislature can pass a bill killing an initiative unless it receives the support of a majority of all registered voters. Because of low voter turnout, the Heritage Fund, while passing, did not have the majority support of the registered voters in the state. As a result, the state legislature could pass a bill that could kill the fund. To date that has not happened, although the threat persists because the state legislature has remained cool to an initiative that took away some of its power to control lottery money.[45]

The Heritage Fund also came with several stipulations. When drafted, Proposition 200 was specific in its allocation of funds. Percentages of the money were automatically earmarked to go for certain projects and issues. Leaders from Game and Fish and Arizona State Parks, who were partners in the campaign to create the Heritage Fund, traded a degree of their decision-making autonomy for a more secure funding source. Matching grants to local, regional, and state parks totaled $3.5 million, or 35 percent, of Arizona State Parks' heritage money. Of the remaining funds, natural areas acquisition, cultural and historic preservation, and state parks acquisition and development each received $1.7 million, or 17 percent, of Arizona State Parks' appropriation. The remainder of Arizona State Parks' money went toward trail development, environmental education, and natural areas management. No Heritage Fund money was specifically designated for salaries or maintenance of the agencies that had to manage these programs, meaning that money for staffing was still an issue.[46]

Even so, staff and board members rejoiced in a source of income that was predictable, substantial, and relatively free from legislative control. As *Arizona Preservation News* once remarked, "With the passage of the Arizona Heritage Fund, we were fortunate to have funds available for the first time to help preserve our state's precious cultural heritage."[47] Within a year, the Heritage Fund was the largest source of income to Arizona State Parks, and its money supported 103 projects statewide.[48]

Heritage Fund money enabled Arizona State Parks to become involved in environmental stewardship to a degree that was not possible in previous years. By the early 1990s, the agency became more interested in the state's rivers and riparian habitats. With the help of the Heritage Fund, staff at Arizona State Parks launched an inventory and evaluation of Arizona's streams and wetlands, the first major survey of its kind conducted since the foundation of the Natural Areas Program in the 1970s. In 1992, the agency used four hundred thousand dollars to acquire riparian habitats for the Verde River Greenway. One major result of the passage of Proposition 200 was that there was finally a known amount of money for acquiring and developing state parks. In the early 1990s, the board used a large portion of its Heritage Fund money earmarked for state parks toward the development of Tonto Natural Bridge and Kartchner Caverns State Parks.

In the years since 1990, the Heritage Fund has remained relatively secure, although the legislature and the governor have made periodic attempts to alter the fund. The legislature has periodically challenged the Heritage Fund and attempted to seize part of the Heritage Fund money for other purposes. So far, these moves have failed. Governor Symington proposed eliminating Arizona State Parks entirely from the legislature's general fund, making the agency solely dependent on Heritage Fund money. After considerable public protest, this move failed. Recently, fluctuations in lottery sales have affected the amount of money in the fund. It remains to be seen whether the Heritage Fund will continue to support the many programs of Arizona State Parks. In the 1990s, at least, the creation of the fund was one of the most significant improvements to happen to Arizona State Parks.[49]

Sonoita Creek

The new environmental sentiment, financed through lottery dollars, led to the creation of the second natural area under the authority of the Arizona State Parks Board: Sonoita Creek. By the 1990s, the land around Patagonia Lake State Park began to be developed. As housing tracts and commercial development encroached around the park, riparian areas and grassy hills that had inspired Western film producers four decades earlier seemed doomed to fall to the bulldozer. One of these parcels was nearly five thousand acres, just downstream from the lake, around a place known as Fresno Canyon. Relatively intact, the area was rich in vegetation as well as birds and other wildlife. In 1994, the owner of the parcel was a development company called the Rio Rico Investment Limited Partnership. The land seemed ready to develop. Taking advantage of Heritage Fund money, the Arizona State Parks Board stepped in and purchased the tract for $2.8 million. Rio Rico, which owned other parcels nearby, concluded that the value of having such an open space would actually enhance the quality of life, and hence the property values, of the other developments in the vicinity. The land acquired became Sonoita Creek State Natural Area. In 1999, the board acquired several smaller lots to add to the natural area. The Sonoita Creek State Natural Area, however, was not contiguous with Patagonia Lake State Park, separated from each other by more than three thousand acres of state trust land. In 1995,

San Rafael Ranch Natural Area represents a new ethic in park development. The ranch buildings stand on what became state land but the bulk of the ranch remains as a conservation easement. Other parties possess the land but Arizona State Parks owns the use of it.

the board applied for the purchase of this land. Once opened, Sonoita Creek would offer opportunities for hiking, bird watching, and other low-impact forms of recreation in contrast to the boating and picnic facilities at Patagonia Lake, reflecting the shift in resource stewardship over the past thirty years.[50]

San Rafael Ranch

The Heritage Fund also helped finance the creation of one of the newest state parks—and one of the largest: San Rafael Ranch. Adjacent to the Mexican border, in the broad, grassy Santa Cruz River Valley, the ranch was also one of the most remote in the system, accessible only through rough, unpaved Forest Service roads. In its day, however, the ranch was one of the finest in Santa Cruz County, the legacy of cattle baron Colin Cameron, who came to southern Arizona in the 1880s. The ranch was part of the Spanish San Rafael de la Zanja land grant, extending six miles along the San Pedro. At twenty-two thousand acres, the ranch was the largest private parcel of land in the area. Although the ranch's two-story main house burned under mysterious circumstances in 1899, Cameron was undaunted and built an even bigger, grander house, which doubled as the ranch headquarters. With its raised main floor atop an above-ground basement, large hipped roof, surrounding verandah, and Victorian detailings, the house looked more like a plantation in Louisiana than a ranch in Arizona. Cameron only lived in the house a short time. He had faced constant legal battles with neighbors over land rights. When he went to court and lost in 1903, he decided the ranch was not worth the hassle and sold it to the equally colorful copper magnate William C. Greene.[51]

During the twentieth century, the ranch was the home of the Greene Cattle Company. In the 1910s, Pancho Villa occasionally raided the ranch for horses. In the 1950s, the ranch gained national fame as the setting for the movie version of the musical *Oklahoma!* After searching throughout the state, the movie's producers decided that the wide grasslands looked more like Oklahoma than Oklahoma itself. By this time, the ranch was the property of Greene's daughter, Florence Sharp, who became the matriarch of the family. The ranch had ceased being the major enterprise that it once was, however, and by the late 1950s, there was a growing concern in the family about the massive estate taxes that the ranch would bring once San Rafael passed to the next generation.

The Sharps were not alone in their concerns. Their neighbors in that part of Santa Cruz County, and a number of other individuals around the state, also wondered what would become of the ranch. In the 1970s, the Arizona State Parks Natural Areas Committee considered the San Rafael Valley to be one of the outstanding natural areas of the state. Ever since, groups such as the Nature Conservancy sought ways to protect this resource. Not long afterward, the conservancy's William Roe began working with the Sharps to find a way to preserve their land. The Sharps had long understood the environmental value of their land. Florence Sharp became especially interested in the ecology of the riparian areas when she met a graduate student who visited the ranch to study the endangered topminnow. As research in the valley continued, it became clear that several rare species of salamanders, snakes, and desert fish existed in greater numbers on the ranch than anywhere else in Arizona. Ken Travous once noted that it was the "mother lode of natural areas." The Sharp's grazing did not seem to dramatically impact the resources on the ranch. Subdivision and uncontrolled development probably would. Something had to be done to make sure that San Rafael Ranch stayed in its present condition.[52]

The local community of ranchers was tight-knit. They enjoyed the rural living that the region afforded and did not want the development that was happening elsewhere in Santa Cruz County to ruin the San Rafael Valley. In 1994, the

Sonoran Institute, a newly established organization that worked with communities to preserve local ecology and still maintain economic needs, arranged for a workshop of local landowners to discuss possible solutions for their valley, of which the Sharps's ranch was a central part. Locals did not want the ranch to be broken up among the Sharp children, which might lead to unwanted development in the area. The best chance for the future was to work while the ranch was still in one piece. However, the locals were equally wary of turning over the ranch to either the federal government or the state because so much of the area was already owned by a public entity. Simply making the ranch a big park ran the risk of destroying the area's ranching character and, in the words of one resident, would "pickle" rather than "preserve" their beloved valley.

The most agreeable solution seemed to be a compromise centering on acquiring a conservation easement instead of the land itself. Whoever purchased the easement would control the use of the land without actually changing the ownership. Moreover, the land under such an easement could not be subdivided.[53] Out of that workshop came the San Rafael Valley Land Trust, which began setting up conservation easements in the area.

Florence Sharp died shortly after the meeting, and the family found that they had to sell part of the ranch to handle estate taxes. The family hoped that selling the conservation easement to the ranch would pay for these taxes and looked for a potential buyer. They worked with William Roe, a long-time acquaintance and member of the Arizona State Parks Board. With his help, the Sharps and the Nature Conservancy put together a proposal so that the Arizona State Parks Board, which now had the benefit of money from the Heritage Fund, could purchase the easement. Such a collaborative partnership would provide Arizona State Parks with a new site, would preserve the ecological integrity of the ranch, and would help the Sharps with their financial problems.

In early 1998, the Sharp family and the Nature Conservancy went before the Arizona State Parks Board with the proposal. Although the board was already embroiled in a feverish attempt to complete Kartchner Caverns, San Rafael Ranch seemed promising. The board members especially liked the combination of public and private ownership. In addition, the agency was again under pressure to create more parks. A new state audit suggested that the agency do more to acquire park sites—especially with Heritage Fund money available. Meanwhile House Bill 2177, which would have abolished the State Parks Board and created an agency under a director appointed by the governor, appeared in the legislature but did not pass. The board began the process of earmarking $6 million from the

Heritage Fund to acquire the easements to San Rafael and perhaps a few parcels of the land itself.

The move received support from the community near the ranch. A supporter with the Brush Hill Land and Cattle Company noted, "I've seen most of my beloved state destroyed forever by development. With every tract of land that died under the bulldozers, a part of me seems to die top. Now I, nor any one else, will have to see this particular Eden destroyed." Ironically, fifty years earlier the cattle industry fought a fierce battle to prevent state park acquisitions from taking land out of what it saw as productive use. Now, a state park was going to become a tool for ranching families to preserve their way of life.[54]

Within a few months, however, this optimistic scenario changed when the Sharp family came back to the board and said that because of problems with the estate tax issue, the conservation easement would not remedy their situation as they had hoped. In July 1998, they proposed abandoning the conservation easement idea and have the Arizona State Parks Board simply acquire the land outright—for a price of about $11 million. That price was too much for State Parks, and the Sharps put the ranch up for sale on the open market. Roe and the staff of the Nature Conservancy moved quickly, however, and managed to marshal the funds to purchase the ranch. Then the board agreed to purchase a smaller section of the lands on the ranch, with a conservation easement on the rest of the property. Not everyone agreed, however. Some of the landowners in San Rafael Valley felt that the Sharps and Arizona State Parks had simply ignored the agreement the various parties had committed to earlier in the year. Some were concerned that establishing a park, even on just part of the ranch, would come closer to "pickling" rather than "preserving" the place. Even so, with members of the Nature Conservancy, Arizona State Parks, and the Sharp family still interested, the arrangements proceeded quickly. In late 1998, the Nature Conservancy purchased the San Rafael Cattle Company from the Sharp family. In January 1999, the Arizona State Parks Board agreed to allocate $8.6 million to purchase a combination of land parcels and conservation easements on San Rafael. The purchase included 3,557 acres on the southern part of the ranch, including the ranch house. The conservation easement consisted of 17,570 acres in the northern part of the ranch, which the Nature Conservancy had purchased from the Sharps.

The hope was to find a conservation rancher who would continue to operate a ranch on the site but with the care and consideration that the Sharps had. The thought of having cattle, which have ruined so many acres elsewhere in the

A recent Arizona State Parks project was at Spur Cross Ranch, north of Phoenix. Technically a unit of the Maricopa County Regional Park System, Spur Cross Ranch Conservation Area was a cooperative venture among local, county, state, and national organizations.

West, as tools for conservation at San Rafael may have struck some as odd. Others held that having cattle graze on the grassland of the ranch would help reduce the fire danger. The ranch represented a new form of stewardship for Arizona State Parks. The public and private partnership through conservation easements was a far cry from the direct acquisitions of the 1950s, making partners out of interests that would have been opponents in earlier years.[55]

Spur Cross

Arizona State Parks' most recent project was as complex as San Rafael Ranch. Spur Cross Ranch consisted of 2,200 acres of Sonoran desert north of Cave Creek. A place of both natural and archaeological value, the ranch contained the last year-round, spring-fed stream in Maricopa County as well as more than ninety Hohokam archaeological sites. The land was private, with ownership primarily split between the Cincinnati-based Great American Life Insurance Company (70 percent) and the Dreiseszun family (30 percent), who had been involved with the place for decades.

By the late 1980s, the ranch that was once an isolated spot well north of Phoenix was threatened by encroaching development. Governor Babbitt learned of efforts to save the archaeological resources on the property late in his administration. By 1996, however, a Scottsdale developer proposed turning Spur Cross into a planned community with more than six hundred houses, a resort, and an eighteen-hole golf course. Citizens in the nearby town of Cave Creek were concerned about the loss of such a large stretch of open land and tried to make it a city-run park.

Efforts on the part of Cave Creek to annex the ranch failed, and the project took on additional significance when several political figures got involved. Herbert Dreiseszun and local officials had approached the Arizona State Parks Board in 1997 about making Spur Cross a state park. Meanwhile, U.S. Senator John McCain got involved in an effort to get Spur Cross incorporated into the adjacent Tonto National Forest. Stung by his reputation as being cool to environmental issues, McCain saw Spur Cross as a way to show that he was sensitive to the environment. Envisioning a Babbitt-like land swap, McCain proposed that Great American give Spur Cross to the USFS in exchange for land elsewhere in Arizona. There were, however, several problems with the proposal. The heads of Tonto National Forest didn't want Spur Cross. Also, communities from Flagstaff to Scottsdale were concerned that valuable natural areas near them would get swapped to save the Cave Creek property. With no clear goal of what would be traded and with a deep concern over whether this endeavor would actually make environmental sense, groups including the Arizona Game and Fish Department, the Arizona League of Conservation Voters, the Arizona Horseman's Association, and the Sierra Club, Grand Canyon Chapter, came out against the trade. By the end of 1998, the land trade idea seemed unworkable.

The Spur Cross issue reemerged, however, in 1999 when Governor Jane Dee Hull (with the support of McCain, Great American, the mayor of Cave Creek, and other influential state and local officials) supported a bill to make Spur Cross a state park. In her State of the State speech in January 1999, Hull expressed hope that creating Spur Cross State Park would be "one of the greatest legacies of the 44th legislature." It paid to have the support of the governor. The board and staff of Arizona State Parks already had a lot to do. They were in the final stages of opening Kartchner Caverns, working out arrangements for the Sonoita Creek State Natural Area, reopening Yuma Crossing, and negotiating the conservation easements at San Rafael. Even so, the support of the governor ensured that Spur Cross was to be acquired in an arrangement between the state and Maricopa County. In May 1999, Hull and others persuaded the Arizona state legislature to pass a bill allocating $3.25 million out of the general fund for the purchase of the park, with the provision that the money revert to the general fund if not spent by 2003. The rest of the estimated $15 million to purchase Spur Cross would come from the State Park portion of the Heritage Fund ($3.5 million) and from Maricopa County chipping in $7.5 million. However, an unexpected twist threatened to kill everyone's efforts to preserve Spur Cross. Herbert Dreiseszun, patriarch of the family who owned the 30 percent interest, announced publicly that his portion was worth more than previously determined. Suddenly the state and county were short by almost $7 million, with no prospect of raising the funds from existing coffers. The crisis was solved with the birth of a unique partnership between the state, Maricopa County, and the Town of Cave Creek. Cave Creek came to the rescue by proposing and getting voter approval of a $6.7 million bond measure, the first tax the townspeople had ever imposed on themselves. These funds made it possible for the town to purchase the Drieseszun interest in Spur Cross. The resulting partnership involved the Maricopa County Parks Department providing operational management. Operational revenues would be generated at the gate along with a percentage of the Cave Creek bed tax. The state would hold conservation easements over the entire property to provide the safety net for the protection of the site.[56]

Shifts in Attitude and Tactics

When House Bill 72 first created the Arizona State Park Board, the intent was for the institution to acquire and manage sites as parks for the enjoyment of Arizona's residents and visitors. It was a time when outdoor recreation still had the reputation of being a benign presence on the land. As a park, a location could, ideally, preserve natural beauty and allow people to enjoy it as well. This was just before the wilderness movement of the 1960s and the development of ecology in the 1970s and 1980s reshaped how parks functioned and were perceived. Preservation and recreation, once nearly synonymous, became separate, even competing concepts. The change affected even the interior West, with its strong tradition of recreation-oriented state parks. Although Arizona State Parks still had a recreation focus, as evidenced by the Fool Hollow Project, the agency now had responsibilities to care for significant natural features, such as Kartchner and Tonto, rather than just provide access to them. By the 1990s, it was also clear that parks could be overused and that some places needed to be preserved through limiting the number of people on the land. Kartchner Caverns, Sonoita Creek State Natural Area, San Rafael Ranch State Park, San Rafael Ranch Natural Area, and Spur Cross Ranch illustrate this shift in attitude. These were places whose value rested in their natural features more than in how many people could visit them.

The staff and leadership of Arizona State Parks still faced some of the same challenges that they had in earlier years, but there were new tactics to overcome them. Partnerships among federal, state, and local bodies helped establish facilities such as Yuma Crossing, Fool Hollow, and Spur Cross Ranch. Meanwhile, new sources of funding, such as the ability to keep park admissions or the creation of the Heritage Fund, helped in the acquisition of parks and natural areas.

This influx of money, however, has not entirely freed Arizona State Parks from financial problems. Budgetary constraints in the early 1990s, for example, forced the state to consider cutting back on funding for state parks and the agency that ran them. Recent years have brought renewed budget issues. In June 2002, cutbacks again prompted the Arizona State Parks Board to announce the potential closure of parks. When the legislature announced a 41 percent budget cut for the agency for the 2002–2003 fiscal year, Travous announced that the only way to handle that shortfall was to close parks. This time eleven parks were listed: Lyman Lake, Fool Hollow, Homolovi Ruins, Tonto Natural Bridge, Catalina, McFarland, Lost Dutchman, Oracle, Picacho Peak, Roper Lake, and Tubac. During the months that followed, the agency and other bodies in state government worked on new financial arrangements to keep at least some of those parks open. At least for the short term, the closures were avoided, although the larger issues that prompted the move remain.[57]

Conclusion
Finding the Right Niche

By the time Arizona created its state park system, most of the major recreational, cultural, and natural sites were already on federal land or managed by a county, local, or private entity. This did not necessarily mean the arrangement was ideal. After all, some areas of habitat or of scenic beauty were on federal land that was being submerged under vast reservoirs. Many private and local museums were small and poorly funded.

Arizona State Parks was a latecomer, however, and had to compete with agencies and organizations that were much larger and had decades of experience with state and federal politics. Once a parcel of land was in the federal domain, taking it out of that domain to become a state park was often problematic. The agencies that ran these sites, particularly the BLM and the USFS, had no interest in relinquishing their major sites to the state, let alone to a small, underfunded upstart of an agency. Aravaipa Canyon, Baboquivari, Sabino Canyon, and Horsethief Basin failed to become state parks in large part because they were already on federal land. This was an era when recreation had become a major industry in the interior West and an important use for public lands. The Forest Service and other agencies were, themselves, trying to meet the growing need for recreation as well. Those places that the federal government was not managing on its own were already leased out to other entities, as the BLM did with Lake Pleasant. Federal agencies did not want to ruin their established relationships with cities and counties.

The state-level situation was not much better. Arizona State Parks emerged in an already crowded arena with players who had vaguely defined and overlapping responsibilities. Sites not protected by the federal government were often already the responsibility of another entity such as cities, counties, or Arizona Game and Fish. The AHS attempted to become a steward of cultural sites as well. Moreover, the SLD had operated for decades with a mandate to make state lands profitable, which usually meant supporting industries such as cattle grazing. In a state with less than 20 percent of the land in private hands, any agency looking to the private sector for parcels to acquire was starting with a limited base. As it was, landowners and agencies that wanted to sell or transfer their holdings had a number of local, state, federal, and private entities to choose from. If Arizona State Parks was not careful, another agency or organization could get there first, whether it was the AHS and the Calabasas *visita* or certain landowners donating their holdings, such as the Aravaipa donation to the Defenders of Wildlife.

Caught between federal, state, and local agencies known for their territorial nature and a legislature beholden to the cattle industry, or at least to low taxes, state parks needed to gain the support of powerful and vocal figures who could marshal public support on their behalf. Most of the general public barely understood the different responsibilities of the various federal, state, and local agencies, much less cared about who owned what. Who operated a given site was irrelevant so long as important natural or cultural resources got protection and there was access to popular recreational spots.

These dynamics tended to shape Arizona State Parks into a manager of sites rather than an owner of them. Although far-sighted landowners such as the Kartchners, Calvin Ireys, and the TRC saw creating a state park as a benevolent way to preserve a site for future generations, most state parks in Arizona were places whose owners preferred not to manage or could not manage on their own. Many natural or recreational parks, including Roper Lake, Oracle, Boyce Thompson Southwestern Arboretum, Lost Dutchman, and Fool Hollow had previous lives of being "protected" by public or private organizations. Historic sites such as Tubac, Tombstone, Yuma Prison, Fort Verde, and parts of Yuma Crossing began as museums owned by a local group or community. These places were already "saved" from development and destruction. All that changed was who was responsible for operating the site.

Yet when the Arizona State Parks Board tried to acquire major federal holdings, such as Aravaipa Canyon, the agencies that managed those areas resisted. Acquisition of land was problematic.

When the board and staff of Arizona State Parks worked to develop partnerships, the situation was different. The development of lake-based recreation proved to be one of the agency's more successful endeavors. Working with the BOR, BLM, and the U.S. Army Corps of Engineers, members of Arizona State Parks were able to lease space for campsites, parking, and boat ramps, taking advantage of federal moneys such as the LWCF. A large portion of Lyman Lake was a lease from a water company. Alamo Lake's lease was from the U.S. Army Corps of Engineers as was the lake portion of Painted Rocks. Later on, Catalina was a lease from the USFS (having been transferred from the SLD). The results were some of the state's most visited parks. Cooperative arrangements worked at other parks as well. Roper Lake, Boyce Thompson, and Fool Hollow were created by cooperative agreements with other agencies. A large section of San Rafael Ranch was a conservation easement. Spur Cross Ranch was a complex cooperative venture with county and municipal jurisdictions.

In several instances, the prominent feature for which a given park was noted did not even fall within the park boundaries. Catalina, for example, was in the shadow of dramatic mountains under the jurisdiction of the USFS. The actual slide rock that makes Slide Rock State Park so popular is just outside the park boundary on USFS land as well. Jerome State Park consisted of a mansion outside the main downtown of Jerome. Buckskin Mountain was not actually in Buckskin Mountain State Park. The dramatic cliffs of Picket Post that inspired Colonel William Boyce Thompson were just outside of Boyce Thompson Southwestern Arboretum. The rounded formations around Sedona were visible from, but not part of, Red Rock State Park. Lost Dutchman State Park had wonderful views of the Superstitions but was outside the national forest that contained the mountains. Assuming it actually existed, the fabled mine of Lost Dutchman Jacob Walz was almost certainly outside of the park that bore his name. In each of these cases, the Arizona State Parks Board did not actually acquire the dramatic features that people came to see. Rather, the agency managed access points to these landmarks and provided essential visitor facilities such as parking lots, campgrounds, restrooms, and trailheads.

Federal agencies such as the USFS came to rely on state parks to manage public access to some of its lands. State Parks could then do its job without getting into futile land acquisition attempts. In a region where the national government owned the majority of the land, state park systems had to develop partnerships with federal agencies or risk being left behind. Partnerships proved beneficial, if sometimes awkward, to both sides.

Arizona State Parks had to develop these partnerships because of dynamics common to state parks in the intermountain West. In the East or on the West Coast, state parks were often the primary vehicle for park development, with national parks managing the most spectacular or significant places. Although all states have small state parks of mainly local or regional interest, many state parks east of the Rocky Mountains are large and significant, such as the Adirondacks or Niagara Falls in New York, Mount Katahdin in Maine, Itasca State Park in Minnesota, and the Palo Duro Canyon in Texas. In these places, a site often gets preserved as a state park or it does not get preserved at all.

This is exactly the opposite situation in the intermountain West, where state parks are sandwiched amid a prominent federal system of parks, forests, historic sites, preserves, natural areas, and wildernesses, and a parallel array of county and local entities. With small populations (until recently) and large federal land holdings, western states have relied on national parks and forests to provide most of their outdoor recreation. National parks and monuments also preserved most of the region's significant historic, scenic, natural, and archaeological sites. City, county, and private sites handled local needs. Early on, sites that became state parks tended to be those that did not achieve or maintain federal status. Supporters of Lake Chatcolet in Idaho, for example, hoped to make the site a national park but had to settle for state-level status, establishing Heyburn State Park in 1909. Arizona's Papago Park started as a national monument before becoming a state park.

Some individual state parks were established in the 1920s. States such as New Mexico and Montana created state parks in connection with New Deal projects, but most state park systems and the vast majority of state parks in the region emerged after World War II. This was the era when demand for outdoor recreation reached unprecedented levels and when more people took notice of the problems of development. Parks of all levels were developing into major recreational and tourist spots, where the population could "get away from it all" with as much comfort and convenience as possible. Recreation increasingly became a major use of resources, first accompanying and then even supplanting industries such as cattle and timber. States took advantage of federal programs, such as the LWCF, to provide facilities for the growing numbers who inundated recreational sites, especially lakes. Even so, extractive industries remained significant and powerful contributors to the political process, requiring compromises to be made.

State park systems in the region were also vulnerable to changes in federal policies. Parks such as Goblin Valley or Kodachrome Basin in Utah started as BLM facilities that the state government later acquired. By contrast, Lake Havasu State Park emerged out of the federally sponsored planning efforts only to lose most of its land when the BLM reassessed its interest in the area. Several national monuments in New Mexico, such as the missions of Pecos, Abo, and Quarai, started as state-operated facilities. Creating state parks was more often a case of determining who managed a site than saving it from destruction from unscrupulous extractive industries. State park systems in the West have been in constant competition—not just with unresponsive private landholders but with other agencies as well.

In the 1970s and 1980s, a new attitude toward resource stewardship had emerged. Supporters of the new environmental West, such as Bruce Babbitt, worked with and around existing political arrangements to provide recreational space, preserve habitat, and protect cultural resources such as archaeological ruins. More recently, state parks professionals have had to become savvy with developing partnerships and even rethinking what a state park is. Today's conservation easements are a far cry from the "catfish farms, ponds, and boat docks" of a previous generation.

In the interior West, state parks agencies have had to adapt. Arizona State Parks did so by emphasizing partnerships over acquisitions. Over its history Arizona State Parks transformed itself from competitor to partner with the other federal, state, local, and private entities. That transition was sometimes painful and was not always easy. Nor is it complete. It is an ongoing process of redefinition. Changes in land ownership, financial opportunities or restrictions, and demographic changes will likely reshape state parks in the future. For the leadership and staff of Arizona State Parks, being stewards of a constantly changing collection of recreational, natural, and cultural sites has its challenges. Each board member and each member of the agency will have to be creative as they decide who manages the parks, how the parks are maintained, at what cost, and for what purposes. Arrangements, ownership, and funding may change but one need remains: to enable people to experience Arizona's natural, cultural, and recreational resources in ways that ensure the continued survival of those resources.

Appendix A

Arizona State Officials

State Parks Directors

Dennis McCarthy, 1957–1976
Michael Ramnes, 1976–1985
Donald Charpio, 1986–1987
Kenneth Travous, 1987–present

State Parks Deputy/Assistant Directors

Paul Crandall, 1966–1969
Wallace Vegors, 1970–1978
Roland Sharer, 1978–1986
Kenneth Travous, 1986–1987
Courtland Nelson, 1987–1993
Charles Eatherly, 1993–1998
Jay Ziemann, 1998–present

State Historic Preservation Officers

Dennis McCarthy, 1967–1976
Dorothy Hall, 1972–1979
James Ayres, 1979–1981
Ann Pritzlaff, 1981–1982

Donna Schober, 1983–1987
Shareen Lerner, 1987–1992
James Garrison, 1992–present

Note: Dorothy Hall oversaw activities related to the National Historic Preservation Act, although Dennis McCarthy was officially State Historic Preservation Officer until 1976.

Appendix B
Five-Year Plan, 1960–1965 (as Proposed in 1959)

Proposed State Scenic Areas

Tonto Natural Bridge State Park
Cochise Stronghold State Park
Lower Sycamore Canyon State Park
Meteor Crater State Park

Proposed State Recreation Areas

Horsethief Basin Recreation Area
Hualapai Mountain Recreation Area
Camp Tuthill Recreation Area
Selected Game and Fish Department lakes

Proposed State Monuments

Mining Town of Jerome State Historical Monument
Territorial Governor's Mansion Historical Monument
Forts Crittenden and Buchanan Historical Monuments and/or
Fort Bowie Historical Monument

Proposed State Landmarks

"Seventy State Landmarks commemorating historical and prehistorical events, persons, areas, sites and structures."

Source: Arizona State Parks Board, *Annual Report,* 1958–1959, 17–19.

Appendix C

Ten-Year Plan, 1965–1975 (as Proposed in 1959)

Proposed State Scenic Areas

A mesquite forest
A palo verde forest
A natural desert area
Palms Canyon
Southwestern Arboretum
Baboquivari Peak area
Picacho Peak
Aravaipa Canyon
Texas Canyon
Monument Valley
Dinosaur Canyon
Tisnasbas
Bottomless Pit
Crystal Caves
Cave of the Bells
Coconino Caverns

Proposed State Recreation Areas

Selected campgrounds
Selected Colorado River recreation areas

Appendix C

Selected Arizona Game and Fish lakes
Selected U.S. Army Corps of Engineers flood-control projects
Selected Arizona Power Authority dams
Selected Salt River Project lakes
Stoneman Lake
San Carlos Lake
Granite Dells, Watson Lake area
Winter sports areas in northern and southern Arizona

Proposed Historical Monuments

Fort Apache
Camp Verde
Barth Hotel
Zane Grey's cabin
San Xavier Del Bac
Awatovi
Guevavi and Quiburi
Maricopa Wells stage stop
A ghost town

Proposed Prehistoric Monuments

Kinishbah
Besh-ba-Gowah
Pueblo Grande Museum
Long Wall Ruins
Malpais Fort
Sierra Ancha cliff dwellings
Snaketown Ruins
Catlin Ruins
Clear Creek Ruins
Elden Ruins
Adamsville Ruins
Reserve Monument Number 1
Chavez Pass
Picture Rocks
Painted Rocks
St. John's Ruins
University Indian Ruins

Source: Arizona State Parks Board, *Annual Report,* 1958–1959, 17–19.

Notes

Abbreviations Used in the Notes

ACGA	Arizona Cattle Growers Association
ADS	Arizona Daily Star
AHS	Arizona Historical Society
AHS-T	Arizona Historical Society, Tucson
AHS-Y	Arizona Historical Society, Yuma
AORCC	Arizona Outdoor Recreation Coordinating Commission
AR	Arizona Republic
ASPA	Arizona State Parks Association
ASPB	Minutes of the Arizona State Parks Board
BFP	Bert Fireman Papers
BLM	Bureau of Land Management
BTSWA	Boyce Thompson Southwestern Arboretum
CCC	Civilian Conservation Corps
CVHS	Camp Verde Historical Society
DLAPR	Arizona State Department of Library and Archives
ECW	Emergency Conservation Work Program
FVSHP	Fort Verde State Historic Park
LCRLUP	Lower Colorado River Land Use Plan
LLSP	Lyman Lake State Park
LWCF	Land and Water Conservation Fund
MSHP	McFarland State Historic Park

MSPP	Governor Ernest McFarland Papers, McFarland State Park
NACP	National Archives, College Park Site, Maryland
NAU	Northern Arizona University
OSP	Oracle State Park
PCHS	Pinal County Historical Society
PG	Phoenix Gazette
PJFP	Paul Jones Fannin Papers
SES	Southern Environment Service
SHPO	State Historic Preservation Officer
SLD	State Land Department
SLIF	State Lake Improvement Fund
TCSHP	Tombstone Courthouse State Historic Park
TPSHP	Tubac Presidio State Historic Park
TRC	Tombstone Restoration Commission
UA	University of Arizona
USFS	United States Forest Service
USFS-AS	United States Forest Service, Apache Sitgreaves National Forest
YCSHP	Yuma Crossing State Historic Park
YDS	Yuma Daily Sun
YTPSHP	Yuma Territorial Prison State Historic Park

Introduction

1. Wrobel and Long, *Seeing and Being Seen;* Pomeroy, *In Search of the Golden West;* Runte, *National Parks;* Rothman; *Devil's Bargains;* Junkin, *Lands of Brighter Destiny.*

2. Newton, *Design on the Land,* 517.

3. Hays, *Beauty, Health, and Permanence,* 436–440; Thomas, ed., *Politics and Public Policy in the Contemporary American West.*

4. For this work, "Arizona State Parks," or "State Parks," refers to the combination of the Arizona State Parks Board and agency. If the board works alone, it is referred to as simply "the board." Agency staff or units, when working alone, will be designated as such.

Chapter 1. From Dream to Reality

1. Meyer, *Everyone's Country Estate*; Thompson, "Politics in the Wilderness"; Terrie, "The Adirondack Forest Preserve"; Graham, *The Adirondack Park*; Conard, "Hot Kitchens in Places of Quiet Beauty" and *Places of Quiet Beauty.*

2. "U.S. General Service Administration Table: Comparison of Federally Owned Land with Total Acreage by State as of September 30, 1999," http://www.blm.gov/natacq/pls00/pdf/part1-3.pdf. For details on Arizona's land use, see Walker and Bufkin, *Historical Atlas of Arizona*; Baker, *Timeless Heritage.* See also Thomas, ed., *Politics and Public Policy in the Contemporary American West,* 417–497; Junkin, *Lands of Brighter Destiny.*

3. Cox, "Before the Casino," 336.

4. Thomas, ed., *Politics and Public Policy in the Contemporary American West*; Hays, *Beauty,*

Health and Permanence, 435–440; Cox, "Before the Casino" and "Weldon Heyburn, Lake Chatcolet, and the Evolving Concept of Public Parks"; Kleinsorge, *Exploring Colorado State Parks*; Conklin, "The Long Road to Riches"; quote from Woods, "The Role of Federal Dollars and the Economics of Recreation in the Development of Idaho's State Parks," 18; Petersen and Reed, "'For All the People, Forever and Ever.'"

5. Goff, *Arizona Civilization,* 99, 205–208; Murdock, *The Constitution of Arizona,* 198–201; Taylor, *Public Administration in Arizona,* 53–55; Van Petten, *The Constitution and Government of Arizona,* 144–146; Mason and Hink, *Constitutional Government in Arizona,* 55–58.

6. For this book, *interior West* and *Intermountain West* are used interchangeably to refer to a region of eight states: Arizona, Colorado, Idaho, Montana, Nevada, New Mexico, Utah, and Wyoming.

7. Rothman, *America's National Monuments;* King, ed., *Arizona's National Monuments;* Arizona Game and Fish Commission, *Arizona Game and Fish: 30 Years of Progress,* special edition of *Wildlife Views* 7 (January 1960).

8. Torrey, *State Parks and Recreational Uses of State Forests in the United States,* 71.

9. Nelson, *State Recreation Parks, Forests and Game Preserves.*

10. Quoted in "State Parks Are Not Needed: U.S. Forest Service Better Qualified," *Arizona: The State Magazine* 14 (February 1925): 5.

11. Ibid.

12. Tilden, *The State Parks,* 486.

13. Williams interview and Woodruff interview; Cox, "Before the Casino."

14. National Park Service, *A Study of the Park and Recreation Problem of the United States.*

15. Bureau of Census, *1940 Population Census;* Arizona Resources Board, *Arizona: Park, Parkway and Recreational Area Plan, Progress Report,* 111–128.

16. Richardson, "The Civilian Conservation Corps and the Origins of the New Mexico State Park System"; Lowitt, *The New Deal and the West;* McClelland, "A New Deal For State Parks, 1933–1942," 229–255; Conklin, "The Long Road to Riches"; Cox, "Before the Casino"; Petersen and Reed, "For All the People, Forever and Ever."

17. Aaron L. Citron to R. A. Vetter, October 11, 1935, National Park Service Papers, National Archives, College Park Site, Maryland, hereafter referred to as NACP.

18. Narrative Report of Camp SP-11-A, Records of the Brand of Recreation, Land Planning, and State Cooperation, Project Reports on CCC Projects in State and Local Parks, 1933–37; Letter from Herbert Evison to Dr. Alfred Atkinson, December 3, 1940; Aaron L. Citron, Assistant to Procurement Officer, ECW, to R. A. Vetter, October 11, 1935, NACP; Paige, *The Civilian Conservation Corps and the National Park Service, 1933–1942,* 182–183; Rothman, *America's National Monuments,* 10; Arizona Resources Board, *Arizona: Park, Parkway and Recreational Area Plan, Progress Report,* 111–128; "Arizona" in H. James, ed., *25th Anniversary Year-book;* Gart, "Let's Meet At the Hole in the Rock," 47–66; Clemensen, *Cattle, Copper, and Cactus,* especially 148–155.

19. H. James, ed., *25th Anniversary Year-book,* 29–30; K. C. Kartchner to Conrad L. Wirth, December 20, 1940, NACP; Arizona Resources Board, *Arizona: Park, Parkway and Recreational Area Plan, Progress Report,* 115–116; Gart, "Let's Meet at the Hole in the Rock," 67; *House Bill 247,* cited in Arizona Legislature, *Journal of the House,* 20th Legislature, 1st Regular Session and 1st Special Session, Phoenix, 1951, 993–994; Ben Avery, "Rod and Gun," *Arizona Republic*

(AR), February 18, 1955; "City Applies for Papago Park Lease," *AR*, April 15, 1955; National Park Service report to the Arizona State Parks Board, in Minutes of the Arizona State Parks Board (hereafter referred to as ASPB), March 31, 1958, 15–21; Joseph Pendergast, director of the National Recreation Association, to Dennis McCarthy, November 15, 1957, in ASPB, December 16, 1957.

20. Richards, *History of the Arizona State Legislature, 1912–1967*, vol. 8, 5; R. A. Vetter to James B. Williams, September 15, 1936; A. E. Demaray, associate director, National Park Service, to superintendent, Southwestern National Monuments, October 26, 1936; Hugh M. Miller, acting director, Southwestern Monuments, to Paul Keefe, president, Arizona State Senate, February 11, 1937; A. E. Demaray, acting director, National Park Service, to Governor R. C. Stanford, May 14, 1937, NACP; Arizona Legislature, *Journal of the House*, 13th Legislature, Phoenix, 1937, 209, 222; ibid., *Journal of the House*, 15th Legislature, Phoenix, 1941, 974; Aaron L. Citron to R. A. Vetter, October 11, 1935, NACP; Arizona Resources Board, *Arizona: Park, Parkway and Recreational Area Plan, Progress Report*, 116–119; H. James, ed., *25th Anniversary Year-book*, 29–30.

21. Ben Avery, "Yes, These, Also, Are Desert Sports," *This is Arizona*, 514.

22. See Luckingham, *The Urban Southwest* and *Phoenix*; Melnick and Roepke, *Urban Growth in Arizona*; Wiley and Gottlieb, *Empires in the Sun*; Bureau of Census, *1940 Census of Population* and *1960 Census of Population*. See also Hays, *Beauty, Health, and Permanence*, 1–39, 527–543; Wrobel and Long, *Seeing and Being Seen*; and Aron, *Working at Play*.

23. Rothman, *Devil's Bargains*; Wrobel and Long, *Seeing and Being Seen*; Shaffer, *See America First*; Norris, *Discovered Country*; Pomeroy, *In Search of the Golden West*; Jennings, *Roadside America*.

24. Stanley Womer to Ernest W. McFarland, August 15, 1956, Arizona State Parks Association Papers, Arizona State Archives, Phoenix, hereafter referred to as ASPA papers; "To Relax in the Sun, $66 Million," *Arizona Days and Ways, AR*, March 4, 1956, 86–89; "Lake Mead Draws 2 Million Visitors," *AR*, February 4, 1955; "Tourist Travel Into State Establishes March Record, *AR*, April 15, 1955; "Canyon Visitors Spend $19 Million," *AR*, April 22, 1955; Roger Lewis, "Word of Valley's Charm Gets Around," *AR*, May 13, 1955; "Visitors to Grand Canyon Increase 7 Per Cent in '57," *AR* August 31, 1958; "Canyon Visitors Spend $19 Million," *AR*, April 22, 1955; "Saguaro Park Draws 77,000 Sight Seers," *Arizona Daily Star (ADS)*, January 9, 1956; Burke Johnson, "From All Over the World–Millions of Visitors," in *AR, This is Arizona*, 338–348; Conrad Wirth, "An Adequate National Park System for 300 Million People," *American Planning and Civic Annual* (1955): 1–8; Richard E. McArdle, "Recreational Uses of National Forests," *American Planning and Civic Annual* (1955): 8–14.

25. "State Shares in Park Plan," *AR*, February 5, 1956; "Park Service Speeds Program of Expansion at Grand Canyon," *AR*, August 31, 1958; United States Department of the Interior, *Annual Report*, 1956; Hatfield Chilson, "The Department of the Interior and Its National Park Service," *Planning and Civic Comment* (June 1957): 3–7; National Park Service, "Mission 66— Our New National Parks Program," *Arizona Recreation Bulletin* 4 (December 1956): 7; Runte, *National Parks*, 170–173; Arizona Game and Fish Department, *Arizona Game and Fish: 30 Years of Progress*, special edition of *Wildlife Views* 7 (January 1960); Ben Avery, "Rod and Gun" series in *AR*, 1955–1957.

26. Cosco, *Echo Park*; Brower, *For Earth's Sake*.

27. Stewart L. Udall, "Arizona, Its Promise and Challenge" in *AR, This Is Arizona,* 354–355.

28. See, for example, "City Survey of Culture Ordered," *ADS,* September 29, 1954; "Work Starts on Razing of Building," *AR,* August 7, 1955; "Pictographs on Display," *AR,* January 2, 1955. See also Roger A. Brevoort, "Historic Preservation: An Agenda for Keeping Arizona History Tangible for the Future," in Luey and Stowe, *Arizona at Seventy-Five,* 173–210; Sigurd F. Olsen, "The Challenge of Our National Parks," *National Parks Magazine* 28 (April–June 1954): 51–52, 85; Richard E. McArdle, "Recreational Use of National Forests," *American Planning and Civic Annual* (1955), 8–14; C. J. Olsen, "Integration of Outdoor Forest Recreation Potential with Public Park Programs," *American Planning and Civic Annual* (1956): 106–111; *Arizona Days and Ways, AR,* April 3, 1955, 2; Fred M. Packard, "Grand Canyon Monument in Danger," *National Parks Magazine* 23 (July–September 1949): 3–8, and "Grand Canyon Park and Dinosaur Monument in Danger," *National Parks Magazine* 23 (October–December 1949): 11–13; Luckingham, *Phoenix,* 136–176 and *The Urban Southwest,* 75–94; Richardson, *Dams, Parks, and Politics.*

29. Ernest W. McFarland to the Second Regular Session of the Twenty-Second Legislature, January 9, 1956, Governor Ernest McFarland Papers, McFarland State Park, hereafter referred to as MSPP.

30. See Don Dedera, "Good Morning!," *AR,* November 12, 1959; Ben Avery, "Rod and Gun," *AR,* January 14, 1955; Reg Manning, cartoon in *AR,* July 3, 1955; "Arizona Warned Against Pollution of the Air," *AR,* February 5, 1956; Ben Avery, "Rod and Gun," *AR,* September 4, 1955; Ben Avery, "Rod and Gun," *AR,* June 3, 1955; Hehr K. Steyart, "West Without Coyote Viewed as Colorless, Flat," *AR,* January 15, 1955.

31. Cox, "Before the Casino," 347.

32. Arizona Legislature, *Journal of the House,* 20th Legislature, 2nd Regular Session, Phoenix, 1952, 699; *Journal of the House,* 21st Legislature, 1st Special Session and 2nd Regular Session, Phoenix, 1954, 901; *Journal of the House,* 22nd Legislature, 1st Regular Session, Phoenix, 1955, 905–906.

33. Ben Avery, "Rod and Gun," *AR,* January 14, 1955.

34. "State Park System Legislation Urged," *AR,* December 4, 1955; "State Park System Called For," *ADS,* December 4, 1955; Dale King to General Superintendent, August 29, 1955, Bert Fireman Papers (hereafter referred to as BFP), Arizona Historical Foundation, Arizona State University, Tempe.

35. Arizona Development Board, *Preliminary Survey and Recommendations Relating to the Establishment of a State Parks and Recreation Board,* 8.

36. Ibid.; "State Park System Called For," *ADS,* December 4, 1955.

37. Cox, *The Park Builders,* 79–103; Tilden, *The State Parks,* 485–488; "Role Call of the States," *American Planning and Civic Annual* (1955), 75–77; Young, *The State Parks of Utah, The State Parks of Arizona,* and *The State Parks of New Mexico;* Kleinsorge, *Exploring Colorado State Parks.*

38. Ben Avery, "Rod and Gun," *AR,* April 24, 1956.

39. Ernest W. McFarland to the 2nd Regular Session of the 22nd Legislature, January 9, 1956, MSPP; *Journal of the House,* 22nd Legislature, Phoenix, 1956, 292–293, 910–913; Joseph F. Carithers to Ben Avery, April 17, 1956, ASPA papers, Arizona State Archives, Phoenix.

40. Barry Burkhard, "Conservation Pioneer Ben Avery Dies," *AR,* May 10, 1996.

41. "J. F. Carithers Appointed to NPA Staff," *National Parks Magazine* 31 (April–June 1957): 79; Fred M. Packard, "Joseph F. Carithers Heads Western Office," *National Parks Magazine* 32 (April–June 1958): 79. Carithers eventually became the western representative of the National Parks Association and wrote essays on the national parks.

42. Joseph F. Carithers to Ben Avery, May 2, 1956, ASPA papers. Carithers interview.

43. For example, representatives of the Central Arizona Project had strong reservations about Joseph Carither's agitation against dam construction in Arizona. See "Cease Fratricidal Strife, Conservation Units Urged," *ADS*, January 20, 1955; "Two Conservation Films Labeled Propaganda," *ADS*, January 11, 1955; "City Survey of Culture Ordered," *ADS*, September 29, 1954; "Conservation Unit Selects Officers," *ADS*, January 27, 1955; Ben Avery, "Rod and Gun," *AR*, December 16, 1955; Roger Lewis, "Scenic Lovers Organize," *AR*, November 11, 1959; ASPB, March 31–April 1, 1958.

44. Minutes of the Preliminary Organization Meeting of Arizona Parks Association, June 22, 1956, and Registered Attendance At Preliminary Meeting, June 22, 1956, ASPA papers; "Arizona Parks Victory Predicted At Meeting," *AR*, June 23, 1956; "Recreation Group Being Organized," *ADS*, June 22, 1956; "J. F. Carithers Heads Up New Park Group," *ADS*, June 23, 1956; *Highway Spotlight* 1 (December 13, 1955): 2; *Highway Spotlight* 2 (April 3, 1956): 1; *Highway Spotlight* 2 (October 16, 1956): 2; Letter from Charles J. Reitz to Joseph F. Carithers, June 19, 1956, ASPA papers. See "Arizona State Parks Association States Purpose," *Arizona Recreation Bulletin* 4 (December 1956): 3; Bert Fireman, "Recollections of Arizona: A Personal Perspective," *The Journal of Arizona History* 23 (spring 1982): 81–102, 98–100.

45. Stanley Womer to Ernest W. McFarland, August 15, 1956, 24–25, 32; ASPA, "Organization Growing" and "Bill Drafting" *News Bulletin* (October? 1956): 2, ASPA papers (The question mark here and in all references to the ASPA bulletin refers to the probable month. The bulletin does not include dates.) Arizona Development Board, *Preliminary Survey*, 1–2.

46. ASPA, "The Arizona State Parks Association Constitution and By-Laws, Adopted August 10, 1956"; Registered Attendance at Organization Meeting, August 10, 1956; ASPA, "State Park Association is Formed," *ADS*, August 11, 1956; "New Park Emphasis," *Phoenix Gazette (PG)*, August 10, 1956.

47. Robert M. Jaap to officers and board members, ASPA, September 5, 1956; Joseph F. Carithers to Stewart Udall, June 4, 1956; J. E. Thompson, Jr. to Bert Fireman, July 30, 1956; W. Taylor Marshall to Bert Fireman, July 27, 1956, ASPA papers; Harald K. Jensen to Bert Fireman, September 8, 1956; Arizona Development Board, *Preliminary Survey*, 3–8; ASPA, *News Bulletin* (October? 1956), ASPA papers; ASPA, *News Bulletin* (November? 1956), ASPA papers; ASPA, *News Bulletin* (December? 1956), ASPA papers; ASPA, "Proposed Drive Asked for Parks," *ADS*, September 15, 1956; "State Parks System Needs Own Setup," *PG*, May 9, 1956; Ben Avery, "Rod and Gun," *AR*, April 24, 1956; Jaap interview; Earley interview.

48. Arizona Cattle Growers Association, Minutes of the Quarterly Directors' Meeting, June 9, 1954, Arizona Cattle Growers Association Papers (hereafter referred to as ACGA), Arizona Historical Foundation, Arizona State University.

49. Minutes of the ASPA, September 14, 1956, ASPA papers.

50. Smithee interview; ASPA, *News Bulletin* (October? 1956), ASPA papers; ASPA, *News Bulletin* (November? 1956), ASPA papers; ASPA, *News Bulletin* (December? 1956), ASPA papers.

51. Joseph F. Carithers to Robert M. Jaap, February 28, 1957, ASPA papers.

52. ASPB, May 27, 1957.
53. Quote from ASPB, May 27, 1957. See also Jaap to Officers and Board Members, September 5, 1956, ASPA papers.
54. State of Arizona, *House Bill 72,* 23rd Legislature, 1st Regular Session.
55. Quote from ASPB, May 27, 1957.
56. Smithee interview.
57. Quote from ASPB, May 27, 1957.
58. "Parks Assn., Cattlemen Agree On Commission," *ADS,* January 19, 1957; "State Parks Bill Readied," *ADS,* January 28, 1957; ASPA, "We Had to Act—And Did," *News Bulletin* (March? 1957): 2, ASPA papers; form letter from Bert Firemen to the members of the legislature, January 30, 1957, ASPA papers; Smithee interview; Ben Avery, "Rod and Gun," *AR,* March 17, 1957; "State to Embark on Park Development," *ADS,* April 25, 1957; "Parks Department Bill Becomes Law," *AR,* March 26, 1957.
59. Nelson, *State Recreation,* 7.
60. *House Bill 72,* 23rd Legislature, 1st Regular Session, 1957.
61. Arizona Cattle Growers Association, Minutes of the Quarterly Directors Meeting, June 9, 1954, ACGA.
62. Obed M. Lassen to Ernest W. McFarland, January 23, 1957, Papers of the State Land Commissioner, Arizona State Archives; press release from Governor McFarland's office, April 23, 1957, ASPA papers; "Ricki Rarick Appointed to Parks Board,' *ADS,* April 24, 1957; Ben Avery, "Move Grows to Draft Lassen for Governor," *AR,* December 12, 1957.
63. Joseph F. Carithers to Wayne Early, September 11, 1957, ASPA papers.
64. ASPB, September 8, 1957, 3–4; Smithee interview.
65. ASPA, *Newsletter,* November 3, 1958, ASPA papers.
66. Odd S. Halseth, President's report, cited in ASPA, *Report* (December? 1959): 44–45, ASPA papers.
67. ASPA, *Newsletter* (May 1959): 2; *Newsletter* (October 1958): 3–9; and *Newsletter* (January 1959): 1; Robert M. Jaap to Odd S. Halseth, February 11, 1959; Kenneth J. Smithee to Devens Gust, January 14, 1963, ASPA papers. Ben Avery, "Rod and Gun," *AR,* March 17, 1957; Earley interview; report of the meeting of the State Parks Association, December 2, 1958, Paul Jones Fannin Papers, hereafter referred to as PJFP.
68. Ben Avery, "Rod and Gun," *AR,* February 18, 1955; ASPB, 1957–1959; Arizona State Parks Board, *Annual Report,* 1957–1958, 1958–1959, 1959–1960, and 1960–1961. See especially ASPB, May 27, 1957; June 17, 1957.
69. Dennis McCarthy to Ernest Allen, July 3, 1958, in ASPB, August 13, 1958.
70. Arizona State Parks Board, *Annual Report,* 1958–1959, 11; *Annual Report,* 1957–1958, 16–28; *Annual Report,* 1958–1959, 10.

Chapter 2. Local Landmarks under New Management

1. Murtagh, *Keeping Time,* 51.
2. Brownell, *They Lived in Tubac*; Wormser, *Tubac*; Spooner, *Tubac*; "Tubac: Little Town With a Big History," *Arizona Highways (AH)* (February 1957): 36–39; "Tubac: Where Time Is

Many Tomorrows," *AH* (March 1966): 31–38.

3. "Move for Tubac Sparked by Newcomers," *Nogales International (NI)*, January 10, 1958; *Weekly Arizonian* 1, no. 1 (fall 1957).

4. Brownell, *They Lived in Tubac,* 173–181; ASPB, March 31–April 1, 1958, and November 16, 1957; Arizona State Parks Board, *Annual Report,* 1958–1959, 12; Morrow interview; "Old Tubac Gets New Life," *AR,* October 2, 1958; "Tubac: Arizona's First State Park," *AH* (September 1958): 36–39; Santa Cruz County Supervisor's Minutes, December 12, 1958; Santa Cruz County Recorder's Office Docket 8, p. 15, Brownell Notes, Tubac Historical Society.

5. Arizona State Parks Board, *Annual Report,* 1960–1961, 15–16; "Tubac Historical Museum Completed," *Tucson Citizen (TC),* January 16, 1964; "Tubac: Where Time Is Many Tomorrows," *AH* (March 1966): 31–38; "Presidio Monument Dedicated as Dignitaries Crowd Tubac," *ADS,* February 3, 1964; "Standing Room Only in Tubac as Governor Opens Museum," *Green Valley News,* February 6, 1964; Museum Dedication Program, Tubac Presidio State Historic Monument, February 2, 1964, Tubac Historical Society; "Reach Tubac Plans Accord," *NI,* June 20, 1962; "Worth Restoring," *PG,* December 29, 1960; Chamber of Commerce Bulletin III, no. 1 (January 1962), Brownell notes; Young, *The State Parks of Arizona,* 178–187.

6. ASPB, December 7–8, 1964; March 30, 1966; May 18–19, 1966; August 25, 1966; February 23, 1967; April 20–21, 1967; August 12, 1969; March 17, 1970; July 21, 1970; June 16, 1971; May 31, 1973; "Battle Lines Drawn in Fight to Save Old School," *AR,* March 19, 1967; "Tubac Residents Hope to Preserve Old Structure as Historic Park Site," *TC,* March 27, 1967.

7. Quit Claim Deed between Cochise County and the City of Tombstone, January 5, 1942; Faulk, *Tombstone,* 186–209.

8. State of Arizona, Arizona Corporation Commission, Articles of Incorporation of the Tombstone Restoration Commission, December 19, 1949, located at Tombstone Courthouse State Historic Park, hereafter TCSHP; Speech from TRC (speaker unknown), December 21, 1950, TCSHP. See also undated "Comments By Individuals Who Are Deeply Interested in Tombstone Restoration," TCSHP.

9. *Annual Report of the Tombstone Restoration Commission,* January 30, 1957, TRC; Richard H. Howland, president, National Trust for Historic Preservation, to executive director, Arizona Park Board, June 6, 1958, TCSHP; "Tombstone Restoration Museum in New Location," *ADS,* October 25, 1957; TRC *Annual Report,* January 30, 1957, and Landin to Charles Bloomquist, October 5, 1957, TRC.

10. "Mrs. Tombstone," *AH* (October 1962): 32–34.

11. Landin to the TRC membership, November 2, 1959, TRC.

12. Landin to A. R. Spikes, state senator from Cochise County, January 9, 1957; Landin to Charles Bloomquist, October 5, 1957; Landin to Barry Goldwater, March 4, 1958; Landin to Senator Ernest McFarland, September 1955; Bloomquist to Landin, October 12, 1957; Jules Klegge to Bloomquist, October 11, 1957; Spikes to Landin, March 12, 1957; all documents are from TRC.

13. Agreement of Conveyance between the City of Tombstone and the Arizona State Parks Board, August 1, 1959. For discussion leading up to the creation of the park, see ASPB, March 31–April 1, 1958; Arizona State Parks Board, *Annual Report,* 1958–1959, 13. See also, Landin to membership, November 2, 1959; Landin to Dennis McCarthy, June 28, 1959; McCarthy to Landin, April 3, 1958; Landin to McCarthy, April 1, 1958; Landin to Governor Ernest

McFarland, March 4, 1958; Landin to Odd Halseth, January 22, 1959; Landin to A. R. Spikes, May 16, 1957; all from TRC. McCarthy to Landin, June 1, 1959; Minutes of the Meeting of the Executive Board, Tombstone Restoration Commission, including Landin to Dennis McCarthy, May 14, 1959; Tombstone Restoration Commission, *Annual Report,* January 29, 1959; McCarthy to Landin, May 6, 1959; report of May 20, 1958. See also TRC meeting to Dennis McCarthy and Howard L. Cox, Arizona State Parks Board landscape architect, March 2, 1959; Landin to McCarthy, October 27, 1958; McCarthy to Landin, September 17, 1958; McCarthy to Landin, June 24, 1958; Landin to L. Max Connolly, chair, Arizona State Parks Board, April 2, 1958; Landin to McCarthy, March 5, 1958, TCSHP; Landin to Governor Paul Fannin, January 9, 1959, PJFP; Young, *The State Parks of Arizona,* 166–177.

14. Trafzer and George, *Prison Centennial*; Murphy, *The Prison Chronicle*; Robert Woznicki, *The History of Yuma and the Territorial Prison*; Yuma Territorial Prison State Historic Park Statement of Management.

15. Notes taken from Minutes of the Yuma City Council, at Yuma Territorial Prison State Historic Park, hereafter YTPSHP; Yuma City Resolution 557 A, April 1, 1941; "Restoration of Old Prison Is Sought by VFW Committee, *Yuma Daily Sun (YDS),* March 22, 1937; "VFW to Seek Federal Funds for Restoring Territorial Prison," *YDS,* November 3, 1937; "Renew Efforts to Convert Old Prison Into Historical Museum, Public Park," *YDS,* March 8, 1939; "May Get NYA Project for Prison Re-Construction, Committee Told," *YDS,* April 27, 1939; "NYA Approves Prison Hill Project: Museum Planned May Start Work Monday," *YDS,* September 14, 1939; "Plan Dance June 1 to Raise Funds for Additional Work at Territorial Prison Museum, Nearing Completion," *YDS,* May 17, 1940; Westover, *Yuma Footprints,* 22–27.

16. See materials on Clarissa Winsor at the Arizona Historical Society–Yuma branch collection; "Historic Desert Alcatraz Is Now Museum," *Los Angeles Times,* August 25, 1966.

17. City of Yuma Ordinance 808, September 6, 1960; ASPB, June 7, 1960; Arizona State Parks Board, *Annual Report,* 1959–1960, 12–13; Young, *The State Parks of Arizona,* 188–198.

18. ASPB, December 9, 1968; August 26, 1968; "Historic Resources, Office of Depot Quartermaster," Yuma Crossing State Historic Park.

19. "Historic Land," *The Jerome Chronicle* (summer 1999); "Happy Birthday to the Jerome Historical Society," *The Jerome Chronicle* (spring 1988); Jerome Historical Society bulletins for 1955; Minutes of the Jerome Historical Society, 1955–1965; "Tumbledown Town With a Love of Life," *AH* (May 1976): 40–45; Young, *The State Parks of Arizona,* 56–73.

20. Laura Williams, secretary-treasurer, Jerome Historical Society, Inc., to Mary Dennis, secretary to the board, August 9, 1957, ASPB, August 11–12, 1957; Quit Claim Deed for the Douglas Mansion, August 27, 1962, in Statement of Management for Jerome State Historic Park; "Mr. Douglas of Arizona, Friend of Cowboys and Kings," *AH* (September 1953): 2–11; Dennis McCarthy to Thomas J. Allen, June 14, 1960, PJFP; Arizona State Parks Board news release, in ASPB, December 12, 1963.

21. Quoted in *The Jerome Chronicle* (August 1963).

22. "Verde Valley Welcomes Jerome State Historic Park," *Verde Valley Independent (VI),* October 14, 1965; includes several smaller articles, such as "Jerome Park is Credit to Work of Valley Folks," "Entire Verde Valley Top Attraction," "Mining History Told By Displays"; "Douglas Memorial Mining Museum," Jerome Historical Society *News Bulletin,* fall and winter 1966–1967, 6.

23. Ringer, *Engagement at Picacho Pass*; Martin Hardwick Hall, "The Skirmish of Picacho," *Civil War History*, 4 (1958): 27–35; United States Department of the Army, *The War of the Rebellion*, 1049.

24. Later excavations around the monument found a coffin, but the body was of a woman who died c. 1900. Some archaeological excavations suggest that the 1862 encounter might have taken place a mile to the north at a watering hole used by Butterfield Overland Mail.

25. L. Boyd Finch, "Sanctified by Myth"; "Picacho Pass Monument Honors Casualties of Civil War Skirmish," *AR*, April 28, 1985; Edna Evans Hoffman, "The Civil War in Arizona," *AH* (June 1962): 30–37; Dennis McCarthy to Thomas J. Allen, June 14, 1960, PJFP.

26. ASPB, July 30–31, 1962; January 21, 1963, including a letter from Raymond Cleghorn, acting state director for BLM, to Dennis McCarthy, November 29, 1962; June 25–26, 1963; December 17, 1965; March 30, 1966; Session Laws of Arizona, 1965, chapter 78; Young, *The State Parks of Arizona*, 142–149; Session Laws of Arizona, 1970, chapter 157; 1974, chapter 10.

27. The ownership and dates of transfer for all the buildings are summarized in a compilation of Yavapai County, Arizona Deeds, done in 1977, Fort Verde State Historic Park (FVSHP); "Camp Verde, Fort Apache, Outposts in the Wilderness," *AH* (June 1982): 12–15.

28. "Camp Verde Enhances Future By Preserving Past," *VI*, November 18, 1965; Sharlot Hall Award Nomination Form for Margaret Hallett, Camp Verde Historical Society (CVHS).

29. "Opening of Fort Verde Museum Scheduled Tomorrow," *VI*, November 22, 1956. Deed for administration building, CVHS; "Historic Fort Verde Comes Alive through Efforts of Today's Pioneers," *The Arizonian*, April 24, 1969; Constitution of the Fort Verde Museum, CVHS; *Master Plan Narrative, Fort Verde Museum, Chapter I*, January 1965; "History of Fort Verde—1665–1891, Camp Verde Arizona," n.d.; "Fort Verde Museum," c. early 1957, with second part c. 1964, and third part c. 1967, CVHS.

30. "Summary of Points Brought Up in Discussion of Fort Verde Museum Becoming a Part of the State Parks System," October 14, 1969, CVHS.

31. ASPB, September 17, 1969; Deed for Fort Verde to Arizona State Parks Board, August 18, 1970, FVSHP; Certification of resolution from Fort Verde Museum Board from August 26, 1970, and dedication program for Fort Verde State Historic Park, October 10, 1970, CVHS; "Word on Making Old Fort Verde into a State Historical Park," *VI*, June 18, 1970; Dennis McCarthy to Craig Jackson, October 21, 1969, in ASPB, December 9, 1969.

32. "In the Matter of an Open Public Meeting Regarding State Parks Board's Relationship with Camp Verde Historical Society," November 24, 1975, CVHS, p. 11.

33. Ibid; quotes from p. 30 and p. 25, respectively. See also, "Fort Verde Attached as Group Faults Plan," *VI*, November 26, 1975.

34. Deeds for surgeon's quarters, November 2, 1972, and parade ground parcels, May 28, 1971, FVSHP; "Future Bright for Fort," *VI*, November 16, 1972; Memo from John Schreiber, supervisor, Fort Verde, to Wallace Vegors, assistant director, September 16, 1974, FVSHP; "Fort Verde State Historic Park," *Arizona Preservation News* 3 (December 1972); Young, *The State Parks of Arizona*, 43–55; Ryden Architects, *Fort Verde State Historic Park Twenty-Year Master Plan*, January 1990; *Fort Verde State Historic Park Master Plan*, March 1978.

35. ASPB, November 20, 1960.

36. Bert Fireman may have also been a significant factor in the board's acceptance of the act. Fireman was well known in the state for his work in preserving and promoting Arizona

Notes to Pages 46–53   **193**

history and was involved in a variety of historical organizations, including the Arizona Pioneers Historical Society and the Arizona Historical Foundation at Arizona State University. A persuasive influence on the board, it is probable that the move for the board to implement the National Historic Preservation Act was at least partly his doing.

37. Dennis McCarthy to Samuel P. Goddard, October 21, 1966; Dennis McCarthy to Bert Fireman, August 4, 1969, BFP; *Arizona Preservation News* 7 (July 1977).

38. *Arizona Preservation News* 7 (July 1977).

39. ibid.

40. ASPB, May 19, 1965; Vegors interview; Dennis McCarthy to Jack Williams, March 30, 1970, in Arizona State Parks Board, *Annual Report,* 1968–1969; ASPB, June 16, 1971; July 20, 1976; *Arizona Preservation News* 2 (October 1972); 3 (December 1972); 4 (March 1973); 7 (July 1977).

41. Ellinwood, *The Arizona Historical Society Today.*

42. ASPB, December 21, 1970; February 26, 1971.

43. Letter to the chair and members of the Senate Natural Resources and Environment Committee, March 25, 1975, in ASPB, March 25, 1975.

44. AHS quote from "Parks Board Slaps Historical Society," *TC,* October 30, 1974; ASPB, February 13, 1969; December 21, 1970; February 26, 1971; February 27, 1974; October 29, 1974; T. G. Chilton to Dell Trailor, November 4, 1974, in ASPB, December 10, 1974; Dennis McCarthy to Jack Williams, March 6, 1974, and Jack Williams to Dennis McCarthy, February 11, 1974, John R. "Jack" Williams Papers. See also "Babbitt Boosts History Society Bill," *AR,* May 15, 1975; ASPB March 25, 1975, and September 19, 1975.

45. ASPB, December 9, 1969; July 21, 1970; February 26, 1971; August 19–20, 1971; October 25, 1971.

46. ASPB, January 14, 1972; August 9, 1972; November 13–14, 1972; December 21, 1972.

47. ASPB, March 7, 1973; May 31, 1973; November 19, 1973; Text of *Senate Bill 1136* in ASPB, October 5, 1973.

48. ASPB, January 23, 1967; March 13, 1972; March 28, 1972; July 27, 1973; June 22, 1977.

49. ASPB, October 2–3, 1966; August 19–20, 1971; December 15, 1978.

50. Arizona Register of Historic Places nomination form, March 1972; *Interpretive Plan, McFarland Historical State Park,* January 1990, McFarland State Historic Park (MSHP); Sorbin, ed., "Florence Townsite, A. T.," final report of Florence Townsite Historic District study.

51. For a personal account of this career, see McFarland's autobiography, *Mac,* published by McFarland in 1979. See also the section on Ernest McFarland in J. Myers, ed., *The Arizona Governors.*

52. Ernest McFarland to Dennis McCarthy, December 15, 1972, in ASPB, December 21, 1972; Quote from ASPB, July 20, 1976.

53. "McFarland Outlines Details in Gift of Pinal Courthouse," *Tri-Valley Dispatch,* January 8–9, 1975; ASPB, May 31, 1973; December 4, 1974; February 20, 1976; July 20, 1976.

54. ASPB, March 25, 1977; "McFarland Park Will Be Opened Here in 1977," *Florence Reminder and Blade Tribune,* January 6, 1977; "State Park Now Officially Open," *Florence Reminder and Blade Tribune,* February 1, 1979; Young, *The State Parks of Arizona,* 108–125.

55. "Paying a Call on the Riordans," *AH* (August 1993): 18–23; Miscellaneous items from Blanche Riordian Chamber Collection, Special Collections, Northern Arizona University (NAU), Flagstaff.

56. Riordan Mansion State Historic Park Statement of Management, including Gift and Warranty Deed from Blanche and Robert Chambers dated November 15, 1978; Miller interview; "Flagstaff Estate to Open as Park after Restoration," *AR*, June 6, 1982; Blanche Riordan Chambers Collection, Special Collections, NAU; Janet Webb Farnsworth, "The Riordan Mansion," *True West* (October 1995): 6–8; ASPB, August 24, 1972; September 23, 1977; December 9, 1977; press release, "Riordan State Historic Park Opens," July 25, 1983, Bruce Babbitt Papers, Arizona State Department of Library and Archives, hereafter referred to as Bruce Babbitt Papers, DLAPR; Young, *The State Parks of Arizona*, 150–159.

57. See, for example, Freed, *Preserving the Great Plains and Rocky Mountains*; Delahanty, *Preserving the West*; Rothman, *Devil's Bargains*; Murtagh, *Keeping Time*; Hosmer, *Preservation Comes of Age*; Wilson, *The Myth of Santa Fe*; Bodnar, *Remaking America*; Kammen, *In the Past Lane* and *Mystic Chords of Memory*; Thelan, "Memory and American History"; Coyne, *The Crowded Prairie*; Fenin and Everson, *The Western*; Hitt, *The American West from Fiction (1823–1976) into Film (1909–1986)*. For the role of women in preservation and community development, see, for example, P. Miller, *Reclaiming the Past*, and Howe, "Women in Historic Preservation."

Chapter 3. Water in the Desert

1. Reisner, *Cadillac Desert*; Baker, *Timeless Heritage*, 121–143; Makowski, "Scenic Parks and Landscape Values"; Doell and Fitzgerald, *A Brief History of Parks and Recreation in the United States*, Clawson and Van Doren, *Statistics on Outdoor Recreation*.

2. National Park Service, *Parks for America*; House Committee on Interior and Insular Affairs, *Land and Water Conservation Fund*, 88th Cong., 1st sess., 1963, H. R. 1960–1967, 13–22; *Land and Water Conservation Fund*, 88th Cong., 2nd sess., 1964, H. R. 1639–1711, 2–34; ASPB, May 4–5, 1964; T. G. Smith, "John F. Kennedy, Stewart Udall, the New Frontier Conservation."

3. Myers and Green, *State Parks in a New Era*.

4. ASPB, January 21–22, 1963; March 9, 1965; Arizona Outdoor Recreation Coordinating Commission, *Arizona State Lake Improvement Fund Plan*.

5. Ben Avery, "Water Sport Fans Edge Out Anglers," *AR*, April 24, 1956.

6. *Arizona State Lake Improvement Fund Plan*, 3–4. In the early 1980s, the legislature created an additional fund, the Boating Law and Safety Enforcement Fund, which provided state money to State Parks and Game and Fish to promote water safety issues. See ASPB, March 21, 1980; January 30, 1981.

7. Avery interview.

8. Dennis McCarthy to Governor Paul Fannin, February 6, 1965, PJFP; ASPB, May 4–5, 1964; April 23–24, 1963; Dennis McCarthy to Paul Fannin, May 1963, in ASPB, June 25–26, 1963.

9. Arizona Game and Fish Department, *Annual Report*, 1963–1964 and 1964–1965; Smithee interview.

10. Smithee interview; Dennis McCarthy to John M. McGowan, October 17, 1963, in ASPB, December 12, 1963.

11. Ben Avery, "All Must Help on Water Plan," *AR*, June 17, 1967.

12. ASPB, January 14, 1965; Dennis McCarthy to Governor Paul Jones Fannin, February 6, 1964; Dennis McCarthy to Wendell Swank, February 6, 1964; Dennis McCarthy to Paul Fannin, May 2, 1963, PJFP.

13. Smithee interview; "Arizona Outdoor Agency Created by Governor Fannin," *ADS*, October 1, 1963.

14. ASPB, April 16–17, 1962; July 19, 1967; Ben Avery, "Haters Kill Boating Bill," *AR*, March 19, 1967; "Stoops Tells Boat Views," *AR*, March 23, 1967; AORCC, *State Lake Improvement Fund Plan*, 3–6, 74–76.

15. "Lyman Dam, Monument to Mormon Pioneer Courage and Industry," *AH* (September 1965): 43–47; "State Repairs Lyman Dam," *AH* (January 1932): 6–7.

16. Arizona State Parks press release, c. June 1961; ASPB, October 3, 1960; Dennis McCarthy to Thomas J. Allen, June 14, 1960, PJFP.

17. ASPB, April 23, 1963; clippings files, Lyman Lake State Park (LLSP); brochure, "Interpreting the Prehistory of Lyman Lake State Park, Peninsula and Ultimate Petroglyph Trail Guides" and Memorandum of Agreement Between National Park Service, Intermoutain Cultural Center Conservation Program, and St. Johns Chamber of Commerce and Arizona State Parks, 1996, LLSP; Kaisa Barthouly, *Lyman Lake State Park, Rattlesnake Point Pueblo Stabilization Report*.

18. "Havasu" is the Havasupai word for "blue-green." It was an ironic yet appropriate designation for a stretch of river that, because of the dam, changed color from its earlier silt-laden red-brown ("Colorado" means "red" in Spanish) to brilliant blue.

19. In the days of the riverboats, Pittsburg Point was the location Liverpool Landing, a supply port to some nearby mining towns; Sherman and Sherman, *Ghost Towns of Arizona*, 137.

20. "Lake Havasu," *AH* (April 1949): 8–13.

21. Lower Colorado River Land Use Advisory Committee, United States Department of the Interior, *Lower Colorado River Land Use Plan*, hereafter referred to as LCRLUP, 23.

22. "Havasu Lake National Wildlife Refuge," *The Reclamation Era* (February 1959): 5–8.

23. ASPB, February 2, 1964; May 4–5, 1964; March 30, 1966, January 23, 1967; February 23, 1967; April 20–21, 1967; "Parker, Arizona—the Heart of the River County," *AH* (February 1966): 32–36, 38; Young, *The State Parks of Arizona*, 28–33.

24. Wood's father gave C. V. initials instead of a first name.

25. "How to Build a River in the Arizona Desert to Flow Under the London Bridge," *Esquire* (February 1969): 79–83, 138, 140.

26. ASPB, December 12, 1963; May 4–5 1964; September 10, 1964; March 9, 1965; "Parks Board Fails to Back Poston Park," *ADS*, February 4, 1964; Young, *The State Parks of Arizona*, 74–91; Dennis McCarthy to C. R. Krimminger, September 11, 1968, Jack Williams Papers; news release, August 10, 1966, BFP; United States Department of the Interior, Bureau of Reclamation, Lease of Land to the State of Arizona for Park and Recreational Purposes, Contract Number 14-06-300-1533, February 1, 1965.

27. ASPB, August 25, 1966; January 23, 1967; April 20–21, 1967; July 19, 1967. For a discussion of the concessionaire system, see "Business in State Parks," *PG*, August 12, 1970.

28. Bert Fireman to State Parks Board, May 8, 1968, Jack Williams Papers.

29. Miller interview.

30. ASPB, December 9, 1968, including "Fact Sheet, London Bridge at Lake Havasu State Park; ASPB reports, December 10, 1976; "Lake Havasu City," *AH* (February 1966): 2–7; "London Bridge has Fallen Here," *AH* (January 1972): 6–11; Malach, *Lake Havasu City*; ASPB, February 13, 1969; "A Bridge Too Far," *Preservation* (July/August 2001): 62–66.

31. Priscilla Robinson to Bruce Babbitt, December 8, 1982, Southern Environment Service (SES), Special Collections, University of Arizona, Tucson.

32. Lake Havasu State Park Statement of Management; Memorandum of Agreement Regarding the Disposal of Federal Lands At Lake Havasu City Among the U.S. Department of the Interior, Bureau of Land Management, Arizona State Land Department, Arizona State Parks Board, and Lake Havasu City, November 1985, in Statement of Management.

33. U.S. Senate Subcommittee on Oversight and Investigations, Commission on Energy and Natural Resources, *Hearing on the Propriety of a Commercial Lease issued by the Bureau of Land Management at Lake Havasu, Arizona,* 104th Cong., 2nd sess., August 1, 1996; Travous interview.

34. "Bill Williams River and Tributaries, Arizona," *Letter from the Secretary of War,* 78th Cong., 2nd sess., H. Doc. 625; Turhollow, *A History of the Los Angeles District,* 251; Bureau of Reclamation, *The Colorado River,* 170; *Annual Report of the Chief of Engineers on Civil Works,* 1967, 1336–1337; 1973, p. 33–10.

35. "Alamo Reservoir Project, 2 June 1964," located at Alamo Lake State Park, documents from the Alamo Lake State Park Statement of Management, including the Department of the Army Lease for Public Park and Recreational Purposes, April 30, 1969, and Memorandum of Understanding; ASPB, January 21, 1963; March 30, 1966; February 13, 1966; April 16, 1969; April 29–30, 1969; September 17, 1969; Young, *The State Parks of Arizona,* 8–19.

36. ASPB, April 16, 1976; May 31, 1977, LCRLUP.

37. Young, *The State Parks of Arizona,* 164.

38. In 1964, a state senator informed the board that he was drafting a piece of legislation creating a state recreational area near Safford at a place called Cluff Ranch. State parks looked into the matter and concluded that the area would be more suitable as a regional or county park than as a state park. Eventually, State Parks proposed the site be developed by the county with aid of Land and Water Conservation Fund money. See ASPB, February 2, 1964; May 4–5, 1964; September 10, 1964.

39. ASPB, May 23, 1972.

40. Dennis McCarthy to the Hon. Boyd Tenney, December 18, 1972, in ASPB, December 21–22, 1972; May 23, 1972; Session Laws of Arizona, 1972, chapter 209.

41. Robert Jantzen and Bob Curtis, Arizona Game and Fish Department, to Dennis McCarthy, April 13, 1973, in ASPB, May 21, 1973; Wally Vegors to Dennis McCarthy, October 1, 1973, in ASPB, October 5, 1973; ASPB, May 23, 1972; May 31, 1973; July 27, 1973; March 27, 1974; December 10, 1974; Session Laws of Arizona, 1974, chapter 202.

42. ASPB, July 27, 1973; March 27, 1974; April 16, 1976; May 27–28, 1976; Session Laws of Arizona, 1974, Chapter 202.

43. ASPB, March 30, 1966; September 17, 1969; November 13–14, 1972.

44. "Impressions of Santa Cruz County," *AH* (February 1968): 10–11, 38–39; "$1.2 Million for Patagonia Lake," *NI,* May 19, 1967; "Well, Pop Said It Looks Like a Natural, So Dig!," *AR,* June 25, 1968; "New Lake Beginning to Fill," *ADS,* October 27, 1968; "Lake Patagonia

Ready to Open," *ADS*, September 2, 1970; "New Recreational Lake 'Discovered,'" *Tucson Daily Citizen (TDC)*, September 8, 1970.

45. ASPB, November 14, 1972; December 21, 1972; March 7, 1973; "Arizona State Parks Board, Patagonia Lake, Santa Cruz County," in ASPB, October 5, 1973.

46. ASPB, December 21, 1972; March 7, 1973; December 19, 1973; January 30, 1974; October 29, 1974; December 10, 1974; February 7, 1975; March 25, 1975; Lake Patagonia State Park Statement of Management; Arizona Session Laws, 1974, chapter 156; "Patagonia Lake, Santa Cruz County," in ASPB, December 19, 1973.

47. The site's name is misleading. There are many petroglyphs of figures and symbols inscribed in the patina of a rock but no painted images. They are not painted on. The Spanish named the site *Piedras Pintadas,* or Painted Rocks, which some scholars speculate meant that at one time, the site also contained pictographs—figures and designs painted on rocks. No one knows for sure.

48. Noble, *Ancient Ruins of the Southwest*; Wasley and Johnson, *Salvage Archaeology in Painted Rocks Reservoir, Western Arizona*; *Painted Rock Reservoir Project Phase 1.*

49. ASPB, April 23, 1963; February 2, 1964; May 4–5, 1964; July 2, 1964; August 9, 1972; March 9, 1975.

50. *Gila River and Tributaries Below Gillespie Dam, Ariz: Letter from the Secretary of the Army,* 81st Cong., 1st sess., H.Doc. 331; *Annual Report of the Chief of Engineers on Civil Works Activities,* 1960, 1570–1571; *Annual Report of the Chief of Engineers on Civil Works Activities,* 1968, 1014.

51. Dick Wright to Governor Paul Fannin, June 2, 1960; John M. McGowan to Dennis McCarthy, June 16, 1960; Dennis McCarthy to John McGowan, June 16, 1960; Dennis McCarthy to Thomas J. Allen, June 14, 1960, PJFP; ASPB, March 30, 1966; May 31, 1977; Arizona Department of Game and Fish, *Wildlife Views,* annual report issue, 1960–1961, 28.

52. Dennis McCarthy to Jack Williams, April 27, 1973, in ASPB, May 31, 1973.

53. ASPB, June 16, 1971; May 31, 1973; December 10, 1974; Dennis McCarthy to Col. H. M. Roger, U.S. Army Corps of Engineers, May 1, 1973, and April 25, 1973, both in ASPB, May 31, 1973.

54. ASPB, December 10, 1976.

55. ASPB, March 25, 1977; March 17, 1978.

56. ASPB, December 10, 1976; March 25, 1977; May 31, 1977; March 17, 1978; June 28, 1978; December 15, 1978; January 27, 1979; August 3, 1979; September 14, 1979; Session Laws of Arizona, 1978, chapter 96; Young, *The State Parks of Arizona,* 126–133.

57. ASPB, November 18, 1988; March 17, 1989; February 2, 1990; July 30–31, 1990; Kathleen Stanton, "Welcome Fishermen! (But Don't Eat the Fish)," *New Times* 26 (October–November 1988); Eatherly interview.

58. ASPB, May 31, 1973.

59. ASPB, March 17, 1970, includes letter from F. L. Caughlin to Dennis McCarthy, March 10, 1970; May 6, 1970; June 16, 1971, includes letter from George Ricca to Dennis McCarthy, May 27, 1971; August, 19–20, 1971.

60. Ben Avery, "Three Blows for Wildlife," *AR,* November 1, 1973.

61. ASPB, March 13, 1972; March 28, 1972, includes Roger Garrett, legal counsel to the majority leader, to Dennis McCarthy, February 1, 1972; May 23, 1972; August 9, 1972; No-

vember 13–14, 1972; December 21, 1972; March 7, 1973; May 31, 1973; November 19, 1973; December 19, 1973. Quote from "County Raps State Parks Land Plans," *PG*, November 8, 1973. Bivens and Associates, "Philosophical Aspects, Proposed Transfer, Maricopa County, Lake Pleasant Regional Park to Arizona State Parks Board," November 28, 1972; "State, County Officials Meet Again on Transfer of Lake," *PG*, October 23, 1973; "County balks at transfer of lake to state," *PG*, November 7, 1973.

62. ASPB, January 30, 1974; February 27, 1974; March 27, 1974; December 10, 1974; February 7, 1975.

Chapter 4. Ambitions and Setbacks

1. Quoted in Tilden, *The State Parks*, 8–9.
2. Conklin, "The Long Road to Riches," 3.
3. Cox, "Before the Casino," 336–337.
4. Hays, "The New Environmental West," and *Beauty, Health, and Permanence*; R. Nash, *Wilderness and the American Mind* and *American Environmentalism*, 187–348.
5. ASPB, April 16, 1976.
6. "State Starts Trimming Requests," *PG*, November 7, 1967; Miller interview.
7. ASPB, reports, February 6–7, 1958.
8. "State Parks Board Suspends Director," *AR*, January 21, 1976; "State Parks Chief Is Fired after 19 Years in Position," *AR*, March 6, 1976; Williams interview.
9. ASPB, December 16, 1957; June 6, 1960; October 3, 1960; January 21, 1963; April 23, 1963; Dennis McCarthy to Thomas J. Allen, June 14, 1960, PJFP.
10. ASPB, August 20–21, 1963; May 4–5, 1964; March 30, 1966; April 20–21, 1967; January 31, 1968; March 27, 1974.
11. ASPB, December 12, 1963; October 25, 1971; December 13, 1971; March 13, 1972; Dennis McCarthy to Laurence Bloom, January 20, 1972, Jack Williams Papers; Joseph Fallini, state director, Bureau of Land Management, to Andrew Bettwy, state land commissioner, January 28, 1972, in ASPB, May 23, 1972; "Aravaipa May Become Park," *AR*, July 30, 1972; "Adventuring in Aravaipa," *AH* (March 1979): 35–41; Hadley, *Environmental Change in Aravaipa, 1870–1970*, 286–291; Bureau of Land Management, *Wilderness Management Plan for the Aravaipa Canyon Wilderness, Arizona*, 2–3.
12. Dennis McCarthy to Norman Weeden, forest supervisor, Coronado National Forest, October 24, 1957, in ASPB, October 21, 1957; Weeden to McCarthy, November 13, 1937, in ASPB, November 16–17, 1957; ASPB, October 21, 1957; November 17, 1957; July 10–11, 1961; August 30, 1961; May 4–5, 1964; December 7–8, 1964; March 30, 1966.
13. "Tonto Natural Bridge," *AH* (April 1966): 29.
14. "Tonto Natural Bridge," *AH* (March 1939): 12–13; "Tonto Natural Bridge," *AH* (September 1946): 26–28; "From Payson to Camp Verde," *AH* (April 1959): 36–39; Tonto Natural Bridge State Park Statement of Management; "Tonto Natural Bridge," in Northern Gila County Historical Society, *Rim Country History*, 54–56.
15. ASPB, April 20–21, 1967; August 25, 1967; August 26, 1968, including Dennis McCarthy to Stan Womer, June 12, 1968; Arizona State Parks Board Priority Project Number 1, Tonto Natural Bridge, in ASPB, December 9, 1968.

16. ASPB, February 13, 1969; April 16, 1969; August 12, 1969, including Dennis McCarthy to Huey Johnson, July 23, 1969; December 9, 1969; March 17, 1970; May 6, 1970; "Tonto Bridge Site Sold, State Caught with Plans Down," *PG*, July 17, 1970; "After Two Failures, State Again Plans Effort to Rescue Tonto Natural Bridge," *TDC*, August 9, 1971; "Legislature May Enable Tonto Bridge Land Swap," *TC*, March 6, 1972.

17. Session Laws of Arizona, 1969, Chapter 63; "Suit Filed over Tonto Bridge," n.d., ASPB reports, May 23, 1972; "Legislature May Enable Tonto Bridge Land Swap," *TC*, March 6, 1972; ASPB, December 9, 1969; March 13, 1972; August 9, 1972; December 21, 1972; November 19, 1973; January 30, 1974; September 19, 1975; February 20, 1976.

18. The details for this section come especially from Ireys interview. See also Miller interview.

19. That same law also authorized a land transfer in Graham County for the creation of a recreational lake and to purchase three hundred acres along the Hassayampa River below Wickenburg.

20. At the same time that the Dead Horse Ranch project emerged, the owners of five hundred acres along the river south of Wickenburg approached Dennis McCarthy about creating a state natural area at the site. The parcel contained a significant stretch of riparian habitat, not unlike that found along Sonoita Creek and the Verde River. However, finding money to acquire the property proved difficult. State Parks was unable to acquire LWCF funds for the purchase. Thus, Arizona State Parks went to the legislature and managed to include $167,524 to buy the Hassayampa lands in the Dead Horse Ranch bill. Even though the bill passed, it took more than a year to come up with matching federal funds for the project and for the acquisition process to start. By then, the owner of the property began to reconsider the asking price. Negotiations over the amount deteriorated until the board decided to abandon the project in December 1975. See ASPB, December 13, 1971; March 13, 1972; November 13–14, 1972; December 21, 1972; March 27, 1974; October 29, 1974; September 19, 1975; December 12, 1975. See especially Dennis McCarthy to Boyd Tenney, December 18, 1972, in ASPB, December 21, 1972.

21. ASPB, October 25, 1971; December 13, 1971, including Dennis McCarthy to Calvin Ireys, November 4, 1971; January 14, 1972; May 23, 1972; Session Laws of Arizona, 1972, chapter 209; "Dead Horses Survive," *Tombstone Epitaph (TE)*, July 5, 1973.

22. ASPB, June 11, 1974; December 10, 1974; February 7, 1975; September 19, 1975; December 10, 1976; May 31, 1977; September 23, 1977; January 27, 1979; supplement of the ASPB, December 12, 1975; "Dead Horse State Park Seen as Community Service," *VI*, December 3, 1975; "Dead Horse Park Called 'the Best Park' in State," *VI*, December 15, 1976; "Dead Horse Ranch a Full-Fledged Park," *VI*, June 8, 1977; "Dead Horse Ranch State Park Opens," *Arizona State Park News*, July 1, 1977; Ireys interview; Miller interview; Young, *The State Parks of Arizona*, 42–47.

23. Ireys interview.

24. The most detailed account of William Boyce Thompson's life is his sympathetic biography, *The Magnate*, by Hermann Hagedorn. For the opening ceremonies, see Program, Official Opening of the Boyce Thompson Southwestern Arboretum, Saturday, April 6, 1929, and *Boyce Thompson Southwestern Arboretum, Inc., Purpose-History-Dedication*, Arizona Historical Society, Tucson (AHS-T).

25. "Symphony in Tree Major" *AH* (April 1940): 18–19, 37–39; "Col. Wm. Boyce Thompson," *AH* (December 1945): 20, 33; "Garden in the Desert," *AH* (June 1952): 28, 33–35; "Desert Garden at Superior," *AH* (January 1967): 3–4, 8–9; "Boyce Thompson's Curious Garden in the Desert," *AH* (April 1978): 6–11; Thompson's Marvelous Garden in the Desert," *AH* (June 1989): 4–5, 8–10.

26. Correspondence files of E. Lendell Cockrum, Boyce Thompson Southwestern Arboretum BTSWA; *Annual Report, Desert Biology Station for Period 15 May 1965 through 31 May 1967; Report of E. Lendell Cockrum for Period 1 June 1965 to 28 February 1966; Report 1 March 1966 to 28 February 1967,* all at BTSWA.

27. E. Lendell Cockrum, Memorandum Concerning Visit to Dennis McCarthy, director, State Parks Board, August 18, 1965, BTSWA; ASPB, August 31, 1965.

28. Director's report for BTSWA, 1969, 1970, 1971 at BTSWA; ASPB, May 31, 1973; December 19, 1973; January 30, 1974.

29. Shortly after the agreement had been made, the University of Arizona officially changed the administration of the arboretum from the department of Liberal Arts to the College of Agriculture, with the department of Plant Sciences being the principal source of contact.

30. Memorandum of Agreement, March 30, 1976, from Boyce Thompson Southwestern Arboretum Statement of Management; report for BTSWA, 1973, 1974, January 1, 1976 to June 30, 1977, Special Collections, University of Arizona (UA); "Staff Report: Boyce Thompson Southwestern Arboretum Tripartite Management Agreement," in ASPB, March 25, 1975; ASPB, May 20, 1975; December 12, 1975; February 20, 1976; April 16, 1976; May 27–28, 1976; June 22, 1977. Address given by Richard Wellman, October 25, 1978, Pinal County Historical Society (PCHS); Young, *The State Parks of Arizona,* 20–27.

31. The legend of the Lost Dutchman Mine centers on the figure of Jacob Walz, who was actually German, not Dutch. In 1864, Walz and five other prospectors came across a very promising gold deposit near the Superstition Mountains. Two days later, however, Apaches attacked the party, with only Walz and one other person surviving. Walz later settled in Phoenix and, by 1891, lived in a small shack behind the store of a local businesswoman, Mrs. Julia Thomas. In the summer of that year, he mentioned to Thomas that the location of the mine site was "a short distance back from the western end of the main Superstition Mountain." Walz died before he could show where the site was. Ever since, people have tried to follow Walz's cryptic clues in search of a treasure in the Arizona desert.

32. Fred C. Scott, "Homeless—The Heart of the Matter," *Arizona Desert Sun,* March 11, 1987; ASPB, January 16, 1976.

33. ASPB, January 19, 1976; February 11, 1977; June 22, 1977; August 5, 1977; *Arizona Preservation News* (June 1977); Burgbacher quote from ASPB, January 16, 1976; Young, *The State Parks of Arizona,* 92–101.

34. *Arizona Preservation News* (June 1977).

35. ASPB, May 31, 1973; July 27, 1983.

36. ASPB, October 5, 1973; November 19, 1973; December 19, 1973; "State Cools, Pima Warms to Rancho," *TDC,* October 3, 1973; Miller interview.

37. Minutes of the Oracle Road Greenbelt Committee, 1973–1974, UA.

38. ASPB, March 27, 1974; Session Laws of Arizona, 1974, chapter 65.

39. "Planning Started at Catalina Park, *TDC,* May 27, 1974; County Agrees to Buy 2,000

Acres of Rancho, *ADS,* April 30, 1975; "Rancho Romero Land Swap Sours," *TDC,* September 24, 1975; "Catalina Park . . . with a Hole in It," *TDC,* October 2, 1975.

40. "On the Trail," *ADS,* December 7, 1975; ASPB, September 19, 1975, includes Jarrett S. Jarvis to Dennis McCarthy, July 29, 1975, and Ron Asta to Dennis McCarthy, August 27, 1975; ASPB, October 29, 1975.

41. ASPB, April 16, 1976; September 19, 1975; October 29, 1975; May 20, 1975. Supplement of the ASPB, December 12, 1975; "State Park Plan to Be Discussed," *ADS,* December 5, 1975; "Arizona State Parks Board Okayed Catalina State Park," *ADS,* December 14, 1975; "Rancho Romero to Be Included in State Park," *ADS,* December 13, 1975; Young, *The State Parks of Arizona,* 34–41; Eatherly interview; Miller interview; "Catalina Park Plan 'Moving,'" *TDC,* April 16, 1976; "Catalina State Park Boundaries Decided," *ADS,* April 17, 1976; Director's reports, SES.

42. SES Director's report, February 14, 1978; Wesley Bolin to Katie Dusenberry, et al, February 24, 1978, SES; "Catalina Park Bill a Political Pawn," *TDC,* May 18, 1978; "Sawyer Shift Leaves Impasse in Legislature," *ADS,* May 24, 1978; Session Laws of Arizona, 1978, chapter 101; Director's reports (1975–1988), SES. ASPB, March 17, 1978.

43. State Land Department, *Annual Report,* 1980–1981, 21; ASPB, November 2, 1979; press release, Catalina State Park Dedication, May 10, 1983, Bruce Babbitt Papers, DLAPR; "Land Swap Moves Catalina Park One Step Closer," *ADS,* August 15, 1979; "Catalina State Park," *Bridle and Bit* (January 1981); "Swap Clears Final Block to Catalina Park," *ADS,* February 20, 1981; State Land Department Recreational Lease, 27-81883, August 24, 1981; Arizona State Parks news release, July 25, 1983; Arizona State Parks news release, May 10, 1983; Michael Ramnes to Jane Rosenbaum, February 8, 1983; Lloyd W. Golder, III, to Charles Eatherly, March 2, 1982; Bruce Babbitt to Jane Poston, June 24, 1980; Jane Poston to Bruce Babbitt, n.d.; Jim Matthews to Bruce Babbitt, February 4, 1980, Bruce Babbitt Papers. "State's First 'Great Urban Park' Opens," *ADS,* May 26, 1983; director's reports (1975–1988), SES. Young, *The State Parks of Arizona,* 34–41.

44. "Catalina State Park, Going Once, Going Twice . . ." *City Magazine,* March 10, 1987

45. In this arrangement, the state of Arizona traded parcels of lands in Catalina State Park, the Black Canyon archaeological area, Lake Pleasant, Arivaca Lake, and several other locations to various agencies in the federal government in return for federal land, including the Santa Rita Experimental Range, several parcels in Mesa, and land along the Colorado River.

46. The agreement was one of the last activities of the SES, which shut its doors in March 1988.

47. "State, U.S. Are Negotiating Exchanges of 99,900 Acres," *ADS,* July 12, 1987; "Fed Seeking Catalina Park," *Catalina Oracle,* August 7, 1987; "Big Swap of State Land for Federal Sites Urged," *AR,* November 11, 1987; press release, SES, January 20, 1988; "Environmental Groups Back Land Swap, Say It Protects Range, Park," *TDC,* January 21, 1988; "Land Swap, Including Catalina State Park, Gets Support, *ADS,* January 21, 1988; "Ugly Baggage: Land Swap Is Tainted by Telescope Maneuver," *ADS,* September 25, 1988; "Supreme Court Decision on Land Exchanges Puts Swap on Hold, Leaves Much in Doubt," *Territorial,* October 5, 1988; State Land Department, *Annual Report,* 1990–1991, 2; Session Laws of Arizona, 1988, chapter 76; Travous interview.

48. Quoted in "Udall Hits State Park System," *TC,* November 20, 1961.

49. Ibid.; "State Starts Trimming Requests," *PG,* November 7, 1967.

50. Supplement of the ASPB, December 12, 1975.

Chapter 5. The Babbitt Era

1. Nash, *American Environmentalism,* 256.

2. Thomas, ed., *Politics and Public Policy in the Contemporary American West,* 253–281, 417–452; Cawley, *Federal Land, Western Anger.*

3. Biographical note, Finding Aid, Bruce Babbitt Papers, Special Collections, Northern Arizona University, hereafter referred to as Bruce Babbitt Papers, NAU; "Governor to Receive Conservation Award," *Arizona Wildlife News* (March 1983); "The Life and Improbably Good Times of Bruce Babbitt," *Notre Dame Magazine* (February 1983): 36–38; Bruce Babbitt, *Color and Light* and *Grand Canyon.*

4. Quoted in speech to Governor's Conservation Awards Banquet, March 10, 1982, Bruce Babbitt Papers, NAU.

5. Quoted in "The Life and Improbably Good Times of Bruce Babbitt," 37.

6. Samuel P. Hays, "The New Environmental West" and *Beauty, Health, and Permanence.*

7. "Arizona, Long a Straggler on State Parks, Rushes to Catch Up," *New York Times,* December 7, 1985.

8. P. Myers and Green, *State Parks in a New Era.*

9. ASPB, March 16, 1979; Arizona State Parks Board, *Arizona State Parks Plan,* 1980; "The Arizona State Parks Plan," Natural Resources Issue Brief, June 19, 1980; Parks Acquisitions, Natural Resources Issue Brief, June 19, 1980, Bruce Babbitt Papers, DLAPR.

10. See various appointments in Bruce Babbitt Papers, NAU, and Bruce Babbitt Papers, DLAPR.

11. State-Federal Land Selection and Exchange Program 1978–Present, c. 1987, and State/Private Exchanges Completed 1978–Present by Fiscal Year, c. 1987; Arizona State Land Department, *Transition Report, Review Draft,* n.d.; Governor's office press release regarding appointment of Joe Fallini, April 10, 1979; Governor's office press release regarding appointment of Robert Lane, January 6, 1983, Bruce Babbitt Papers, NAU; State Land Department, *Annual Report,* 1978–1988.

12. Schober was the third Babbitt appointee to be SHPO. After Dorothy Hall left in 1978, Babbitt appointed Jim Ayres, who served until 1981. The second appointee, Ann Pritzlaff, served until 1982.

13. Eatherly interview; Peter Goudinoff to Bruce Babbitt, December 19, 1979; William Roe to Bruce Babbitt, December 5, 1979; David Yetman to Bruce Babbitt, November 29, 1979; press release, "New State Historic Preservation Officer Appointed," May 7, 1981; press release, "Arizona State Parks Selects New State Historic Preservation Officer," n.d., Bruce Babbitt Papers, DLAPR.

14. Arizona State Parks Board, *Arizona State Parks Transition Report,* 1987; ASPB, August 13, 1982; January 21, 1983; December 9, 1983; January 17, 1984; April 25, 1984; Mary Alice Bivens to Ruth Hamilton, September 1, 1981, and Arizona Outdoor Recreation Coordinating Commission Summary, c. 1980, Bruce Babbitt Papers, DLAPR; Eatherly interview.

15. An advisory group usually brought together ten to fifteen influential or local leaders

to propose alternatives or solutions for a particular course of action. A task force consisted of twenty to thirty members derived from various interest groups, sometimes with competing views, to analyze and resolve issues. *Arizona State Parks Transition Report*; James Matthews to Bruce Babbitt, et al., October 9, 1980; Wayne O. Earley to Bruce Babbitt, December 7, 1981, Bruce Babbitt Papers, DLAPR.

16. Elizabeth F. Ruffner to Bruce Babbitt, August 18, 1980; Patricia Bergthold, Draft of Document on Historic Preservation Organizations in Arizona, October 6, 1980, Bruce Babbitt Papers, DLAPR. Governor's Task Force on Historic Preservation, *Report of Preliminary Findings and Recommendations,* January 1981, in ASPB, January 30, 1981; *Findings and Recommendations,* August 3, 1981, in ASPB, August 21, 1981; Memorandum from Heritage Foundation of Arizona to Governor Babbitt regarding Heritage Conservation Section Staff Shortage, August 1980; Memorandum from Heritage Foundation of Arizona to Governor Babbitt regarding State Program for Heritage Conservation, August 1980; Arizona Historic Preservation Work Program, Bruce Babbitt Papers, DLAPR; *House Bill 2435,* in ASPB, February 19, 1982; Howard H. Chapman to Bruce Babbitt, June 23, 1982; Billy G. Garret to Bruce Babbitt, July 21, 1982, Bruce Babbitt Papers, DLAPR. ASPB, January 7, 1982; Governor's Task Force on Recreation on Federal Lands, *Final Report,* June 1986, Bruce Babbitt Papers, NAU.

17. Governor's Task Force on Parks and Recreation in Arizona, *Final Report,* February 1982; Arizona State Parks press release, February 11, 1982; Arizona State Parks press release, June 15, 1981, Bruce Babbitt Papers, NAU. See also ASPB, July 10, 1981; February 19, 1982; "Babbitt Says Recreation up to State," *VI,* August 9, 1981. For the AORCC study, see AORCC, *A Report to the Governor on Potential Water-Based Recreation Sites in Arizona.*

18. For this study, "Homol'ovi" will refer to the ruins, themselves. "Homolovi Ruins" is the name of the park.

19. National Register of Historic Places Nomination Form for Homol'ovi I, II, and III, NAU; Adams, *Homol'ovi* and "The Homol'ovi Research Program"; Walker, *Homol'ovi*; Lange, "Survey of the Homolovi Ruins State Park"; Adams and Hays, eds., *Homol'ovi II*; Larkin, "The Homol'ovi Project," 20–37.

20. "Raiders of the Ruins," *AH* (September 1987): 26–29.

21. Adams, *An Archaeological Assessment of Homolovi I Ruin*; Weaver, Dosh, and Miller, *An Archaeological Assessment of Homolovi II Ruin,* Larkin, "The Homol'ovi Project," 37–44, 70–83; ASPB, September 15, 1978; October 31, 1980.

22. Andrews, *An Archaeological Assessment of Homolovi III and Chevelon Ruins*; Hantman, *A Long Term Management Plan for Significant Sites in the Vicinity of Winslow, Arizona*; Larkin, "The Homol'ovi Project," 37–44, 83–101.

23. Larkin, "The Homol'ovi Project," 101–102. Quote from ASPB, September 15, 1978.

24. Draft Memorandum of Understanding Creating Homolovi Management Board, March 14, 1983, Bruce Babbitt Papers, DLAPR; State Land Department, *Annual Report,* 1982–1983, 24; 1983–1984, 34; ASPB, August 10, 1984; August 5, 1985; Larkin, "The Homol'ovi Project," especially 37–49.

25. "Arizona, Long a Straggler on State Parks, Rushes to Catch Up," *New York Times,* December 7, 1985. See also "State Parks Receive No Respect—But Really Should," *AR,* January 24, 1986; Minutes, Arizona Parklands Foundation Board of Directors Meeting, July 22, 1986, Bruce Babbitt Papers, DLAPR.

26. "From Hopi Pueblo to Spanish Presidio: A Wish List for More State Parks," *AH* (January 1986): 16–23, 16; ASPB, August 10, 1984.

27. Ibid.

28. ASPB, October 25, 1985; January 20, 1986; May 9, 1986; November 9, 1986; Woodbury, *Sixty Years of Southwestern Archaeology,* 411. Quote from "New State Parks, Save What's Left of Sites Marking Early Inhabitants," *ADS,* January 10, 1985. "Babbitt Seeks New Destiny for Quiburi," *ADS,* January 9, 1985; "A Worrisome Idea," *ADS,* September 4, 1985; Cabot Sedgwick to Bruce Babbitt, October 29, 1980; Bruce Babbitt to Winifred G. Meskus, September 20, 1985; "Homolovis," "Cerro Prieto," "Quiburi," "Empire Ranch," attached to Lynn Larson to Marilyn Seyman, February 20, 1986, Bruce Babbitt Papers, DLAPR.

29. Session Laws of Arizona, 1986, chapter 396; "200 See Gov. Babbitt Sign Bill for New Park," *Holbrook Tribune-News,* May 28, 1986; "Ruins Linked to Hopis Get State Protection," *AR,* May 22, 1986; "San Pedro Riparian National Conservation Area," U.S. Senate Reports 100–525, September 22, 1988; Arizona State Parks Expansion Program, November 15, 1984, Bruce Babbitt Papers, NAU; ASPB, May 9, 1986.

30. Statement by Bruce Babbitt before the President's Commission on Americans Outdoors, February 20, 1986, Bruce Babbitt papers, NAU; Bruce Babbitt, "Saving Habitat in the Desert," *Defenders* (September/October 1986): 20–33; U.S. Senate, "San Pedro Riparian National Conservation Area," Senate Reports 100–525, September 22, 1988; "BLM Obtains San Pedro Refuge Land," *ADS,* March 8, 1986; "San Pedro River Area Approved for Swap, *TC,* March 3, 1986; "Friends of the San Pedro River," http://www.theriver.com/public/fspr/, October 2000; "Empire-Cienega Resource Conservation Area," http://azwww.az.blm.gov/lascienegas/lascieneg.htm, May 2003; "The Empire Ranch, A Brief History," http://www.empireranchfoundation.org/BLMHist.htm, May 2003; ASPB, May 9, 1986.

31. ASPB, August 21, 1985; July 16–17, 1987; Application for Institutional Taking, 89-96378, May 26, 1989, State Land Department; documents from Homolovi Ruins Statement of Management; State Land Department, *Annual Report,* 1985–1986, 19.

32. Adams, "The Homol'ovi Research Program"; Lange, "Survey of the Homolovi Ruins State Park"; "Homolovi," *AH* (March 1991): 12–17; ASPB, January 15, 1993.

33. For more information about the Fryes, see "History of Old Smoke Trail Ranch," n.d., volunteer class handout (Red Rock State Park); Jean Strong to Judith Bemis, May 20, 1996; and clippings files, all at Red Rock State Park.

34. From a draft of a piece for *Parks and Recreation Magazine,* August 21, 1985, Bruce Babbitt Papers, NAU.

35. Ibid.

36. Session Laws of Arizona, 1981, chapter 274; "Oak Creek Area Part of Twin Buttes Trade," *Anamax Grapevine* (July 1981); "Trade for Sedona Land Still at Square One," *VI,* April 28, 1981; "Sedona Park Trade Final Thursday," *VI,* August 5, 1981; Lower Oak Creek Land Near Sedona Acquired in Trade," *Verde View,* August 13, 1981; Arizona State Parks, *A Report for a Potential State Park on Lower Oak Creek,* December 1981; State Land Department, *Annual Report,* 1980–1981, 21.

37. "Lower Oak Creek Land Near Sedona Acquired in Trade," *Verde View,* August 13, 1981; "Committee Reviews Plans for State Park," *VI,* October 2, 1981; "Sedona State Park

Plan Is Unveiled," *Verde View,* November 27, 1981; "Oak Creek Park Plan Gets Favorable Response," *VI,* November 25, 1981.

38. American Planning Association, Arizona Chapter, *A Proposed Concept Plan for Lower Oak Creek State Park Based upon an On-site Charette,* October 23–30, 1983; Memorandum of Agreement Regarding the Disposal of Federal Lands At Lake Havasu City Among the U.S. Department of the Interior, Bureau of Land Management, Arizona State Land Department, Arizona State Parks Board, and Lake Havasu City, November 1985, all in Lake Havasu State Park Statement of Management. Michael Ramnes to Mr. and Mrs. Roger Harter, April 28, 1983; Cabot Sedgwick to Bruce Babbitt, October 29, 1980, Bruce Babbitt Papers, DLAPR. Red Rock State Park Statement of Management; ASPB, November 7, 1986; "State Park to Be Open in '90" *VI,* February 15, 1990; "Newest State Park May Be Loveliest," *AR,* March 6, 1992; "Sneak Preview: Red Rock State Park," *Sedona Magazine* (summer 1990): 26–33.

39. Quoted in Bruce Babbitt to Dave Diamond, n.d., Slide Rock/Pendley Collection, NAU. All direct quotes from Babbitt in this section come from this letter.

40. The best and most thorough discussion of the creation of Slide Rock's history, including its transition into a state park, is David Diamond's paper, "The Pendley Homestead and the Creation of Slide Rock State Park." This discussion owes much of its detail to Diamond's hard work. See also National Register of Historic Places Nomination Form, Pendley Homestead Historic District, NAU.

41. ASPB, February 27, 1974.

42. Minutes, Arizona Parklands Foundation Board of Directors Meeting, November 10, 1983, Bruce Babbitt Papers, DLAPR.

43. Arizona State Parks Expansion Program, November 15, 1984, Bruce Babbitt Papers, NAU; ASPB, June 1, 1984.

44. Untitled, undated brochure of AZ Parklands Foundation; Bylaws and Articles of Incorporation of the Arizona Parklands Foundation, Bruce Babbitt Papers, NAU; Bruce Babbitt to David Diamond.

45. Bruce Babbitt, speech to the 37th legislature, January 14, 1985, Bruce Babbitt Papers, NAU; Memorandum of a Telephone Conversation by David Diamond, December 3, 1999, Slide Rock/Pendley Papers, NAU; "Babbitt Optimistic on Proposed Park," *AR,* December 8, 1984; "Park Near Slide Rock?" *VI,* February 15, 1985; "Pendley Property Sold to Parklands Foundation for $3.6 MIllion, *Sedona Red Rock News,* February 20, 1985; Miller interview; Session Laws of Arizona, 1985, chapter 322.

46. Memorandum of Understanding Between Coconino National Forest, U.S. Department of Agriculture, and the Arizona State Parks Board, December 24, 1986, found in Slide Rock State Park Statement of Management; Deborah Howard to Bruce Babbitt, August 8, 1985, and Deborah Howard to Bruce Babbitt, November 15, 1985, Bruce Babbitt Papers, DLAPR.

47. "Six New Areas to Join Park System," *The Territorial,* June 27, 1985; "From Hopi Pueblo to Spanish Presidio: A Wish List for More State Parks," *AH* (January 1986) 16–23, 19–20; "New State Park Proposed Includes Picket Post House, Arboretum," *Superior Sun,* May 22, 1985; ASPB, July 9, 1985; August 28, 1986.

48. Just before the Kannally donation, the Defenders received several large parcels in Aravaipa Canyon adjacent to the BLM holdings. Aravaipa received an extensive review in

Defenders magazine that listed the story of its acquisition and the many types of wildlife that lived there. Oracle, by contrast, was a relatively small parcel of former ranch land that barely received mention in the footnotes of the Defenders' annual report. Oracle was nice to have but it was no Aravaipa Canyon. "Arizona Oasis," *Defenders* 60 (January/February 1985): 38–39; "Mr. and Mrs. George Whittell," *Defenders* 51 (June 1976): 197–198; Hadley, *Environmental Change in Aravaipa, 1870–1970.*

49. Schifano, *Oracle Speaks*; Last Will and Testament of Lucille Kannally, Report to the Board of Directors of Defenders of Wildlife on the Kannally Bequest by Special Committee, October 1976, records at Oracle State Park, hereafter referred to as OSP. Quote from "Reactions Are Mixed to Plans for Oracle's 4,000-Acre Wildlife Refuge," *ADS*, October 26, 1985.

50. Deed for Oracle, November 9, 1985, OSP; "4000-acre Park Planned Near Oracle," *San Manuel Miner*, May 15, 1985; "T-C Invited to Oracle 4000-Acre Park Dedication," *San Manuel Miner*, October 16, 1985; "Oracle Ranch May Be Park," *TDC*, April 30, 1985; "Kannally family's gift of 4,000 Acres Near Oracle to Become State Park," *ADS*, May 8, 1985; "$15 Million Oracle Park Plan Unveiled," *San Manuel Miner*, October 30, 1985.

51. Quotes from "Reactions Are Mixed to Plans for Oracle's 4,000-Acre Wildlife Refuge" and "Protesters Question Oracle State Park Development and Entry," *San Manuel Miner*, November 8, 1989. See also, "Oracle Park Will Fit Community," *San Manuel Miner*, November 20, 1985; "Plan for Oracle Park Worrying Neighbors," *AR*, January 26, 1986, and "A Look Back at . . . The Dedication," *Oracle Magazine* (November 1990).

52. ASPB, Oracle State Park Ad Hoc Committee Report, January 7, 1987; McGann and Associates, *Master Plan, Arizona State Parks Oracle Center for Environmental Education*; "Protesters Question Oracle State Park Development and Entry," *San Manuel Miner*, November 8, 1989. Woodruff interview.

53. "Fortifying the Ranch House: Face Life at State Park's Kannally House," *Pinal Ways*, winter 1995/1996, 32–35; "Friends of Oracle State Park," http://www.azstarnet.com/nonprofit/fosp/, October 2000.

54. University of Arizona Cooperative Extension Service, *Recreation Resources of the Verde River, Cottonwood Reach.*

55. Worden, de Kok, and Esparanza, *The Tourist and Recreational Economy of the Verde Valley, Arizona*, 3.

56. U.S. Forest Service, Coconino, Prescott and Tonto National Forests, *Verde River.*

57. Quote from "Babbitt Promotes Greenway," *Verde Valley Journal*, November 12, 1986.

58. Robert K. Lane to Bruce Babbitt, October 23, 1985, Bruce Babbitt Papers, DLAPR.

59. ASPB, May 9, 1986.

60. Dan Campbell, president, Arizona Nature Conservancy, to Don Charpio, April 21, 1986; John B. Nutter, western regional director, the Nature Conservancy, to Bruce Babbitt, February 21, 1986, Bruce Babbitt Papers, DLAPR; "Babbitt Promotes Greenway," *Verde Valley Journal*, November 12, 1986.

61. *Verde River Greenway Management Plan*; ASPB, July 15, 1988; *Diversity*, 1 (December 1992): 15, 18–19; (March 1993): 13–14, 17; (June 1993): 15; Jerry Kammer, "Banking on It Business, Environmental Factions Celebrate Glories of Verde River," *AR*, September 29, 1991; Travous interview; ASPB, May 9, 1986; August 28, 1986; November 7, 1986; July 15, 1988;

May 14, 1992; "Verde River Greenway Nearly a Reality," *Sedona Times,* November 12–November 18, 1986; Verde River Greenway Statement of Management.

62. Quoted in "Arizona Lacks State Parks, Report Says," *PG,* April 13, 1987.

63. Representative Art Hamilton and Senator Alan Stephens, "For the Good of Arizona Democrats: No Retreat From Growth," *AR,* February 8, 1987.

64. The ruling built on a 1968 U.S. Supreme Court case, *Lassen v State Highway Department.* In that instance, the court found that because of the wording of Arizona's 1910 Enabling Act, the SLD could not dispose of school lands without compensation except in extremely limited conditions. Ironically, the case involved the transfer of lands at Papago Park. ASPB, December 9, 1969; State Land Department, *Annual Report,* 1988–1989, 3; 157 Ariz. statute 537.

65. State Land Department, *Annual Report,* 1989–1990, 3; 1990–1991, 2.

66. Arizona State Office of the Auditor General, *Performance Audit: Arizona State Parks Board,* 8.

Chapter 6. New Directions and Old Challenges

1. *Diversity* 1 (December 1992): 2.

2. Travous interview.

3. Ibid.

4. Hose and Pisarowicz, "Kartchner Caverns—Research Symposium," 40–120.

5. A friend of Tenen and Tufts who visited the cave proposed calling the caverns Xanadu after the beginning of the poem by Samuel Taylor Coleridge: "In Xanadu did Kubla Khan a stately pleasure dome decree." The cavern's great column, Kubla Khan, received its name from that poem as well.

6. Quoted in Cheek, "The Secret of Kartchner Caverns: Dramatic Find Is Saved for All," 38.

7. Quoted in Ken Travous, "Welcome to Kartchner Caverns," *AH* (September 1995): 4–13, 9–10.

8. Tufts and Tenen, "Discovery and History of Kartchner Caverns, Arizona"; "Rare Cave is Overnight Sensation," *PG,* May 3, 1988; "Benson Bonanza," *PG,* August 11, 1988; "Colorful, Virgin Cave May Have Big Impact on Benson's Economy," *AR,* August 25, 1988; "Underground Wonders," *AR,* December 24, 1989; "Pair 'Felt A Breeze,' Then Spent 14 Years Guarding Secret of Cave," *AR,* December 17, 1989; Cheek, "The Secret of Kartchner Caverns: Dramatic Find Is Saved for All"; "Cave Discovery Led to Preservation," *AR,* October 31, 1999; "Kartchner Caverns: Arizona's Newest State Park," *AH* (March 1989): 4–8; Arizona State Parks press release, "The Story of Kartchner Caverns State Park," n.d.; Negri, *Kartchner Caverns*; ASPB, May 20, 1988; June 3, 1988; Eatherly interview; Travous interview.

9. ASPB, January 30, 1997; "Construction Difficult at Kartchner Caverns," *Rocky Mountain Construction Journal,* June 13, 1997, 10–13; "Cave Discovery Led to Preservation," *AR,* October 31, 1999; "Construction a Carefully Measured Process," *AR,* October 31, 1999; McGann and Associates, Inc., *Above-ground Master Plan for Kartchner Caverns State Park*; Travous interview.

10. ASPB, October 16, 1997; November 20, 1997; "Kartchner Caverns State Park Latest Gem," *AR*, October 31, 1999.

11. ASPB, January 21, 1999.

12. Travous interview.

13. *Arizona Preservation News* 8 (January 1991): 10; Bob Hirsch, "Tonto Bridge Pine Creek Wonder Is Latest Addition to State Parks List," *PG*, September 27, 1990; "Tonto Bridge Is Dedicated as 26th State Park," *AR*, June 30, 1991; "Arch Support: Tonto Bridge Park Set to Open," *PG*, June 24, 1991; ASPB, March 16, 1990; April 23, 1990; Travous interview.

14. Although sometimes referred to as Apache-Sitgreaves National Forest, technically the jurisdiction consists of two separate forests operated as a single unit.

15. "Fool Hollow Lake Recreation Area Design Narrative," United States Forest Service, Apache Sitgreaves National Forest (USFS-AS); United States Forest Service, Southwest Region, *Apache Sitgreaves National Forests Plan*, 7, 45–63.

16. ASPB, February 20, 1987.

17. ASPB, January 9, 1987; February 20, 1987; February 19, 1988; May 12, 1989.

18. Meeting Notes from Fool Hollow Project's June 29, 1989, meeting, USFS-AS.

19. By 1998, the USFS had spent almost $4.8 million on Fool Hollow. Arizona State Parks spent $100,000 but also contributed $2 million as part of a partnership with the Arizona Department of Transportation for road construction. SLIF funds, managed by the City of Show Low, amounted to nearly $3 million. "Fool Hollow Lake Recreation Area—$'s Spent as of June 1, 1998," USFS-AS.

20. Session Laws of Arizona, 1994, chapter 19; Memorandum of Understanding Between the U.S. Department of Agriculture, Apache Sitgreaves National Forest, Arizona State Parks, Arizona Game and Fish Commission, the City of Show Low, Arizona Public Service Company, and McCarty Construction Company, 1991; U.S. Forest Service, Apache Sitgreaves National Forest, *Fool Hollow Recreation Area Development Environmental Assessment*, May 3, 1990; Minutes of Steering Committee Meeting of May 25, 1990, all USFS-AS, with copies of some documents at Arizona State Parks. "Recreation Future Set for Lake," *White Mountain Independent*, September 18, 1990; Travous interview.

21. Because of the partnership involved, it could not be named Fool Hollow Lake State Park, although it is sometimes called that by mistake.

22. "Important Information About the Fool Hollow Lake Recreation Area," March 31, 1995, USFS-AS.

23. Yuma Quartermaster Depot Statement of Management, files on individual buildings at Yuma Crossing State Historic Park, hereafter referred to as YCSHP.

24. ASPB, July 24, 1976; September 23, 1977; November 2, 1979.

25. Quoted in "BLM Completes Proposals for River Crossing Park," *YDS*, June 14, 1981.

26. "In the Beginning: The Roots of Yuma Crossing Park," *At the Crossing* 1 (February/March 1988); "Riverfront Park: Twists, Turns and Pitfalls Fill Yuma's Road to Realizing a Dream: A Historic Park on the Colorado River," *YDS*, July 22, 1983; "State Shows Interest in Park," *YDS*, August 21, 1981; "Need to Find Reasons behind the 'No' Votes," *YDS*, October 2, 1980; ASPB, January 25, 1980. See also "Chronology of Yuma Crossing State Park," an undated paper at YCSHP.

27. An Agreement for the Establishment of the Yuma Crossing State Park, located at City of Yuma; "Babbitt Brings Good News on River Park," *YDS,* October 5, 1982; "Babbitt Expects Major State Role in Yuma Park," *YDS,* October 6, 1982.

28. Yuma Crossing has been one of several historic sites that has used the "Williamsburg of the West" moniker.

29. Gerald A. Doyle and Associates, *A Master Plan for the Yuma Crossing National Historic Landmark,* 1984, YCSHP; "Yuma Crossing, Williamsburg of the West," *AH* (November 1984): 10–15.

30. Mark T. Swanson and Jeffrey H. Altschul, draft, "Cultural Resources Investigations of the Yuma Quartermaster Depot, AZ X:6:12 (ASM), Yuma, Arizona," 1989; ASPB, November 7, 1986; program from groundbreaking ceremony for the office of the depot quartermaster, October 29, 1986, Arizona Historical Society at Yuma, hereafter referred to as AHS-Y; "Crossing Park Groundbreaking Grand Ceremony," *YDS,* October 20, 1986.

31. "From the Desk of the Director," *At the Crossing* 2 (June/July 1989); "Group Wants Steamboat Replica Built," *YDS,* September 17, 1986; Hitchcock, *Yuma Crossing;* "Foundation Begins Operating Quartermaster Depot," *At the Crossing* 3 (October/December 1990); "From the Desk of the Executive Director," *At the Crossing* 3 (April/June 1990).

32. "Foundation Selects New Executive Director," *At the Crossing* 4 (April/May 1988); Agreement between the City of Yuma and the Yuma Crossing Foundation, June 24, 1988, City of Yuma records.

33. "2% Election Passes," *At the Crossing,* 6 (October/December 1993).

34. Quotes taken from City of Yuma Regular Council Meeting Minutes, May 1, 1996.

35. "From the City Administrator," *Yuma Advantage,* April 25, 1996; "Council Looks at Termination of Crossing Park Lease," *YDS,* April 15, 1996; "Council Will Look at Ending Crossing Park Agreement," *YDS,* April 29, 1996; City of Yuma Ordinance Number 096-46, May 1, 1996; Travous interview.

36. ASPB, January 30, 1997; March 20, 1997. Quote from ASPB, June 18–19, 1997. Arizona State Parks news release, "Yuma Crossing State Historic Park Grand Re-Opening," August 7, 1997; "Grand Re-Opening of the Yuma Crossing State Park," *The Calendar* (July–September 1997): 2; "Park Efforts to Cross from Planning to Heavy Work," *YDS,* October 23, 1996; "State Excited about Future of River Park," *YDS,* June 16, 1996; ASPB, May 16, 1996. Application for Obtaining Property for Historic Monument Purposes, March 20, 1997; Intergovernmental Agreement between the City of Yuma and the Arizona State Parks Board, KR96-1978LNR, August 1, 1996, YCSHP. Travous interview.

37. ASPB, January 20, 1985; March 13, 1987.

38. ASPB, January 18, 1991; May 17, 1991; July 9–10, 1991; "Plans to Close Tubac Presidio Incites Debate," *NI,* April 24, 1991; "More than 300 Turn Out to Protest Plan to Close Park," *Green Valley News,* April 24, 1991; "Valley Rallies to Save State's Oldest Park from Closing," *The Monthly Arizonian* (May 1991); "Rule Change to Allow Presidio to Stay Open," *Southern Arizona Trails,* May 14, 1991; Cynthia Krug to Charles Eatherly, July 9, 1991; Cynthia Krug to Fran Appleyard, Tubac Historical Society, December 8, 1991, Tubac Presidio State Historic Park (TPSHP); "Ft. Verde Among Parks Considered for Closure," *The Bugle,* April 12, 1991; "State Parks Will Be Back to Cry Wolf Another Day," *The Journal,* May 15, 1991; "State

Parks to Keep Fort Verde Open," *The Journal,* Camp Verde, May 15, 1991; "Fort Verde Remembers . . ." *Prescott Sun,* April 26, 1991; ASPB, January 18, 1991; May 17, 1991; July 9–10, 1991; January 17, 1992; July 9–10, 1992; July 15–16, 1993.

39. P. Myers and Green, *State Parks in a New Era,* 3.

40. Arizona was not the first to use lottery money to support parks and recreation. By 1990, states including Florida and Minnesota also used lottery money for parks and related projects. See Joel Nilsson, "Position 200: A Vision for the Future of State's Resources," *AR,* September 29, 1990.

41. "Rhode Island's Red Ink Shuts State Government," *AR,* March 9, 1991; "Budget Crises Big Headaches in Some States," *AR,* July 5, 1991; William B. Lowry, "Nature Under Siege," *State Government News* (January 1995): 8–11; P. Myers, *State Grants for Parklands,* 19–21; "Alternative Funding Sources," in ASPB, March 13, 1987; National Park Service, Preservation Planning Series, *FY 82 State Program Overviews; Performance Audit: Arizona State Parks Board,* Table 13.

42. "Foes Unite to Boost Parks, Babbitt, Goldwater Seek Cut of Lottery for Outdoors," *AR,* May 16, 1990; ASPB, September 14, 1990.

43. Mutter, "Interest Group Influence in the Development and Implementation of State Recreation Policy."

44. "Legislature's Day 170: 'There's No News Around Here'," *AR,* June 27, 1990; "Foe Issues Warning on Parks Fund Initiative for the Propositions: Environment," *PG,* October 25, 1990; Initiative Would Aid Parks, Wildlife Habitat," *AR,* October 31, 1990.

45. *Arizona Heritage News* 7 (July 1990): 2; "Heritage Plan on the Right Track," *PG,* May 24, 1990; "Heritage Fund: Sign Up," *PG,* May 29, 1990; "Preserving Arizona's Beauty, Animal Life Important to State's Future," *AR,* June 1, 1990; "Legislature's Day 170: 'There's No News Around Here'," *AR,* June 27, 1990; "Ex-Aide Hits Babbitt on Parks Plan," *PG,* September 5, 1990; "Upkeep of Hiking Trails Important," *AR,* September 21, 1990; "Goddard, Symington Vie to See Who's 'Greener': Environment Looms Large in Governor's Race Election '90," *AR,* October 14, 1990; "Proposition 200: Reinvesting for the Future Stripped of Extravagant Rhetoric, the New Fund Represents a Meat-and-Potatoes Strategy Aimed at Preserving Avalon," *AR,* October 28, 1990; "Heritage OK Gives New Life: Lottery Dollars Aid Wildlife Management," *PG,* November 15, 1990; Ben Avery, "Idea for Heritage Fund Good, but Language in Initiative Bad," *AR,* December 14, 1990; "Agency Seeks Use for Funds: Public Opinion Being Solicited," *AR,* December 14, 1990; ASPB, September 14, 1990.

46. ASPB, *Reports,* September 14, 1990; Travous interview.

47. *Arizona Preservation News,* 9 (January 1992): 1.

48. *Diversity,* 1 (March 1993): 18–21, 28–29; 1 (June 1993): 16, 30–34; 2 (December 1993): 21–31; 3 (March 1994): 7–15; 103; ASPB, September 17, 1993.

49. *Arizona Preservation News,* 9 (April 1992): 2; "State Has Tainted Heritage Fund Vote," *AR,* November 18, 1990; "Heritage Fund, Majority Vote Might Be Ignored," *PG,* November 29, 1990; "On Line Agencies Put Heritage Fund Dollars To Use," *PG,* November 14, 1991; "Bill Would Check Bureaucratic Power," *AR,* March 31, 1991; "Game and Fish Becomes Target of Legislature," *AR,* March 3, 1991; "Coalition Reunites to Battle Legislature," *AR,* March 1, 1991; "Spending Cuts Ok'd by Mofford: $94.7 Million Trimmed to Balance '91 Budget," *PG,*

February 5, 1991; "Opinion Gives Heritage Fund Go-Ahead," *AR,* January 11, 1991; "Targeting the Heritage Fund," *ADS,* August 6, 1993.

50. McGann and Associates, *Sonoita Creek Natural Area Management Plan*; "Jewel of the Sonoita," *AR,* April 6, 1994; ASPB, July 14–15, 1994; October 16, 1997; July 15, 1999; Travous interview.

51. Stewart, *Arizona Ranch Houses,* 74–87; "A Round Trip to Santa Cruz," *AH* (September 1953): 28–33.

52. "Oklahoma: A Visit to the Motion Picture Location in Southern Arizona," *AH* (April 1955): 8–11; "Backroad to the Silver King's Ghost Camps of the Patagonias," *AH* (February 1981): 14–21, 20–21; ASPB, November 19, 1998; quote from Travous interview.

53. A press release from the Nature Conservancy defined a "conservation easement" this way: "A conservation easement is the legal tool . . . that allows a landowner to limit certain uses on their property. A landowner can donate a conservation easement to a third party like a state agency or non-profit conservation organization. Conversely, a state agency or non-profit can purchase a conservation easement." An easement is often cheaper than an outright purchase and also allows the land to still be kept on the tax rolls.

54. ASPB, January 15, 1998; February 19, 1998. Quote from Nancy McCuiston to Arizona State Parks Board, n.d., in ASPB, February 19, 1998. "State Moves to Protect Ranchland Development," *ADS,* January 17, 1998; "Preserve San Rafael," *ADS,* January 31, 1998; Arizona State Parks press release, January 15, 1998.

55. ASPB, July 16, 1998; September 17, 1998; November 19, 1998 (with accompanying letters from the community); January 21, 1999; Arizona State Parks press release, January 21, 1999; November 19, 1998; October 15, 1998; September 17, 1998; "A Conservation Victor: Protecting the San Rafael Valley," Nature Conservancy press release, 1998, found on the website for the Nature Conservancy, http://tncnt.tnc.org (relocated at http://nature.org/) , November 1, 2000; Travous interview.

56. Session Laws of Arizona, 1997, chapter 135; ASPB, May 20, 1999; January 21, 1999; "Spur Cross Ranch Is Ours: Invaluable Resource Will Belong to the People Tomorrow," *AR,* January 10, 2001; "Hard Work Pays Off: Spur Cross Park Is Worth the Wait," *AR,* January 9, 2001; "Purchase of Spur Cross Clinched: Preservationists Win 15-Year Fight," *AR,* January 6, 2001; "PAC Tries to Save Spur Cross," *AR,* August 16, 2000; "Arizona State Parks Board Votes to Preserve Spur Cross Ranch," Hopi Tribe press release, June 8, 1999; Jane Dee Hull, Governor of Arizona, State of the State speech, January 11, 1999; "Governor Applauds House on Spur Cross Project," Arizona Office of the Governor press release, April 22, 1999; "Saving Private Interests," *The Phoenix New Times,* August 6, 1998; "Spur Cross Ranch Frequently Asked Questions and Answers," *Cave Creek Connection,* summer 2000; "Governor celebrates Spur Cross Ranch," Arizona Office of the Governor press release, January 12, 2001; Bruce Babbitt to Roger L. Stevenson, October 17, 1986, Bruce Babbitt Papers, DLAPR; Travous interview.

57. "Lawmakers Asked to Tap Parks Fund: Would Ease Shortfall, Keep Facilities Open," *PG,* May 9, 1991;, "Symington Pushes Budget Shift to Avert Park Closings," *AR,* May 9, 1991; "Hearings Set on Proposal to Close 4 State Parks," *AR,* April 17, 1991; "Budget Cuts May Close 8 State Parks," *PG,* April 11, 1991; "4 Parks in State May Shut: Managers Blame

Reduced Budget," *AR,* April 10, 1991; ASPB, January 18, 1991; May 17, 1991; January 17, 1992; "Arizona State Parks Board Votes to Close Eleven State Parks Due to Budget Deficit," Arizona State Parks press release, June 20, 2002; "Arizona State Parks Board Reviews Budget Proposal That Might Help Re-Open State Parks," Arizona State Parks press release, July 22, 2002; "Arizona State Parks Will Open Seven Parks on August 9, 2002," Arizona State Parks press release, August 6, 2002.

Bibliography

Periodicals and Journals

American Planning and Civic Annual (a.k.a. *Planning and Civic Comment*)
Anamax Grapevine
Arizona Daily Star
Arizona Desert Sun
Arizona Heritage News
Arizona Highways
Arizona News: The Arizona Weekly
Arizona Preservation News
Arizona Recreation Bulletin
Arizona Republic
Arizona: The State Magazine
Arizona State Park Quarterly
Bridle and Bit
The Bugle
Calendar
Catalina Oracle
Cave Creek Connection
City Magazine
At the Crossing (newsletter of Yuma Crossing State Historic Park)
Defenders
Diversity: Covering the Spectrum of Programs at Arizona State Parks

Florence Reminder and Blade Tribune
Green Valley News
Highway Spotlight
Holbrook Tribune-News
Jerome Chronicle
The Journal (Camp Verde)
The Monthly Arizonian (Tumacacori)
National Parks Magazine
News Bulletin aka *Newsletter* (Arizona State Parks Association)
News Bulletin (Jerome Historical Society)
New York Times
Nogales International
Oracle Magazine
Phoenix Gazette
The Phoenix New Times
Pinal Ways
Prescott Sun
The Reclamation Era
Rocky Mountain Construction Journal
San Manuel Miner
SCORP News (Arizona Outdoor Recreation Coordinating Commission)
Sedona Magazine
Sedona Red Rock News
Sedona Times
Southern Arizona Trails
State Government News
Superior Sun
Territorial
Tombstone Epitaph
Trends
Tri-Valley Dispatch
True West
Tucson Citizen aka *Tucson Daily Citizen*
Verde Valley Independent
Verde Valley Journal
Verde View
Weekly Arizonian aka *The Arizonian* (Tubac)
White Mountain Independent
Wildlife Views (Arizona Game and Fish Department)
Yuma Advantage
Yuma Daily Sun

Manuscript Collections

Note: Various files, scrapbooks, and ephemera are located at the state parks. In the notes, the term *Statement of Management* refers to the statements of management and other documents on each park that are housed at the Arizona State Parks Board offices in Phoenix.

Arizona Cattle Growers Association. Papers. Arizona Historical Foundation, Arizona State University, Tempe.
Arizona Historical Society, files and ephemera, repositories in Tempe, Tucson, and Yuma.
Arizona State Central Arizona Division Department of Library and Archives. Arizona Historical Foundation, Tempe.
Arizona State Parks Association. Papers. Arizona State Archives, Phoenix.
Babbitt, Bruce Edward. Papers 1978–1987. Governor's Office, Arizona State Archives, Phoenix.
———. Papers 1978–1987. Special Collections, Northern Arizona University, Flagstaff.
Bolin, Harvey Wesley. Papers 1977–1978. Governor's Office, Arizona State Archives, Phoenix.
Chambers, Blanche Riordan. Papers. Special Collections, Northern Arizona University, Flagstaff.
Fannin, Paul Jones. Papers 1957–1965. Governor's Office, Arizona State Archives, Phoenix.
Fireman, Bert. Papers. Arizona Historical Foundation, Arizona State University, Tempe.
Goddard, Samuel Pearson. Papers 1965–1967. Governor's Office, Arizona State Archives, Phoenix.
McFarland, Ernest W. Papers. McFarland State Historic Park, Florence, Arizona.
———. Papers 1955–1957. Governor's Office, Arizona State Archives, Phoenix.
National Park Service. Papers. National Archives, College Park Site, Maryland.
National Recreation and Park Association Archives Collection, Alexandria, Virginia.
Slide Rock/Pendley Collection, Northern Arizona University, Flagstaff.
Southwestern Environmental Service. Special Collections, University of Arizona, Tucson.
State Land Commissioner. Papers. Arizona State Archives, Phoenix.
Tombstone Restoration Commission Records, Tombstone, Arizona.
Williams, John R. "Jack." Papers 1967–1975. Governor's Office, Arizona State Archives, Phoenix.

Interviews

Avery, Ben. Interview by Zona Davis Lorig. Tape recording, September 22, 1994. Arizona Historical Society, Tempe.
Carithers, Joseph. Interview by Jay M. Price. Tape recording, March 9, 1997. Arizona State Parks Board offices.
Clow, James. Interview by Jay M. Price. January 14, 1995. Dead Horse Ranch State Park, Arizona.
Earley, Wayne O. Interview by Jay M. Price. Tape recording, February 22, 1997. Arizona State Parks Board offices.
Eatherly, Charles. Interview by Jay M. Price. Tape recording, August 2, 1995. Arizona State Parks Board offices.
Hagerty, Mildred. Interview by Jay M. Price. Tape recording, June 17, 1996. Arizona State Parks Board offices.

Ireys, Tere. Interview by Jay M. Price. Tape recording, June 9, 2000. Dead Horse Ranch State Park, Arizona.
Jaap, Robert M. Interview by Jay M. Price. Tape recording, February 26, 1997. Arizona State Parks Board offices.
Miller, Duane. Interview by Jay M. Price. Tape recording, March 21, 1997. Arizona State Parks Board offices.
Morrow, William Cadmen. Interview by Betty J. Lane. Tape recording, March 15, 1990. Tubac Historical Society, Arizona.
Pies, Ron. Interview by Jay M. Price. Tape recording, December 3, 1996. Arizona State Parks Board offices.
Smithee, Kenneth J. Interview by Jay M. Price. Tape recording, July 30, 1996. Arizona State Parks Board offices.
Travous, Kenneth. Interview by Jay M. Price. Tape recording, January 5, 2001.
Wallace, Vegors. Interview by Jay M. Price. Tape recording, February 22, 1997. Arizona State Parks Board offices.
Williams, A. C. Interview by Jay M. Price. Tape recording, February 17, 1997. Arizona State Parks Board offices.
Woodruff, Patricia. Interview by Jay M. Price. Tape recording, March 3, 1997. Arizona State Parks Board offices.

Online and Internet Resources

Arizona State Parks. [Website]. [cited April 2003]. Available from http://www.pr.state.az.us
City of Apache Junction. [Website]. [cited April 2003]. Available from http://www.ajcity.net/
Empire-Cienega Resource Conservation Area. [Website]. [cited May 2003]. Available from http://azwww.az.blm.gov/lascienegas/lascieneg.htm
"The Empire Ranch, A Brief History." [Website]. [cited May 2003]. Available from http://www.empireranchfoundation.org/BLMHist.htm
Friends of Oracle State Park. [Website]. [cited October 2000]. Available from http://www.azstarnet.com/nonprofit/fosp/
Friends of the San Pedro River. [Website]. [cited October 2000]. Available from http://www.theriver.com/public/fspr
The Nature Conservancy. [Website]. [cited April 2003]. Available from http://nature.org/
State Parks Online. [Website]. [cited May 2003]. Available from http://www.wxrnot.com/parks/
"U.S. General Service Administration Table: Comparison of Federally Owned Land with Total Acreage by State as of September 30, 1999. [Website]. [cited April 2003]. Available from http://www.blm.gov/natacq/pls00/pdf/part1-3.pdf

Published Sources

Abbott, Carl. *The Metropolitan Frontier: Cities in the Modern American West.* Tucson: University of Arizona Press, 1993.

Adams, E. Charles. *An Archaeological Assessment of Homolovi I Ruin.* Report prepared for the Bureau of Land Management, Phoenix. Flagstaff: Museum of Northern Arizona, 1980.

———. *Homol'ovi: An Ancient Hopi Settlement Cluster.* Tucson: University of Arizona Press, 2002.

———. "The Homol'ovi Research Program." *Kiva* 54 (1989): 175–194.

Adams, E. Charles, and Kelley Ann Hays, eds. *Homol'ovi II: Archaeology of an Ancestral Hopi Village, Arizona.* Anthropological Papers of the University of Arizona, Number 55. Tucson: University of Arizona Press, 1991.

Ahlgren, Carol. "The Civilian Conservation Corps and Wisconsin State Park Development." *Wisconsin Magazine of History.* 71 (1988): 184–204.

Albright, Horace M. *The Birth of the National Park Service: The Founding Years 1913–1933.* Salt Lake City, Utah: Howes Brothers, 1985.

American Planning Association, Arizona Chapter. *A Proposed Concept Plan for Lower Oak Creek State Park Based Upon an On-Site Charette,* October 23–30, 1983.

Andrews, Michael J. *An Archaeological Assessment of Homolovi III and Chevelon Ruins, Northern Arizona.* Report prepared by the Department of Anthropology, Northern Arizona University, for the Arizona State Land Department, Phoenix, 1982.

Arizona Archaeology Commission. *Annual Report of the Arizona Archaeology Commission.* Phoenix: Arizona State Parks Board, 1986.

———. *Annual Report of the Arizona Archaeology Week.* Phoenix: Arizona State Parks Board, 1985–1989.

Arizona Development Board. *Amazing Arizona! Recent Migration.* Phoenix: Author, 1959.

———. *Preliminary Survey and Recommendations Relating to the Establishment of a State Parks and Recreation Board.* Phoenix: Author 1955.

Arizona Game and Fish Department. *Annual Report.* Phoenix: Author, 1950–2000.

Arizona Good Roads Association. *Illustrated Road Maps and Tour Book.* 1913. Reprint, Phoenix: Arizona Highways Magazine, 1987.

Arizona Governor's Office. Governors' "State of the state" speeches before the state legislature, 1956–2001.

———. *Report of the Governor of Arizona.* Phoenix, August 31, 1898.

Arizona Highway Commission. *Better Roads For Tomorrow, Phoenix-Maricopa County Traffic Study, 1956–57.* Phoenix, 1957.

Arizona Legislature. *Journal of the House.* Phoenix, 1930–2001.

———. *Journal of the Senate.* Phoenix, 1930–2001.

———. *Session Laws of Arizona.* Phoenix, 1938–2001.

Arizona Outdoor Recreation Coordinating Commission. *Arizona Off-Highway Vehicle Recreation Plan.* Phoenix, 1993.

———. *Arizona Outdoor Recreation Plan.* Phoenix, 1967.

———. *Arizona State Lake Improvement Fund Plan.* Phoenix, 1973.

———. *Master Plan, Arizona State Parks Oracle Center for Environmental Education.* Phoenix, 1990.

———. *Meeting Arizona's Current Outdoor Recreation Needs.* Phoenix, 1969.

———. *A Report to the Governor on Potential Water-Based Recreation Sites in Arizona,* Phoenix, November 1981.

———. *Statewide Comprehensive Outdoor Recreation Plan.* Phoenix, 1969–2002.
———. *A Summary of the Arizona Outdoor Recreation Plan.* Phoenix, 1973.
Arizona Republic. *This is Arizona: Fiftieth Anniversary.* Phoenix: Author, 1962.
Arizona Resources Board, Arizona State College, Tempe, Arizona. *Arizona: Park, Parkway and Recreational Area Plan, Progress Report.* Phoenix: Arizona Highway Commission, 1941.
Arizona State Historic Preservation Office. *Annual Report of the Arizona State Historic Preservation Office.* Phoenix: Arizona State Parks Board, 1992–2000.
Arizona State Land Department. *Annual Report.* Phoenix, 1930–2001.
Arizona State Office of the Auditor General. *Performance Audit: Arizona State Parks Board.* Phoenix, 1987 and 1997.
Arizona State Parks Board. *1993 Statewide Outdoor Comprehensive Coordinating Plan.* Phoenix, 1989.
———. *1994 Statewide Outdoor Comprehensive Coordinating Plan, Executive Summary.* Phoenix, 1994.
———. *1996 Arizona State Parks Agency Marketing Plan.* Phoenix, 1996.
———. *Annual Report.* Phoenix, 1958–2001.
———. *Arizona Hiking and Equestrian Trails Committee. Adopt-a-Trail Handbook.* Phoenix, n.d.
———. *Arizona Rivers Assessment.* Phoenix, 1990.
———. *Arizona's Other Lakes.* Phoenix, 1988.
———. *Arizona State Parks Three-Year Strategic Plan.* Phoenix, 1993, 1996.
———. *Arizona State Parks Transition Report.* Phoenix, 1987.
———. *Arizona State Trails Guide.* Phoenix, 1989.
———. *Fort Verde State Historic Park Master Plan.* Phoenix, 1978.
———. Minutes of the meetings of Arizona State Parks Board, 1957–2002.
———. *A Report for a Potential State Park on Lower Oak Creek.* Phoenix, December 1981.
———. State Historic Preservation Office collections, Phoenix, Arizona.
Arizona Statewide Planning Section. *Rural Arizona: The Economic Benefit of Recreation: A Summary Analysis of Tourism and Recreation as Factors Influencing State and Local Economies.* Phoenix, 1989.
Armstrong, Chester, comp. *Oregon State Parks, History, 1917–1963.* Salem: Oregon State Highway Department, 1965.
Army Corps of Engineers. *Annual Reports of the Chief of Engineers on Civil Works.* Washington, D.C., 1945–1970.
Army, Department of the. Bill Williams River and Tributaries, Arizona, *Letter From the Secretary of War.* Washington, D.C., 1944.
———. Gila River and Tributaries Below Gillespie Dam, Ariz., *Letter from the Secretary of the Army.* Washington, D.C., 1950.
———. *The War of the Rebellion: A Compilation of the Official Records of the Union and Confederate Armies.* Washington, D.C.: Government Printing Office, 1880–1901.
Aron, Cindy. *Working at Play: A History of Vacations in the United States.* New York: Oxford University Press, 2001.
Association of Southeastern State Park Directors. *Histories of Southeastern State Park Systems.* Association of Southeastern State Park Directors, 1977.

Babbitt, Bruce E. *Color and Light: The Southwest Canvases of Louis Akin.* Flagstaff, Ariz.: Northland Press, 1973.
Babbitt, Bruce E., comp. *Grand Canyon: An Anthology.* Flagstaff, Ariz.: Northland Press, 1976.
Bailes, Kendall E., ed. *Environmental History: Critical Issues in Comparative Perspective.* Lanham, Md.: University Press of America, 1985.
Baker, Robert D. *Timeless Heritage: A History of the Forest Service in the Southwest.* Report prepared for Department of Agriculture, U.S. Forest Service. Washington, D.C.: Government Printing Office, 1988.
Barnes, Will C., et al. *Arizona Place Names.* Tucson: University of Arizona Press, 1988.
Barthouly, Kaisa. *Lyman Lake State Park, Rattlesnake Point Pueblo Stabilization Report.* Prepared for National Park Service, Intermountain Cultural Resource Center Conservation Program, 1996.
Bennett, George. "The National Park Conference at Des Moines, Iowa, 10–11–12 June 1921." *Iowa Conservation.* 5 (1921): 14–25.
Berman, David R. *Parties and Elections in Arizona: 1863–1984.* Public Policy Papers Series, no. 3. Tempe: Morrison Institute for Public Policy, Arizona State University, 1985.
Beyle, Thad, ed. *State Government: CQ's Guide to Current Issues and Activities.* Washington, D.C.: Congressional Quarterly, 1993–1994.
Bivens and Associates. "Philosophical Aspects, Proposed Transfer, Maricopa County, Lake Pleasant Regional Park to Arizona State Parks Board." Report prepared for Maricopa County and Arizona State Parks, Phoenix, November 28, 1972.
Blatti, Jo, ed. *Past Meets Present: Essays about Historic Interpretation and Public Audiences.* Washington, D.C.: Smithsonian Institution Press, 1987.
Boardman, Samuel H. "Oregon State Park System: A Brief History." *Oregon Historical Quarterly.* 55 (1954): 179–233.
Bodnar, John. *Remaking America: Public Memory, Commemoration, and Patriotism in the Twentieth Century.* Princeton: Princeton University Press, 1992.
Boyce Thompson Southwestern Arboretum. *Boyce Thompson Southwestern Arboretum, Inc., Purpose-History-Dedication.* Superior, Ariz., 1930.
Brent, William, and Milarde Brent. *The Hell Hole: The Yuma Prison Story.* Yuma: Southwest Printers, 1962.
Brower, David. *For Earth's Sake: The Life and Times of David Brower.* Salt Lake City, Utah: Peregrine Smith Books, 1990.
Brower, J. V. *Itasca State Park: An Illustrated History.* St Paul: Minnesota Historical Society, 1904.
Brownell, Elizabeth R. *They Lived in Tubac.* Tucson: Westernlore Press, 1986.
Bureau of the Census. *1940 Census of Population.* Washington, D.C., 1940.
———. *1950 Census of Population.* Washington, D.C., 1950.
———. *1960 Census of Population.* Washington, D.C., 1960.
———. *1970 Census of Population.* Washington, D.C., 1970.
———. *1980 Census of Population.* Washington, D.C., 1980.
———. *1990 Census of Population.* Washington, D.C., 1990.
Bureau of Land Management. Department of the Interior. *Annual Reports,* 1960–2000.

———. *Wilderness Management Plan for the Aravaipa Canyon Wilderness, Arizona,* February 16, 1988.

Bureau of Reclamation. Department of the Interior. *The Colorado River: A Natural Menace Becomes a Natural Resource, A Comprehensive Departmental Report on the Development of the Water Resources of the Colorado River Basin for Review Prior to Submission to the Congress.* Washington, D.C., March 1946.

Caperton, Thomas J., and LaRhoda Fry. "Links to the Past: New Mexico's State Monuments." *El Palacio* 83, no. 2 (1977): 2–23.

Carbonneau, Scott. "It's a Party: State Parks Celebrate 50 Years of Fun." *South Dakota Conservation Digest* (May–June 1995): 2–13.

Cawley, R. McGreggor, *Federal Land, Western Anger: The Sagebrush Rebellion & Environmental Politics.* Lawrence: University Press of Kansas, 1993.

Chandler, Robert W. "Robert W. Sawyer: 'He Thought in Terms of Forever.'" *American Forests* 65 (December 1959): 16–17, 44, 46–48.

Cheek, Lawrence W., et al. *Arizona.* 2nd ed. American Compass Guide Series. New York: Fodor's Travel Publications, 1993.

———. "The Secret of Kartchner Caverns: Dramatic Find Is Saved for All." *American West* 25 (October 1988): 38–41, 38.

Clawson, Marion, and Carlton S. Van Doren, eds. *Statistics on Outdoor Recreation: The Record Since 1956.* Washington, D.C.: Resources for the Future, 1984.

Clemensen, A. Berle. *Cattle, Copper, and Cactus: The History of Saguaro National Monument, Arizona.* Denver: National Park Service, Denver Service Center, 1987.

Coggins, Allen R. "The Early History of Tennessee's State Parks: 1919–1956." *Tennessee Historical Quarterly* 43 (1984): 295–315.

Conard, Rebecca. "Hot Kitchens in Places of Quiet Beauty: Iowa State Parks and the Transformation of Conservation Goals." *Annals of Iowa* 51 (1992): 441–479.

———. *Places of Quiet Beauty: Parks, Preserves, and Environmentalism.* Iowa City: University of Iowa Press, 1997.

Conklin, David G. "The Long Road to Riches: The Development of Montana's State Park System." *Montana Outdoors* 9, no. 7 (1978): 2–3, 36–37.

Cosco, Jon M. *Echo Park: Struggle for Preservation.* Published in cooperation with Dinosaur Nature Association. Boulder: Johnson Books, 1995.

Cox, Thomas R. "Before the Casino: James G. Scrugham, State Parks, and Nevada's Quest for Tourism." *Western Historical Quarterly* 24 (1993): 332–350.

———. *The Park Builders: A History of State Parks in the Pacific Northwest.* Seattle: University of Washington Press, 1988.

———. "Weldon Heyburn, Lake Chatcolet, and the Evolving Concept of Public Parks." *Idaho Yesterdays* (1980): 2–15.

Coyne, Michael. *The Crowded Prairie: American National Identity in the Hollywood Western.* London and New York: I. B. Tauris Publishers, 1997.

Cronon, William, George Miles, and Jay Gitlin, eds. *Under an Open Sky: Rethinking America's Western Past.* New York: W. W. Norton & Company, 1992.

Cross, Jack L., Elizabeth H. Shaw, Kathleen Schiefele, eds. *Arizona: Its People and Resources.* Tucson: University of Arizona Press, 1960.

Culverwell, Albert. "State Parks Are Rich in History." *Pacific Northwest Quarterly* 45 (July 1954): 85–90.
Dart, Allen. "Using Historic Contexts in Cultural Resource Management: Some Examples from the Tucson Area and Some Cautions." *Kiva* 54 (1989): 401–414.
Davis, Richard Carter. "Wilderness, Politics, and Bureaucracy: Federal and State Policies in the Administration of San Jacinto Mountain, Southern California, 1920–1968." Ph.D. diss., University of California, Riverside, 1973.
Decker, J. Smith. "History of the Arizona Academy of Science." *Journal of the Arizona Academy of Science.* 7 (June 1972): 31–45.
Delahanty, Randolph. *Preserving the West: California, Arizona, Nevada, Utah, Idaho, Oregon, Washington.* New York: Pantheon Books, 1985.
Diamond, David. "The Pendley Homestead and the Creation of Slide Rock State Park." Unpublished paper, 2000.
Dickens, Roy S., Jr., & Carole E. Hill, eds. *Cultural Resources: Planning and Management.* Social Impact Assessment Series, No. 2. Boulder: Westview Press, 1978.
Dobie, John. *The Itasca Story.* Minneapolis: Ross & Haines, 1959.
Doell, Charles E., and Gerald B. Fitzgerald. *A Brief History of Parks and Recreation in the United States.* Chicago: The Athletic Institute, 1954.
Doell, Charles E., and Louis Twardzik. *Elements of Park and Recreation Administration.* 4th ed. Minneapolis: Burgess Publishing Company, 1963.
Doyle, Gerald A., and Associates. *A Master Plan for the Yuma Crossing National Historic Landmark.* Prepared for the Yuma Crossing Park Council. Phoenix: Author, 1984.
Doyle, Gerald, Lyle M. Stone, and Richard E. Lynch. *Arizona Heritage Fund. Historic Preservation Five Year Plan.* Prepared for Arizona State Parks, Phoenix, 1992.
Dyer, Richard L. "Columbia State Park." *The Pacific Historian* 25 (1981): 46–51.
Dykman, James, and Lawrence B. de Graaf. "Cultural Resource Management: Caring for a Culture's Clutter in the Bureau of Land Management and the National Park Service." *The Public Historian* 9, no. 2 (1987): 154–159.
Ellinwood, Sybil. *The Arizona Historical Society Today.* Tucson: Arizona Historical Society, 1973.
Engbeck, Joseph H., Jr. *State Parks of California from 1864 to the Present.* Portland, Ore.: Belding & Graphic Arts Center, 1980.
Evison, Herbert, ed. *A State Park Anthology.* Washington, D.C.: National Conference on State Parks, 1930.
Farnsworth, Janet Webb. "The Riordan Mansion." *True West* (October 1995): 6–8.
Faulk, Odie B. *Tombstone: Myth and Reality.* New York: Oxford University Press, 1972.
Fenin, George N., and William K. Everson. *The Western: From Silents to the Seventies.* Rev. ed. New York: Grossman Publishers, 1973.
Fewkes, Jesse Walter. "Archaeological Expedition to Arizona in 1895." *17th Annual Report of the Bureau of American Ethnology.* Washington, D.C.: Government Printing Office, 1896.
———. "Two Summers' Work in Pueblo Ruins." *22nd Annual Report of the Bureau of American Ethnology.* Washington, D.C.: Government Printing Office, 1904.
Finch, L. Boyd. "Sanctified by Myth: The Battle of Picacho Pass." *Journal of Arizona History* 36 (1995): 251–265.

Findlay, John M. *Magic Lands: Western Cityscapes and American Culture after 1940.* Berkeley and Los Angeles: University of California Press, 1992.

Fireman, Bert. "Recollections of Arizona: A Personal Perspective." *The Journal of Arizona History* 23 (1982): 81–102, 98–100.

Flader, Susan, ed. *Exploring Missouri's Legacy: State Parks and Historic Sites.* Columbia: University of Missouri Press, 1992.

Foresta, Ronald A. *America's National Parks and Their Keepers.* Washington, D.C.: Resources for the Future, 1984.

Forest Service, United States. Southwest Region. *Apache Sitgreaves National Forests Plan,* August 1987.

———. Coconino, Prescott and Tonto National Forests. *Verde River: Wild and Scenic River Study: Report and Environmental Impact Statement,* April 1981.

Freed, Elaine, and National Trust for Historic Preservation. *Preserving the Great Plains and Rocky Mountains.* Albuquerque: University of New Mexico Press, 1992.

Gart, Jason. "Let's Meet At the Hole in the Rock: A History of Papago Park From 1848 to the Present." Master's thesis, Arizona State University, 1996.

Gillette, Elizabeth R., and Sierra Club. *Action For Wilderness.* Sierra Club Battle Book B-7. San Francisco and New York: Sierra Club, 1972.

Goff, John S. *Arizona Civilization.* 3rd ed. Cave Creek, Ariz.: Black Mountain Press, 1974.

Gower, Calvin W. "The Minnesota State Forestry Board, The Pillsbury Reserve, and Itasca State Park, 1899–1913." *Midwest Review* 9 (1987): 46–58.

Graham, Frank, Jr. *The Adirondack Park: A Political History.* New York: Alfred A. Knopf, 1978.

Gray, David Eugene, and Donald Pelegrino, comps. *Reflections on the Recreation and Park Movement: A Book of Readings.* Dubuque, Iowa: W. C. Brown, 1973.

Hadley, Diana. *Environmental Change in Aravaipa, 1870–1970, An Ethnoecological Survey.* Prepared by Hadley Associates for the U.S. Department of the Interior, September 1991.

Hagedorn, Hermann. *The Magnate.* 1933. Reprint, Superior, Ariz.: Boyce Thompson Southwestern Arboretum, 1977.

Hakola, John W. *Legacy of a Lifetime: The Story of Baxter State Park.* For Baxter State Park Forest Authority. Woolwich, Maine: TBW Books, 1981.

Hall, Martin Hardwick. "The Skirmish of Picacho." *Civil War History* 4 (1958): 27–35.

Hampton, Duane. "Opposition to National Parks." *Journal of Forest History* 25, no. 1 (1981): 36–45.

Hantman, Jeffrey L. *A Long Term Management Plan for Significant Sites in the Vicinity of Winslow, Arizona.* Prepared by Soils Systems, Inc., for the Arizona State Land Department, Phoenix, 1982.

Hardy, Archie. *Recreation Programs in State Park Settings.* Master's thesis, University of Georgia, 1975.

Harvey, Mark W. T. "Echo Park, Glen Canyon and the Postwar Wilderness Movement." *Pacific Historical Review.* 60 (1991): 43–67.

Hays, Samuel P. *Beauty, Health, and Permanence: Environmental Politics in the United States 1955–1985.* New York: Cambridge University Press, 1987.

———. "From Conservation to Environmentalism: Environmental Politics in the United States Since World War II." *Environmental Review.* 6, no. 2 (1982): 14–41.

———. *Conservation and the Gospel of Efficiency: The Progressive Conservation Movement, 1890–1920.* Cambridge: Harvard University Press, 1959.

———. "The Environmental Movement." *Journal of Forest History.* 25 (1981): 219–221.

———. "The New Environmental West." *Journal of Policy History.* 3 (1991): 223–248.

———. "The Structure of Environmental Politics Since World War II." *Journal of Social History.* 14 (1981): 719–738.

Heinemann, Ronald L. "Alphabet Soup: The New Deal Comes to the Relief of Virginia." *Virginia Cavalcade* 33 (1983): 4–19.

Hitchcock, Victress, writer and director. *Yuma Crossing.* 30 min. Chariot Productions, 1989. Videocassette.

Hitt, Jim. *The American West from Fiction (1823–1976) into Film (1909–1986).* Jefferson, N.C.: McFarland & Company, 1990.

Holtaus, Gary, Patricia Nelson Limerick, Charles Wilkinson, and Eve Stryker Munson, eds. *A Society to Match the Scenery: Personal Visions of the Future of the American West.* Boulder: University Press of Colorado, 1991.

Horan, John F., Jr. "Will Carson and the Virginia Conservation Commission, 1926—1934." *The Virginia Magazine of History and Biography* 92 (1984): 391–415.

Hose, Louise D., and James Pisarowicz, eds. "Kartchner Caverns—Research Symposium." *Journal of Cave and Karst Studies* 61 (August 1999): 40–120.

Hosmer, Charles B. *Preservation Comes of Age: From Williamsburg to the National Trust.* Published for the National Trust for Historic Preservation. Charlottesville: University of Virginia Press, 1981.

"How to Build a River in the Arizona Desert to Flow Under the London Bridge." *Esquire* (February 1969): 79–83, 93, 138, 140.

Howe, Barbara J. "Women in Historic Preservation: The Legacy of Ann Pamela Cunningham." *The Public Historian* 12 (winter 1990): 31–61.

Hrebenar, Ronald J., and Clive S. Thomas, eds. *Interest Group Politics In the American West.* Salt Lake City: University of Utah Press, 1987.

Ise, John. *Our National Park Policy: A Critical History.* Published for Resources for the Future. Baltimore: Johns Hopkins University Press, 1961.

Jackson, Kenneth. *Crabgrass Frontier: The Suburbanization of the United States.* New York: Oxford University Press, 1985.

James, Harlean, ed. *Twenty-Fifth Anniversary Year-book: Park and Recreation Progress.* Washington, D.C.: National Conference on State Parks, 1946.

James, James Alton. "The Beginnings of a State Park System for Illinois." *Transactions of the Illinois State Historical Society* (1936): 53–62.

Jennings, Jan. *Roadside America: The Automobile in Design and Culture.* Ames: Iowa State University for the Society for Commercial Archeology, 1990.

Jensen, Clayne R., and Clark T. Thorstenson, comps. *Issues in Outdoor Recreation.* Minneapolis, Minn.: Burgess Publishing, 1977.

———. *Outdoor Recreation in America.* 4th ed. Minneapolis, Minn.: Burgess Publishing, 1985.

Johnson, Ronald W., and Michael G. Schene. *Cultural Resources Management.* Malabar, Fla.: Krieger Publishing, 1987.

Jubenville, Alan. *Outdoor Recreation Planning.* Philadelphia: W.B. Sanders Co, 1976.

Junkin, Elizabeth Darby. *Lands of Brighter Destiny: The Public Lands of the American West.* Golden, Colo.: Fulcrum, 1986.

Kammen, Michael. *Mystic Chords of Memory: The Transformation of Tradition in American Culture.* New York: Vintage Books, 1991.

———. *In the Past Lane: Historical Perspectives on American Culture.* New York: Oxford University Press, 1997.

Karsmizki, Kenneth W. "The Lewis and Clark Caverns: Politics and the Establishment of Montana's First State Park." *Montana* 31 (1981): 32–45.

King, Dale S., ed. *Arizona's National Monuments.* Southwestern Monuments Association Popular Series, No. 2. Santa Fe: Southwestern Monuments Association, 1945.

Kleinsorge, Martin. *Exploring Colorado State Parks.* 2nd ed. Niwot: University Press of Colorado, 1997.

Lange, Richard C. "Survey of the Homolovi Ruins State Park." *Kiva* 54 (1989): 195–216.

Larkin, Robert Abbott. "The Homol'ovi Project: A Model for Decision Making in the Development of Archaeological Theme Parks." Master's thesis, Arizona State University, 1988.

Lazaroff, David. *Sabino Canyon: The Life of a Southwestern Oasis.* Tucson: University of Arizona Press, 1993.

Lindsay, Diana Elaine. *Our Historic Desert: The Story of the Anza-Borrego Desert, The Largest State Park in the United States of America.* San Diego, Calif.: Copley Books, 1973.

Linenthal, Edward. *Sacred Ground: Americans and their Battlefields.* 2nd ed. Urbana and Chicago: University of Illinois Press, 1993.

"The Life and Improbably Good Times of Bruce Babbitt." *Notre Dame Magazine* (February 1985): 36–38.

Lower Colorado River Land Use Advisory Committee. United States Department of the Interior. *Lower Colorado River Land Use Plan: A Report of the Lower Colorado River Land Use Advisory Committee.* Washington, D.C., January 1964.

Lowitt, Richard. *The New Deal and the West.* Norman: University of Oklahoma Press, 1993.

Lowry, William R. *The Capacity For Wonder: Preserving Our National Parks.* Washington, D.C.: The Brookings Institution, 1994.

Lubick, George M. "Forging Ties with the Past: Historic Preservation in Arizona." *Journal of the West* 24, no. 2 (1985): 96–107.

Luckingham, Bradford. *Phoenix: History of a Southwest Metropolis.* Tucson: University of Arizona Press, 1989.

———. *The Urban Southwest: A Profile History of Albuquerque, El Paso, Phoenix, Tucson.* El Paso: Texas Western Press, 1982.

Luey, Beth, and Noel J. Stowe, eds. *Arizona at Seventy Five: The Next Twenty-Five Years.* Tempe: Arizona State University Public History Program and the Arizona Historical Society, 1987.

Lyon Elizabeth A. "Cultural and Environmental Resource Management: The Role of History in Historic Preservation." *The Public Historian* 4 (1982) 86.

———. "Preservation in the States: Utilizing Historic Resources." *State Government News* 31 (1988): 22–23.

Makowski, Ellen Hunning. "Scenic Parks and Landscape Values." Ph.D. diss., University of Illinois, Urbana-Champaign, 1987.

Malach, Roman. *Lake Havasu City: Land of Chemehuevis.* Lake Havasu, Ariz.: London Bridge Rotary Club, 1974.

Mason, Bruce B., and Heinz R. Hink. *Constitutional Government in Arizona.* 4th ed. Tempe: Arizona State University, 1972.

Master Plan, Oracle Center for Environmental Education. Prepared for Arizona State Parks. Phoenix, 1990.

McClelland, Linda Flint. "A New Deal For State Parks, 1933–1942." In *Presenting Nature: The Historic Landscape Design of the National Park Service, 1916 to 1942.* Washington, D.C.: The National Park Service, 1993.

McFarland, Ernest W. *Mac: The Autobiography of Ernest W. McFarland.* Author, 1979.

McGann and Associates. *Above-ground Master Plan for Kartchner Caverns State Park.* Prepared for Arizona State Parks, 1992.

———. *Sonoita Creek Natural Area Management Plan.* Prepared for Arizona State Parks, December 1999.

Melnick, Rob, and Deborah Roepke. *Urban Growth in Arizona: A Policy Analysis.* Tempe: Morrison Institute for Public Policy, School of Public Affairs, Arizona State University, 1988.

Meyer, Roy W. *Everyone's Country Estate: A History of Minnesota's State Parks.* St. Paul: Minnesota Historical Society Press, 1991.

Miller, Char, ed. *American Forests: Nature, Culture, and Politics.* Lawrence: University Press of Kansas, 1997.

Miller, Page Putnam. *Reclaiming the Past: Landmarks of Women's History.* Bloomington: Indiana University Press, 1992.

Mohl, Raymond, ed. *Searching for the Sunbelt.* Knoxville: University of Tennessee Press, 1990.

Muhn, James and Hanson R. Stuart. *Opportunity and Challenge: The Story of the BLM.* Prepared for the U.S. Department of the Interior. Washington, D.C.: Government Printing Office, 1988.

Murdock, John R. *The Constitution of Arizona.* Tempe, Ariz.: W.B. Conkey Company, 1929.

Murphy, Marty. *The Prison Chronicle: Yuma Territorial Prison's Colorful Past: A Visitor's Guide to Yuma Territorial Prison State Historic Park.* Phoenix: Arizona State Parks Board, 1999.

Murtagh, John. *Keeping Time: A History and Theory of Preservation in America.* New York: John Wiley and Sons, 1997.

Mutter, Lawrence R. "Interest Group Influence in the Development and Implementation of State Recreation Policy." Ph.D. diss., Arizona State University, 1994.

Myers, John L. ed. *The Arizona Governors, 1912–1990.* Phoenix: Heritage Publishers, 1989.

Myers, Phyllis. *State Grants for Parklands, 1965–1984: Lessons for a New Land and Water Conservation Fund.* Washington, D.C.: The Conservancy Foundation, 1989.

Myers, Phyllis, and Sharon N. Green. *State Parks in a New Era.* Volume II. Washington, D.C.: The Conservation Foundation, 1989.

Nash, Gerald. *The American West in the Twentieth Century: A Short History of an Urban Oasis.* 2nd ed. Albuquerque: University of New Mexico Press, 1977.

Nash, Gerald, and Richard W. Etulain, eds. *The Twentieth-Century West: Historical Interpretations.* Albuquerque, University of New Mexico Press, 1989.

Nash, Roderick. "The American Wilderness in Historical Perspective." *Forest History* 6 (winter 1963): 2–13.

———. *Wilderness and the American Mind.* 3rd ed. New Haven and London: Yale University Press, 1982.

Nash, Roderick, ed. *American Environmentalism: Readings in the History of Conservation.* (Originally published as *The American Environment.*) New York: McGraw-Hill, 1990.

Nathan, Harriet, ed., and the Public Land Law Review Commission. *America's Public Lands: Politics, Economics, and Administration: Conference on the Public Land Law Review Commission Report, December 1970.* Berkeley: Institute of Governmental Studies, University of California, 1972.

National Park Service. United States Department of the Interior. *FY 82 State Program Overviews.* Preservation Planning Series. Washington, D.C., 1982.

———. *Parks for America: A Survey of Park and Related Resources in the Fifty States, and a Preliminary Plan.* Washington, D.C., 1964.

———. *A Study of the Park and Recreation Problem of the United States.* Washington, D.C., 1941.

"The National Parks: A Forum on the 'Worthless Lands' Thesis." *Journal of Forest History* 27 (1983): 130–145.

National Recreation and Park Association. *Demand for Recreation in America.* Alexandria, Va.: National Recreation and Park Association, 1984.

National Trust for Historic Preservation. *With Heritage So Rich.* Washington, D.C.: The Preservation Press, 1983.

Negri, Sam. *Kartchner Caverns: Nature's Underground Wonderland.* Phoenix: Arizona Department of Transportation, 1998.

Nelson, Beatrice Ward. *State Recreation Parks, Forests and Game Preserves.* Washington, D.C.: National Conference on State Parks, 1928.

Nelson, J. G. "Beyond Parks and Protected Areas: From Public and Private Stewardship to Landscape Planning and Management." *Environment* 21 (1991): 23–34.

Newton, Norman T. *Design on the Land: The Development of Landscape Architecture.* Cambridge, Mass.: Belknap Press, 1971.

Noble, David Grant. *Ancient Ruins of the Southwest: An Archaeological Guide.* Flagstaff: Northland Publishing, 1991.

Norris, Scott. *Discovered Country: Tourism and Survival in the American West.* Albuquerque: Stone Ladder Press, 1994.

Northern Gila County Historical Society. *Rim Country History.* Payson, Ariz.: Northern Gila County Historical Society, 1984.

Olsen, C. J. "Integration of Outdoor Forest Recreational Potential with Public Park Programs." In *American Planning and Civic Annual,* edited by Harlean James. Washington, D.C.: American Planning and Civic Association, 1956.

Oregon. State Parks and Recreation Branch. *Oregon's Beaches: A Birthright Preserved.* Oregon State Parks and Recreation Branch, 1977.

Orser, Edward. "Involuntary Community: Conscientious Objectors at Patapsco State Park During World War II." *Maryland Historical Quarterly* 72 (1977): 132–146.

Paige, John C. *The Civilian Conservation Corps and the National Park Service, 1933–1942: An Administrative History.* Washington, D.C.: United States Department of the Interior, National Park Service, 1985.

Painted Rock Reservoir Project Phase 1: Preliminary Survey and Recommendations. Archaeological Series No 126. Tucson: Arizona State Museum, University of Arizona, 1978.
Peacock, Blanche G. "Reelfoot Lake State Park." *Tennessee Historical Quarterly* 32 (fall 1973): 205–232.
Petersen, Keith, and Mary E. Reed, "'For All the People, Forever and Ever': Virgil McCroskey and the State Parks Movement." *Idaho Yesterdays* 28, no. 1 (1984): 2–15.
Phoenix, City of. *Historic Homes of Phoenix: An Architectural and Preservation Guide.* Phoenix: City of Phoenix, 1992.
Pomeroy, Earl. *In Search of the Golden West: The Tourist in Western America.* Lincoln: University of Nebraska Press, 1990.
President's Commission on Americans Outdoors. *Americans Outdoors: The Legacy, the Challenge.* Washington, D.C.: Island Press, 1987.
Raventon, Edward. *A Piece of Paradise: A Story of Custer State Park.* Helena, Mont.: Falcon, 1996.
Reid, Russell. "The De Mores Historic Site." *North Dakota Historical Quarterly* 8 (1941): 272–283.
———. "Fort Lincoln State Park." *North Dakota Historical Quarterly* 8 (1941): 100–113.
———. "Lake Metigoshe State Park." *North Dakota Historical Quarterly* 9 (1942): 114–124.
———. "The North Dakota State Park System." *North Dakota Historical Quarterly* 8 (1940): 63–78.
———. "Turtle River State Park." *North Dakota Historical Quarterly* 8 (1941): 147–156.
Reisner, Marc. *Cadillac Desert: The American West and Its Disappearing Water.* Revised reprint edition. New York: Penguin, 1993.
Rettie, Dwight F. *Our National Park System: Caring for America's Greatest Natural and Historic Treasures.* Urbana and Chicago: University of Illinois Press, 1995.
Richards, J. Morris. *History of the Arizona State Legislature, 1912–1967.* Phoenix: Arizona Legislative Council, Arizona Department of Library, Archives and Public Records, 1990.
Richardson, Elmo. "The Civilian Conservation Corps and the Origins of the New Mexico State Park System." *Natural Resources Journal* 6 (April 1966): 6–15.
———. *Dams, Parks, and Politics: Resource Development in the Truman-Eisenhower Era.* Lexington: University of Kentucky Press, 1973.
Riggs, Robert E. *The Movement For Administrative Reorganization in Arizona,* Special Studies No. 17. Tucson: Bureau of Business and Public Research, University of Arizona, 1961.
Ringer, Craig. *Engagement at Picacho Pass.* Phoenix: Arizona State Parks, 1996.
Robinson, George W. "Conservation in Kentucky: The Fight to Save Cumberland Falls, 1926–1931." *Register of the Kentucky Historical Society* 81, no. 1 (1983): 25–58.
Rogers, Jerry L. "The National Register of Historic Places: A Personal Perspective on the First Twenty Years." *The Public Historian* 9, no. 2 (1987): 91–104.
Roth, Dennis. "The National Forests and the Campaign for Wilderness Legislation." *Journal of Forest History.* 28 (1984): 112–125.
Rothman, Hal. *Devil's Bargains: Tourism in the Twentieth-Century American West.* Lawrence: University Press of Kansas, 1998.
———. *America's National Monuments: The Politics of Preservation.* (Originally published as *Preserving Different Pasts: The American National Monuments*) Lawrence: Univ. of Kansas Press, 1994.

Runte, Alfred. *National Parks: The American Experience.* Lincoln: Univ. of Nebraska Press, 1979.
Ryder Architects. *Fort Verde State Historic Park Twenty-Year Master Plan.* Prepared for Arizona State Parks, 1990.
———. "Public Lands and Public Lives: Change and Continuity in Environmental History." *The Public Historian* 12, no. 3 (1990): 115–119.
Sale, Kirkpatrick. *The Green Revolution: The American Environmental Movement 1962–1992.* New York: Hill and Wang, 1993.
Scarpino, Philip. "Planning for Preservation: A look at the Federal-State Historic Preservation Program 1966–1986." *The Public Historian* 14, no. 2 (1992): 49–66.
Schifano, Patrick. *Oracle Speaks: A History of the Town, the Kannally Family, and the Park.* Tucson: Spirit Publications, 1998.
Schrems, Susan. "A Lasting New Deal Legacy: The Civilian Conservation Corps, the National Park Service, and the Development of the Oklahoma State Park System." *Chronicles of Oklahoma* 72 (1994–5): 368–395.
Schrepfer, Susan R. *The Fight to Save the Redwoods: A History of Environmental Reform: 1917–1978.* Madison: University of Wisconsin Press, 1983.
Segrest, J. L. "Resume of Alabama State Park History." *Alabama Historical Quarterly* 10 (1948): 77–80.
Semetko, John. "Changing Concepts and Philosophies of State Parks in Texas." Master's thesis, Texas Tech University, 1972.
Shaffer, Marguerite S. *See America First: Tourism and National Identity, 1880–1940.* Washington, D.C.: Smithsonian Institution Press, 2001.
Shaw, Ralph H. "History of the Acquisition of the Butano." *Proceedings of the International Shade Tree Conference* 30 (1954): 293–296.
Shenk, Lynette O., and George A. Teague. *Excavations at the Tubac Presidio.* Archaeological Series Number 85. Tucson: Cultural Resource Management Section, Arizona State Museum, University of Arizona, 1975.
Sherman, James E., and Barbara H. Sherman. *Ghost Towns of Arizona.* Norman: University of Oklahoma Press, 1977.
Shofner, Jerrell H. "Roosevelt's 'Tree Army,' The Civilian Conservation Corps in Florida." *Florida Historical Quarterly* 65 (1987): 433–456.
Smith, Linwood E. *Established Natural Areas in Arizona: A Guidebook for Scientists and Educators.* Prepared by the Arizona Academy of Science for the Arizona Office of Economic Planning and Development, Planning Division. Phoenix, 1974.
Smith, Thomas G. "John F. Kennedy, Stewart Udall, the New Frontier Conservation." *Pacific Historical Review* 64 (1995): 329–362.
Sorbin, Harris J., ed. "Florence Townsite, A.T." Final Report of Florence Townsite Historic District Study, May 1977.
Southern Arizona Environmental Council. *Citizen's Guide to Environment Groups in Southern Arizona, 1974–1975.* Tucson: Southern Arizona Environmental Council, 1975.
Spooner, Jane. *Tubac: Town of 9 Lives.* Tucson, Ariz.: Paragon Press, 1962.
Steely, Jim W. *The Civilian Conservation Corps in Texas State Parks.* Austin: Texas Parks and Wildlife Department, 1986.

Stepenoff, Bonnie. "Archives and Historic Preservation: The Case of the CCC." *Midwestern Archivist* 13 (1988): 77–83.
Stewart, Janet Ann. *Arizona Ranch Houses: Southern Territorial Styles, 1867–1900*. Tucson: University of Arizona Press and the Arizona Historical Society, 1974.
Strong, Douglas R. "Preservation Efforts At Lake Tahoe 1880–1980." *Journal of Forest History* 25 (1981): 78–97.
Sullivan, John J. "The Civilian Conservation Corps and the Creation of the Myakka River State Park." *Tampa Bay History* 9 (1987): 4–16.
Swanson, Mark T., and Jeffrey H. Altschul. "Cultural Resources Investigations of the Yuma Quartermaster Depot, AZ X:6:12 (ASM)." [Draft]. Submitted to Banner Associates, Mesa, Arizona. Technical series no. 21, 1989.
Taylor, Clyde W. *Public Administration in Arizona*. New York: Charles Scribner's Sons, 1942.
Terrie, Philip G. "The Adirondack Forest Preserve: The Irony of Forever Wild." *New York History* 62 (1981): 260–288.
Thelan, David. "Memory and American History." *Journal of American History* 75 (March 1989): 1117–1129.
Thomas, Clive, ed. *Politics and Public Policy in the Contemporary American West*. Albuquerque: University of New Mexico Press, 1991.
Thompson, Roger C. "Politics in the Wilderness: New York's Adirondack Forest Preserve." *Forest History* 6 (1963): 14–63.
Tilden, Freeman. *The National Parks: What They Mean to You and Me*. New York: Alfred A. Knopf, 1951.
———. *The State Parks: Their Meaning in American Life*. New York: Alfred A. Knopf, 1962.
Toney, Sharon Morris. "The Texas State Parks System: An Administrative History, 1923–1984." Ph.D. diss., Texas Tech University, 1995.
Torrey, Raymond H. *State Parks and Recreational Uses of State Forests in the United States*. Washington, D.C.: National Conference on State Parks, 1926.
Trafzer, Cliff, and Steve George. *Prison Centennial, 1876–1976: A Pictorial History of the Arizona Territorial Prison at Yuma*. Yuma, Ariz.: Yuma County Historical Society, 1980.
Trotter, John E. *The State Park System in Illinois*. Ph.D. diss., University of Chicago, 1962.
Tufts, Randy, and Gary Tenen. "Discovery and History of Kartchner Caverns, Arizona." *Journal of Karst and Cave Studies* 61 (August 1999): 44–48.
Turhollow, Anthony F. *A History of the Los Angeles District, U.S. Army Corps of Engineers 1898–1965*. Los Angeles: U.S. Army Engineer District, 1975.
United States House Committee on Interior and Insular Affairs. *Land and Water Conservation Fund*. 88th Cong., 1st sess., 1963.
———. *Land and Water Conservation Fund*. 88th Cong., 2nd sess., 1964.
———. *Theft of Indian Artifacts from Archaeological Sites: Oversight Hearing before the Subcommittee on General Oversight and Investigations of the Committee on Interior and Insular Affairs*. 100th Cong., 1st sess., 1988.
United States Senate Committee on Interior and Insular Affairs. *Preservation of Historic Properties*. 89th Cong., 2nd sess., 1966.
United States Senate Subcommittee on Oversight and Investigations, Commission on Energy

and Natural Resources. *Hearing on the Propriety of a Commercial Lease issued by the Bureau of Land Management at Lake Havasu, Arizona.* 104th Cong., 2nd sess., 1996.

University of Arizona Cooperative Extension Service. *Recreation Resources of the Verde River, Cottonwood Reach.* Cottonwood: Author, 1979.

Van Petten, Donald R. *The Constitution and Government of Arizona.* Phoenix: Sun Country Publishing Company, 1956.

Verando, Denzil. *Big Basin.* Los Altos, Calif.: Sempervirens Fund, 1973.

Wagoner, Jay W. *Arizona's Heritage.* Revised ed. Salt Lake City, Utah: Peregrine Smith Books, 1987.

Walker, Henry P., and Don Bufkin. *Historical Atlas of Arizona.* 2nd ed. Norman: University of Oklahoma Press, 1989.

Walker, William H. *Homol'ovi: A Cultural Crossroads.* Winslow, Ariz.: Arizona Archaeological Society, Homolovi Chapter, 1996.

Waller, Louis K. "A Proposed Operation Manual for State Park Systems." Master's thesis, Southern Illinois University, 1970.

Washington Parks and Recreation Commission. *A History of Washington State Parks: 1913–1988.* Olympia: Washington State Parks and Recreation Commission, 1988.

Wasley, William W., and Alfred E. Johnson. *Salvage Archaeology in Painted Rocks Reservoir, Western Arizona.* Anthropological Papers of the University of Arizona, No. 9. Tucson: University of Arizona Press, 1965.

Waters, Frank. *Book of the Hopi.* New York: Penguin, 1977.

Weaver, Donald E., Jr., Steven G. Dosh, and Keith Miller. *An Archaeological Assessment of Homolovi II Ruin.* Report prepared for the State Historic Preservation Office. Phoenix: Museum of Northern Arizona, 1982.

Weeks, W. William. *Beyond the Ark: Tools for an Ecosystem Approach to Conservation.* Covelo, Calif., and Washington, D.C.: Island Press, 1997.

Welch, Jill Ellen. *Arizona Outdoors: Implementing the Arizona Statewide Comprehensive Outdoor Recreation Plan.* Phoenix: Arizona State Parks, 1989.

Westover, William H. *Yuma Footprints.* Tucson: Arizona Pioneers Historical Society, 1966.

Whipple, Gurth. *A History of Half a Century of the Management of the Natural Resources of the Empire State, 1885–1935.* Albany, New York: Conservation Department and New York State College of Forestry, 1935.

White, Richard. "Historiographical Essay: American Environmental History: The Development of a New Field." *Pacific Historical Review* 54 (1985): 297–335.

Wiley, Peter, and Robert Gottlieb. *Empires in the Sun: The Rise of the New American West.* New York: G. P. Putnam's Sons, 1982.

Wilson, Chris. *The Myth of Santa Fe: Creating a Southwestern Regional Tradition.* Albuquerque: University of New Mexico Press, 1997.

Wolf, Robert Charles. *Iowa's State Parks: Also Forests, Recreation Areas, and Preserves.* Ames: Iowa State University Press, 1991.

Wood, Jack. "Jacob Babler: His Contribution to the State Park Movement in Missouri." *Bulletin of the Missouri Historical Society* 15 (1959): 285–295.

Woodbury, Richard B. *Sixty Years of Southwestern Archaeology: A History of the Pecos Conference.* Albuquerque: University of New Mexico Press, 1993.

Woods, Wilma M. "The Role of Federal Dollars and the Economics of Recreation in the Development of Idaho's State Parks, 1908–1965." *Idaho Yesterdays* (1991): 15–21.

Worden, Marshal A., David A. de Kok, and Adrian Esparanza. *The Tourist and Recreational Economy of the Verde Valley, Arizona.* University of Arizona Cooperative Extension Service, Papers in Community and Rural Development, No. 10. Cottonwood: University of Arizona Cooperative Extension Service, March 1981.

Wormser, Richard. *Tubac.* Tubac, Ariz.: Tubac Historical Society, 1975.

Worster, Donald. *Under Western Skies: Nature and History in the American West.* New York: Oxford University Press, 1992.

Woznicki, Robert. *The History of Yuma and the Territorial Prison.* Tempe, Ariz.: Author, 1995.

Writers' Program of the Work Projects Administration in the State of Arizona, comp. *Arizona: A State Guide.* American Guide series. New York: Hastings House, 1940.

Wrobel, David M., and Patrick T. Long. *Seeing and Being Seen: Tourism in the American West.* Lawrence: University Press of Kansas, 2001.

Young, John V. *The State Parks of Arizona.* Albuquerque: University of New Mexico Press, 1986.

———. *The State Parks of New Mexico.* Albuquerque: University of New Mexico Press, 1984.

———. *The State Parks of Utah: A Guide and History.* Salt Lake City: University of Utah Press, 1989.

Zaslowsky, Dyan, and the Wilderness Society. *The American Lands: Parks, Wilderness, and the Public Lands.* Washington, D.C.: The Wilderness Society, 1986.

Illustration Credits

Note: Photos not listed were taken by the author.

Arizona State Parks

All photographs copyright © 1999 Arizona State Parks.
Map of Arizona State Parks © 2000.
Tubac Presidio State Historic Park. Photograph by Princely Nesadurai.
Tombstone Courthouse.
Yuma Territorial Prison State Historic Park. Photograph by Princely Nesadurai.
Jerome State Historic Park. Photograph by Princely Nesadurai.
Picacho Peak State Park. Photograph by Princely Nesadurai.
Fort Verde State Historic Park.
McFarland State Historic Park. Photograph by Princely Nesadurai.
Riordan Mansion State Historic Park.
Lyman Lake State Park.
Buckskin Mountain State Park. Photograph by Princely Nesadurai.
Lake Havasu State Park.
Alamo Lake State Park.
Roper Lake State Park.
Patagonia Lake State Park. Photograph by Princely Nesadurai.
Tonto Natural Bridge.
Dead Horse Ranch.

Boyce Thompson Southwestern Arboretum. Photograph by Princely Nesadurai.
Lost Dutchman State Park. Photograph by Princely Nesadurai.
Catalina State Park. Photograph by Princely Nesadurai.
Homolovi Ruins State Park.
Red Rock State Park.
Slide Rock State Park. Photograph by Princely Nesadurai.
Ken Travous, director of Arizona State Parks. Photograph by Princely Nesadurai.
Kartchner Caverns State Park. Photograph by Noelle Bonnin-Wilson.
Fool Hollow Lake Recreation Area. Photograph by Princely Nesadurai.

Arizona State Library, Archives, and Public Records, Archives Division, Phoenix

Signing House Bill 72 into law.
Governor Bruce Babbitt. Image number 97-6496.

Index

Adamsville Site, 50, 118
Alamo Lake State Park, 66, 72–74, 87, 153; photo, 73
Anamax Mining Company, 124–26
Apache-Sitgreaves National Forests, 152–55
Aravaipa Canyon, 94, 109, 115, 172, 174
archaeology, 64–65, 114, 116, 122–23, 161–63
Arivaca Lake, 129
Arizona, land use statistics, 4–5, 60
Arizona Auditor General: 1987 audit, 139
Arizona Development Board, 14, 96
Arizona Game and Fish Commission and Department, 7, 12, 61, 66, 117, 173; Alamo Lake and, 74–77; Aravaipa Canyon and, 94, 109; Corps of Engineers flood control projects and, 86; Fool Hollow and, 152–55; Heritage Fund and, 161–63; Homolovi Ruins State Park and, 121; Patagonia Lake and, 78–79; Spur Cross Ranch and, 170; Verde River Greenway and, 134–37
Arizona Highway Commission and Arizona Highway Department, 12, 25
Arizona Highways, 96, 100, 118, 121, 157
Arizona Historical Society, xvi, 21, 44, 56, 122, 173; competition with Arizona State Parks, 45–48; Yuma Crossing and, 158
Arizona Legislative Council, 14
Arizona Legislature, 5, 75, 91–92; Heritage Fund and, 161–63. *See also* individual park projects listed under name of park
Arizona Outdoor Recreation Coordinating Commission (AORCC), 62–63, 115, 117; integration into Arizona State Parks, 116
Arizona Parklands Foundation, xvii, 137–39; Arizona State Parks Expansion Program and, 129; Oracle State Park and, 132–34; Slide Rock State Park and, 127–31
Arizona Preservation News, 46, 162
Arizona Public Service, 153–55
Arizona State Land Department (SLD), 5, 6, 9, 49, 173, 174; Aravaipa Canyon and, 94; Bruce Babbitt and, 115; Catalina State Park and, 107–8; Homolovi Ruins State Park and, 118–23; Historic sites and, 49–50; House Bill 72 and, 18; lakes and, 67, 85; Red Rock State Park and, 124–26;

Supreme Court decision (1988) and, 137; Verde River Greenway and, 135–137
Arizona State Parks Association, 13–25
Arizona State Parks Board: composition of, 21–22, 91–92, 107, 115, 156; creation of, 18–20; finances of, 91–92, 150–60; Heritage Fund creation, xvi, 13–25; Kartchner Caverns and finances of, 147–50; Natural Areas Committee, 165; plans of, 25, 73–74, 96, 115, 117, 152; struggles with legislature, 91–92. *See also* board members, directors, staff members, and state parks by name
Asta, Ron, 104
Atmar, Joe, 155–56
Avery, Ben, 14–15, 48, 61, 62, 81

Babbitt, Bruce, xvii, xviii, 53, 72, 84, 101, 106, 107, 110, 111–39; and Arizona State Parks and state government, 114–17; childhood and upbringing, 112–13, 123, 126–27, 138; Heritage Fund and, 161; Homolovi Ruins State Park and, 119–23, 137–39; impact when no longer governor, 140, 176; Ironwood National Monument and, 123; Kartchner Canverns and, 146; legacy and, 136–39; Oracle State Park and, 132–34, 137–39; photo, 112; political career, 113–14; political style, 114–15; Red Rock State Park and, 124–26, 137–39; as secretary of the interior, 72, 122–23, 138; Slide Rock State Park and, 126–31; Spur Cross Ranch and, 169; task forces, 116–17; Verde River Greenway and, 134-39; Yuma Crossing and, 115, 121, 126, 129, 131
Baboquivari, 94, 115, 129, 172
Bailey, Josephine, 30
banking, interstate, and Slide Rock State Park, 130–31
Bettwy, Andrew, 49, 50, 94, 105, 106
Bill Williams River, 66, 72
Blue, Ted and Associates, 77–79
Bolin, Wesley, 114

Bosh, Joni, 115
Boundary Commission, United States, 36, 155
Boyce Thompson, William, 99–100
Boyce Thompson Southwestern Arboretum, 52, 83, 99–101, 129, 131, 173, 174; photo, 99
Buckskin Mountain State Park, 65–66, 67–68, 160, 174; photo, 67
Bullhead City, 66, 129, 131
Bull Pen Ranch, 129
Burgbacher, Ralph, 91, 102

Calabasas and Guevavi. *See* Guevavi and Calabasas
California, 3, 4, 88, 121, 142, 153
Camp Verde, 135, 136. *See also* Fort Verde State Historic Park
Camp Verde Historical Society, 44–45
Camp Verde Improvement Association, 43–45
Carithers, Joseph, 15–17, 22
Casa Malpais, 129
Castle Hot Springs, 129
Castro, Raul, 106
Catalina State Park, xvii, 49, 52, 83, 103–8, 121, 132, 171, 174; Arizona State Parks Board's resistance and legislative involvement, 105–6; citizens' response to Rancho Romero development, 103–5; land purchases and exchanges and, 107–8; photo, 104; Santa Rita Exchange and, 108, 109–10, 137
Catalina State Park Planning Committee, 107
Cattail Cove, 69–72
cattle industry, xiv–xv; membership on Arizona State Parks Board, 21; reaction to state park movement, 5, 8, 10, 14–20, 173, 176. *See also* Dead Horse Ranch, Empire Ranch, Homolovi Ruins State Park, Oracle State Park, San Rafael Ranch, and Spur Cross Ranch
Cave Creek, 168–70
Ceballos, Lou, 120–21
Cerro Prieto–Pan Quemado, 122–23, 159
Charpio, Don, 142, 146

closing of parks, 84, 160, 171
Cluff Ranch, 94
Cockrum, E. Lendell, 100–101
Coconino Caverns (also known as Grand Canyon Caverns), 93
Colorado, xv, xvi; 5–6, 7, 9, 14, 21, 24, 26, 86, 89, 112; land use statistics, 4, 60
Colorado River, 61, 65–72, 109, 117, 142, 155–59
Colossal Cave, 9, 93, 109
concession arrangements, 67, 69–70, 158
conservation easements, xvii, 166–68, 176
Coronado National Forest, 103–8

Dankworth Ponds, 74–77
Davis Camp, 129, 131
Dead Horse Ranch State Park, 49, 52, 75, 83, 97–99, 160; photo, 97; Verde River Greenway and, 134–37
Deer Valley School District v. State Land Department, 137
Defenders of Wildlife, 94, 132–33, 173
Del Webb Corporation, 117, 127, 132
DiConcini, Dennis, 156, 157
direct stewardship, xvii–xviii
Douglas family, including "Rawhide Jimmy," 36–39
Doyle, Gerald A., and Associates, 157
Dreiseszun family, 168–70

Eatherly, Charles, 102, 143, 146
Eckankar, 123–26
Empire Ranch, 47, 122, 129
Empire Ranch Foundation, 122
environmental movement, 88–92, 111–16, 134, 159, 161–63, 176

Fain Castle and Fitzmaurice Ruins, 49
Fallini, Joseph, 94, 115
Fannin, Paul, 62, 91
federal lands, 3–8, 58–74, 86–87, 88–89, 172–76; Arizona state parks and access to, 174–75
Fireman, Bert, 19, 70, 91; photo, 21

Fool Hollow Lake Recreation Area, 140, 150–55, 170, 171, 173, 174; photo, 151
Fort Verde Museum Association, 44–45
Fort Verde State Historic Park, 25, 42–45, 56, 98, 160, 173; photo, 42
Friends of Kartchner Caverns, 149
Friends of Oracle State Park (FOSP), 134
Frye, Helen, Jack, 123–24

Gatlin Ruin, 49, 81, 82, 129
Gila Bend, 49–50, 81–84
Gila River, 72, 81–84
Giss, Harold, 20, 35, 66
Goblin Valley State Reserve (Utah), 175
Goddard, Sam, 46, 63
Goddard, Terry, 161
Golder, Lloyd, III, 105–8
Goldwater, Barry, 113–14, 161
Graham County, 49, 74–77, 94, 98
greenbelts and greenways, 90, 104–5, 134–37, 155
Griffin, Frank, 29–30, 56
Griffin, Olga "Gay," 29–30, 56
Guevavi and Calabasas, 47–48, 56, 173

Hallett, Harold, 43–45
Hallett, Margaret, 43–45
Hassayampa River, 84; proposed park on, 49, 76, 98, 129
Herberger, Robert, 117, 127, 132–33
Heritage Fund, xviii, 84, 142, 160–63; San Rafael Ranch and, 166–68; Sonoita Creek Natural Area and, 163–64; Spur Cross Ranch and, 169–70; Verde River Greenway and, 162
Heyburn State Park (Idaho), 9, 89, 175
historic preservation and historic sites, xvi, 26–57, 116, 161–63
Homol'ovi (the archaeological site) and Homolovi Ruins State Park, xvii, 50, 65, 116, 117–23, 124, 126, 129, 131, 136, 13–39, 171; photo, 119
Homolovi Management Board (HMB), 121
Hopi Tribe, 117–23

238 Index

Horsethief Basin, 93, 109, 172
House Bill 72, xvi, 18, 21, 24, 89, 129, 170
Hualapai Mountain, 9, 121, 129, 131
Hull, Jane Dee, 169–70

Idaho, xv, 5, 7, 14, 89, 114, 175; land use statistics, 4
indirect stewardship, xvii–xviii
Intermountain West (also called interior West), xvi, 3–10, 14, 24, 58–61, 86–87, 88–90, 170, 172–76; population growth in, 8, 10–11; Sagebrush Rebellion in, 111–12, 114. See also individual states
Iowa, 4, 20, 88
Ireys, Calvin, and family, 97–99, 173
Ironwood National Monument, 123
Itasca State Park (Minn.), 3, 175

Jaap, Robert, 16–17
Jerome State Historic Park, 38–39, 56, 98; photo, 37
Joshua Tree State Park (proposed), 93

Kannally family and ranch, 131–34
Kartchner, James, Lois, and family, 145–47, 173
Kartchner Caverns State Park, xvii, 84, 140, 154, 159, 163, 171; construction of facilities at, 147–50, 166; discovery of, 145; efforts to preserve as park, 146–47; legislation and, 147; opening of, 149, 169; photo, 144
King, Charles, 104–6
Kodachrome State Park (Utah), 175

Lake Carl Pleasant, 83, 85–86, 173
Lake Havasu and Lake Havasu State Park, 65–66, 68–72, 87, 153; land and, 71–72, 126, 138; photo, 69
Lake Havasu City, 68–72, 74
Lake Mead, 12, 59, 65
Lake Powell, 59
lakes, xvi–xvii, 7, 12, 25, 58–87, 174
Lamm, Richard, 112

Land and Water Conservation Fund (LWCF), xviii, 59–63, 89, 98, 160, 174, 176
Landin, Edna Louise, 32–33, 56, 109
Landry, Larry, 115, 127–28, 130
Lane, Robert, 115, 121, 124–25, 135
Lassen, Obed, 50
Lehner Mammoth Kill Site, 129
Lerner, Shareen, 118
Lewis and Clark Caverns (Montana), 9
Lieber, Col. Richard, 88
Linder, M. O., photo, 19
Little Colorado River, 63, 118
London Bridge, 70–71; photo, 69
Lost Dutchman State Park, 83, 101–3, 171, 173, 174; photo, 102
lotteries: Arizona, 160–63; in other states, 161. See also Heritage Fund
Lower Colorado River Land Use Advisory Committee, 66
Lower Colorado River Land Use Office, 66, 67, 69, 70
Lower Colorado River Land Use Plan, 66, 67, 74
Lower Oak Creek. See Red Rock State Park
Lyman Lake State Park, 63–65, 87, 160, 171; photo, 64

Maricopa County. See Phoenix and Maricopa County
McCain, John, 169
McCarthy, Dennis: Alamo Lake and, 74; Arizona Historical Society and, 46, 48; Arizona State Parks Association and, 15; Arizona Outdoor Recreation Coordinating Commission and, 62–63; Boyce Thompson Southwestern Arboretum and, 100–101; Catalina State Park and, 105–7; Colossal Cave and, 93; Dead Horse Ranch and, 98; early activities of, 25; Fort Verde and, 44; hired as parks director, 22–23; Horsethief Basin and, 93; Lake Carl Pleasant and, 85; Lower Colorado River Land Use Advisory Committee and, 66; Lyman Lake and, 64; Painted Rocks

and, 81–82; Michael Ramnes (contrasted with), 92; Sabino Canyon and, 93; termination of, 92; work with cities and counties, 49–50
McCarty Construction Company, 153–55
McCulloch, Robert P., 68–71, 123
McFarland, Ernest, 13, 14, 20, 21, 50–52; photo, 19
McFarland State Historic Park, 50–52, 55, 56, 171; photo, 51
Mechem, Evan, 137
Miller, Duane: Arizona Parklands Foundation and, 127; Arizona State Parks Board and, 91, 109; Catalina State Park and, 105–7; Dead Horse Ranch and, 97–98; Lake Havasu State Park and, 71; Riordan State Park and, 53–54; Yuma Crossing and, 157
mining industry, xiv–xv, 5, 36–37, 75, 148, 152
Minnesota, 3, 4, 160, 175
Mohave County, 85, 129, 131
Montana, xv, 5, 7, 9, 89, 176; land use statistics, 4
Mormon Lake, 7, 16
Muleshoe Ranch, 129
Museum of Northern Arizona (MNA), 119

National Historic Preservation Act of 1966, 46, 55–57
national monuments, xiii, 6; state parks and, 9, 175. *See also* individual monuments by name
national parks, xiii, 3, 6, 89, 148. *See also* individual parks by name
National Register of Historic Places, 150
National Wild and Scenic Rivers Act of 1968, 134
National Wild and Scenic Rivers System, 135
Native American reservations, 4, 5, 12
Native American ruins and petroglyphs, 25, 80, 84, 117–23, 126
The Nature Conservancy: Bruce Babbitt and, 113, 115; Heritage Fund and, 161; Kartch-

ner Caverns and, 146–47; Patagonia Lake and, 77; San Rafael Ranch and, 165–68; Verde River Greenway and, 135, 136
Nevada, xv, 5, 9, 10, 14, 20, 114, 155; land use statistics, 4
New Deal, xv, 8–10, 58, 60, 176
New Mexico, xv, 7, 9, 10, 14, 20–21, 26, 114, 121, 175–76; land use statistics, 4, 60
New Mexico and Arizona Land Company, 121
New York, 3, 4, 160, 175
New York Times, 114, 121
Nick Lause Park, 85

Office of Economic Planning and Development (OEPAD), 115–16, 117, 121
O'Haco, Michael, 119, 121
Old Smoke Trail Ranch. *See* Red Rock State Park
Oracle: community response to Oracle State Park, 132–34
Oracle Center for Environmental Education. *See* Oracle State Park
Oracle Road Greenbelt Committee (ORGC), 104–5
Oracle State Park, 117, 131–34, 137–39, 149, 159, 171, 173; photo, 133
Orme, Charles "Chick," 17–18
outdoor recreation, 5–7, 11–13, 22, 142–43, 170–71, 176
Outdoor Recreational Resources Coordinating Commission (ORRC), 60, 89

Painted Rocks State Park, 50, 63, 81–84, 87, 117–18, 160; closure of, 84, 109; photo, 80
Papago Park, 6, 9, 24, 175
Parker and Parker Dam, 65, 66, 67, 74
partnerships and cooperative agreements, xvii; Fool Hollow and, 150–55, 170; Homolovi Ruins State Park and, 122; lakes and, 86–87; recent importance of, 140–41, 170–71, 174–75; San Rafael Ranch and, 166–68, 170; Spur Cross Ranch and, 169–70

Patagonia Lake State Park, 77–81, 83, 87, 163–64; photo, 78
Patten, Eva, 161
Patterson, Barry, 156, 158
Patterson, John, 157
Pendley, Tom and family, 127–31
pesticides, 84
Phelps Dodge Corporation, 36–37, 75, 152
Phoenix and Maricopa County, xiv, 10; Joni Bosh and, 115; founding of Arizona State Parks Board and, 15, 24, 25; Lake Carl Pleasant and, 85–86, 74; lake recreation and, 62–63, 153; Lost Dutchman State Park and, 101–3; Painted Rocks and, 82–84; Spur Cross Ranch and, 168–70
Picacho Peak State Park, 39, 41–42, 56, 122, 171; photo, 40
Picket Post House, 99–101, 129, 131, 174
Pima County. *See* Tucson and Pima County
Pinal County Historical Society, 51
Pittsburg Point, 65, 66, 68–72; land exchange, 126
"pot-hunting," 118–19, 120
Presidio of Santa Cruz de Terrante. *See* Quiburi

Quiburi, 122–23, 129, 159

Ramirez, Sam, 117
Ramnes, Michael, 50, 83, 116, 142, 146; Arizona Parklands Foundation and, 127; contrasted with Dennis McCarthy, 92
Rancho Romero Coalition (later Catalina State Park Coalition), 103–7
Rarick, Ricki, 22, 91, 93, 98, 105
Ratliff, John, 103–8
Red Rock State Park, 72, 129, 136, 137–39, 174; Bruce Babbitt and, 117, 119–20, 121, 131; land exchanges, 123–26; photo, 125
Reitz, Charles, 21, 23, 35
Rieke, Betsy, 105–7
Riordan State Historic Park, 53–55, 56, 160; photo, 54
Riparian habitats, 75; Heritage Fund and, 162–63; Patagonia Lake and, 77–78, 124; San Rafael Natural Area and, 164–68; Sonoita Natural Area, 163–64; Verde River Greenway and, 134–37
Robinson, Gwen, 115, 155–58
Robinson, Priscilla G., 72, 107, 115
Roe, William, 115, 133, 146, 165–67
Roper, Marie, 75
Roper, Winneford D., 74–75
Roper Lake State Park, 74–77, 87, 98, 153, 160, 171, 173, 174; photo, 75

Sabino Canyon, 93, 105, 109, 172
Sagebrush Rebellion, 111–12
Saguaro Forest State Park, 9
Saguaro National Monument, 9, 104
Salt River Lakes (Saguaro, Canyon, Apache, and Roosevelt), 61, 83, 86
San Francisco River, 129
San Rafael Ranch Natural Area and State Park, xvii, 137, 142, 164–68, 170, 174; photo, 164
San Rafael Valley Land Trust, 167
Santa Rita Exchange, 108, 137
Schober, Donna, 116, 121
Sedgwick, Cabot, 122
Sharp family, 165–67
Show Low, 150–55
Sierra Club, 90, 107, 108, 169
Slide Rock State Park, 126–31, 132, 137–39, 174; photo, 128
Smithee, Ken, 62–63
Sonoita Creek, 77–81
Sonoita Creek Natural Area, xvii, 137, 142, 163–64, 169, 170
The Sonoran Institute, 165–66
Southern Arizona Environmental Council, (SAEC), 103–8
South Mountain Park, xiv, 10
Southwest Environmental Service (SES), 107–8, 115
Spur Cross Ranch, xvii, 142, 168–70, 174; photo, 168
State Historic Preservation Act of 1982, 116

Index **241**

State Historic Preservation Office (SHPO), xviii, 26, 46–47, 116, 118
State Lake Improvement Fund (SLIF), xviii, 61–63, 153
state park movement: early history of, xiv-xvi, 3–10; environmental movement and, xv–xvii, 88–92, 111, 176; lakes and, 58–61; New Deal and, xv, 8–10, 58, 176; in the 1920s, xv, 5–8, 175–76; post–World War II, xv–xvi, 10–12, 14, 20–21, 172–76; recent financial troubles and, 160–61; *See also* individual states and parks
Superstition Mountains, 101–3, 174
Swanson, Robert, 117, 127, 129–30
Symington, Fife, 160, 161, 163

Task Force on Historic Preservation, 116
Task Force on Parks and Recreation, 116–17, 127
Tenen, Gary. *See* Kartchner Caverns State Park
Tenny, Boyd, 98
Texas, 3, 21, 88, 175
timber industry, xv, 5, 8
Tombstone Courthouse State Historic Park, 30–33, 45, 55, 56, 173; photo, 31
Tombstone Restoration Commission, 31–33, 173
Tonto National Forest, 101, 169
Tonto Natural Bridge, xvii, 25, 52, 84, 115, 121, 149, 163; first attempt to make a state park, 94–96; later attempt to make a state park, 129, 140, 150; photo, 95
Travous, Kenneth, 140, 142–43, 160; Kartchner Caverns and, 147–50; photo, 141; San Rafael Ranch and, 165–66
Tubac Presidio State Historic Park, 28–30, 45, 56, 160, 171, 173; photo, 28
Tucson and Pima County, 25; Arizona Historical Society and, 47; Catalina State Park and, 103–8; Colossal Cave and, 9, 93, 109; lake recreation and, 153; Oracle State Park and, 131–32; Red Rock State Park and, 125; Sabino Canyon and, 93, 94

Tucson Mountain Park, 9, 15, 107–8
Tufts, Randy, *See* Kartchner Caverns State Park
Tumacacori, 6
Tuzigoot National Monument, 134, 135

Udall, Morris, 104, 146, 161
Udall, Stewart, 13, 60, 70, 89, 108–9, 117
U.S. Army Corps of Engineers, 6, 59–61; Alamo Lake and, 72–74, 174; Cave Buttes, Adobe, and New River Projects, 86; Painted Rocks borrow pit and, 82–84, 174
U.S. Bureau of Indian Affairs, xiv, 6, 25
U.S. Bureau of Land Management (BLM), xiv, xv, xvii, 5, 6, 12–13, 115, 143, 172–73; Aravaipa Canyon and, 94; Bruce Babbitt and, 109; Colorado River and, 64, 67, 69, 72, 87; Empire Ranch and, 122; Homolovi Ruins State Park and, 119–23; Joshua Tree State Park (proposed), 93; Kartchner Caverns and, 146; land exchange and, 126; Lost Dutchman State Park and, 101–3; Painted Rocks and, 81–84; Picacho Peak and, 41; Utah and, 175
U.S. Bureau of Reclamation, 6, 9, 174; Colorado River and, 65–66, 69, 72, 85, 86, 87; in the West, 59–61; Yuma Crossing State Park and, 155–59
U.S. Environmental Protection Agency, 84
U.S. Fish and Wildlife Service, 6, 65–66
U.S. Forest Service (USFS), and national forests, xiv, xv, xvii, 5, 6, 12–13, 25, 87, 109, 143, 172–74; Catalina State Park and, 108, 115; Fool Hollow and, 151–55; Homolovi Ruins State Park and, 121–23; Horsethief Basin and, 93–94; Lost Dutchman State Park and, 101; Slide Rock State Park and, 126–31; Spur Cross Ranch and, 169; Verde River Greenway and, 134–36
U.S. National Park Service, xiii, xiv, 7, 9, 12, 65–66, 81, 93, 138, 143, 146
University of Arizona, 9, 25, 100–101, 135
Utah, xv, xvi, 5, 6, 7, 14, 20, 86, 114, 121, 175; land use statistics, 4, 60

Vegors, Wallace, 46–47, 49–50, 105
Verde River and Verde Valley, 42–45, 98, 134–37
Verde River Greenway, 117, 134–39, 162
Verde River Greenway Ad Hoc Advisory Committee, 136
Verde River Protection Fund, 136
Verde Valley Recreation Resource Information Group (VVRRIG), 134–37

Walnut Canyon, 6
Walnut Grove, 129
Walz, Jacob, 101, 174
Wilderness Act of 1964, 89
Williams, A. C., 90, 107
Williams, Jack, 48, 71, 91
Windsor Beach, 71–72
Winslow, 116, 120–21
Winsor, Clarissa, 35–36, 56
Wolfswinkel, Clifford, 150

Wood, C. V., 68–71
Wyoming, xv, 7, 14, 15; land use statistics, 4

Xanadu, 145. *See also* Kartchner Caverns State Park

Yuma, 33–36, 115, 155–59
Yuma County Water Users Association, 155–56
Yuma Crossing Foundation, 157–58
Yuma Crossing Park Council, 156–58
Yuma Crossing Park Resource Panel, 156
Yuma Crossing State Historic Park, 36, 140, 142, 149, 170, 173; Arizona State Parks and, 158–59, 169; Bruce Babbitt administration and, 115, 121, 126, 129, 131; first cooperative arrangement, 155–58; photo, 154
Yuma Territorial Prison State Historic Park, 33–36, 45, 155–56, 173; photo, 34

About the Author

Jay M. Price directs the public history program at Wichita State University. He is a native of Santa Fe, New Mexico, and has degrees from the University of New Mexico, the College of William and Mary, and Arizona State University. At Wichita State he teaches classes on public history, the American West, religion in America, and U.S. popular culture. His most recent publication is a photographic history of early Wichita, entitled *Wichita: 1860–1930*. Arcadia Publishing released this book in the spring of 2003. He headed a team of students that produced a second Arcadia book, entitled *Wichita's Legacy of Flight* (forthcoming). His earlier writings include pieces in Old Cowtown Museum in Wichita and a comparative history of the Arizona and New Mexico state capitol buildings.